Pasta & Italian

Pasta & Italian

p

This is a Parragon Publishing Book
This edition published in 2002

Parragon Publishing
Queen Street House
4 Queen Street
Bath BA1 1HE, UK

ISBN: 0-75257-955-X

Printed in China

NOTE

Unless otherwise stated, milk is assumed to be whole fat, eggs are large, and pepper
is freshly ground black pepper.

Recipes using uncooked eggs should be
avoided by infants, the elderly, pregnant women, and anyone
suffering from an illness.

Contents

Soups

Appetizers & Snacks

Fish & Seafood

Fish & Seafood (continued)

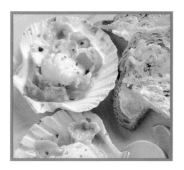

Meat

Chicken & Poultry

Pasta

Pizzas & Bread

Introduction

Italian food, including the many pasta dishes, pizzas, and risottos, as well as the decadent desserts, are enjoyed all around the world. This inspirational cookbook aims to bring a little bit of Italy into your kitchen!

Glorious sunlight, spectacular beaches, luscious countryside, rugged mountains, world-famous museums and art galleries, elegant designer shops, picturesque villages and magnificent cities – if this were not enough, Italy also boasts one of the longest and finest culinary traditions in the whole of Europe.

The ancient Romans loved good food and plenty of it, vying with each other to produce increasingly lavish and outlandish banquets. One of the earliest cookbooks, written by Apicius, a gourmet in the first century, includes an appaling recipe for dormouse stuffed with walnuts! Overseas trade as the Roman empire expanded brought new ingredients, and agriculture began to flourish at home. However, even then, wine production was just as prodigious as it is today.

With the collapse of the Roman empire, the diet returned to plainer fare, relying on the wealth of cereals, fruit, and vegetables that could be cultivated on the fertile plains. However, with the Renaissance, an interest in and enthusiasm for fine food revived and, once again, there were wealthy families who presided over extravagant banquets.

Italian pastry cooks were valued throughout the courts of Europe and were generally acknowledged as the best in the world. When Catherine de' Medici went to Paris to marry the future King Henri II, she took an army of Italian cooks with her and changed French culinary traditions irrevocably. A new middle class developed that also took an interest in eating well, creating a bourgeois cuisine characterized by fresh flavors, and simple, unsauced dishes. The poor, of course, continued with a peasant subsistence.

The very finest produce and freshest ingredients still characterize Italian cuisine as a whole. Although modern transportation makes it possible for more exotic ingredients to travel across the world, Italian

cooking still centers on homegrown produce. Over 60 percent of the land is devoted to crops and pasture. With a climate that ranges from very cold in the Alps and Apennines to semitropical along the coast of the Ligurian Sea, the range of produce is extensive: olives, oranges, lemons, figs, grapes, pomegranates, almonds, wheat, potatoes, tomatoes, sugar beet, corn, and rice.

Livestock includes cattle and buffalo, sheep, goats, pigs, and chickens. In a single year, Italy produces nearly 6.5 million tons of wine, nearly 2.5 million tons of olives, about 500,000 tons of olive oil, over 4.5 million tons of tomatoes, and 120 million chickens. An impressive amount, you'll agree!

The introduction to this book continues to explore Italy, region by region, to discover the different types of food that are identified with a specific area of the country. Seasonal ingredients are also examined to provide the reader with as much insight into the type of produce used by the very discerning people of Italy.

Ragu Sauce

3 tbsp olive oil

3 tbsp butter

2 large onions, chopped

4 celery stalks, thinly sliced

1 cup chopped bacon

2 garlic cloves, chopped

1 lb 2 oz ground lean beef

2 tbsp tomato paste

1 tbsp all-purpose flour

14-oz can chopped tomatoes

⅔ cup beef stock

⅔ cup red wine

2 tsp dried oregano

½ tsp freshly grated nutmeg

salt and pepper

1 Heat the oil and butter in a pan over a medium heat. Add the onions, celery, and bacon and fry for 5 minutes, stirring.

2 Stir in the garlic and ground beef and cook, stirring until the meat has lost its redness. Lower the heat and cook for 10 minutes, stirring.

3 Increase the heat to medium, stir in the tomato paste and the flour and cook for 1-2 minutes. Stir in the tomatoes, stock and wine and bring to a boil, stirring. Season and stir in the oregano and nutmeg. Cover and simmer for 45 minutes, stirring. The sauce is now ready to use.

Regional Cooking

To talk about Italian cuisine is somewhat misleading, as it is not a single entity. The country has been united only since March 17, 1861, and Italians still have a powerful sense of their regional identity.

Regional cuisine is a source of pride and considerable competition. Sicilians are dismissed as *mangimaccaroni* (pasta eaters), while they express their contempt for Neapolitan cooking with the term *mangiafoglie* (vegetable eaters). Each region bases its cuisine on local ingredients, so the best ham comes from the area where pigs are raised, fish and seafood feature in coastal regions, butter is used in dishes from the north of Italy where there is dairy farming, while olive oil is characteristic of southern recipes.

Abruzzi & Molise

This was once a single region and although it has now been divided into two separate provinces, they remain closely associated. Located in northern Italy to the east of Rome, the area is well-known for its high-quality cured meats and cheese. The cuisine is traditional and also features lamb and fish and seafood in the coastal areas. Peperoncino a tiny, fiery hot, dried red chili is from Abruzzi.

Basilicata

If the Italian peninsula looks like a boot, Basilicata is located on the arch of the foot. The landscape is rugged and inhospitable, with much of the region being more than 6,500 feet above sea level.

It is hardly surprising, therefore, that the cuisine is warming and filling, featuring substantial soups in particular. Cured meats, pork, lamb, and game are typical ingredients, and freshwater fish are abundant in the more mountainous areas.

Calabria

In the south, on Italy's toe, Calabria is a region of dramatic contrasts – superb beaches and towering mountains. Excellent fish and seafood typify the local cuisine, which is well known for its swordfish and tuna dishes. Fruit and vegetables are abundant, particularly oranges, lemons, eggplants, and olives. Like other southern regions, desserts are a specialty, often based on local figs, honey, or almonds.

Campania

Naples on the west coast is the home of pizza, now known across the world from Sydney to New York, and the region bases many of its other dishes on the wonderful sun-ripened tomatoes grown locally. Fish and seafood feature strongly in the Neapolitan diet and robust herb-flavored stews, redolent with garlic, are popular. Pastries and fruit desserts are also characteristic.

Emilia-Romagna

A central Italian province, Emilia-Romagna's capital is the beautiful medieval city of Bologna, nicknamed *la grassa*, the fat city, and home to some of the best restaurants in the country. A gourmet paradise, the region is famous for Parmesan cheese and prosciutto from Parma; balsamic vinegar from the area around Modena; cotechino, mortadella, and other cured meats

and, of course, *spaghetti alla bolognese*. Butter, cream, and other dairy products feature in the fine food of the region and a wide range of pasta dishes is popular.

Lazio

Capital of the region and the country, Rome is a cosmopolitan and sophisticated city with some of the best restaurants – and ice cream parlors – in Europe. Fruit and vegetables are abundant and lamb and veal dishes are characteristic of the region, famous for *saltimbocca*, which literally means "jump in the mouth." Here, they have perfected the art of preparing high-quality ingredients in simple, but delicious ways that retain the individual flavors. A Roman specialty is *supplì al telefono* – "telephone wires" – mozzarella cheese wrapped in balls of cooked rice and deep-fried. The mozzarella is stringy, hence the name of the dish.

Liguria

A northern province with a long coastline, Liguria is well known for its superb fish and seafood. It is also said to produce the best basil in the whole of Italy and it is where pesto sauce was created.

The ancient port of Genoa was one of the first places in Europe to import Asian spices and highly seasoned dishes are still particularly characteristic of this area.

Lombardy

An important rice-growing region in northwest Italy, this is the home of risotto and there are probably as many variations of this dish as there

Regional Cooking

are cooks. Dairy produce features in the cuisine, and Lombardy is credited with the invention of butter, as well as mascarpone cheese. Vegetable soups, stews, and pot roasts are characteristic of this region. Bresaola, a cured raw beef, is a local specialty that is often served wrapped around soft goat cheese.

Marches

With its long coastline and high mountains, this region is blessed with both abundant seafood and game. Pasta, pork, and olives also feature and methods of preparation are even more elaborate than those of neighboring Umbria.

Piedmont

On the borders of France and Switzerland, Piedmont in the north-west is strongly influenced by its neighbors. A fertile, arable region, it is well known for rice, polenta, and gnocchi, and is said to grow the finest onions in Italy. Gorgonzola, one of the world's greatest cheeses, comes from this region, although, sadly, the little village that gave it its name has now been subsumed by the urban sprawl of Milan. Piedmontese garlic is said to be the best in Italy and the local white truffles are a gourmet's dream.

Puglia

On the heel of Italy, this region produces excellent olives, herbs, vegetables, and fruit, particularly melons and figs. Fish and seafood are abundant and the region is known for its oyster and mussel dishes. Calzone, a sort of inside out pizza, was invented here.

Sardinia

This Mediterranean island is famous for its luxurious desserts and extravagant pastries, many of them featuring honey, nuts, and homegrown fruit. Hardly surprisingly, fish and seafood – tuna, eel, mullet, sea bass, lobster, and mussels – are central to Sardinian cuisine and spit-roasted suckling pig is the national dish served on feast days. *Sardo* is a mild-tasting pecorino cheese produced in Sardinia.

Sicily

Like their southern neighbors, Sicilians have a sweet tooth, which they indulge with superb cakes, desserts, and ice cream, often incorporating locally grown almonds, pistachios, and citrus fruits. Pasta dishes are an important part of the diet, and fish and seafood, including tuna, swordfish and mussels, feature prominently.

Trentino Alto-Adage

A mountainous region in the northeast, Trentino has been strongly influenced by its Austrian neighbor. Smoked sausage and dumplings are characteristic of the cuisine, which is also well known for its filled pasta.

Tuscany

The fertile plains of Tuscany are ideal for farming and the region produces superb fruit and vegetables. Cattle are raised here and both steak and veal dishes feature on the Tuscan menu, together with a wide range of game. Tripe is a local specialty and *Panforte di Siena*, a traditional Christmas cake made with honey and nuts, comes from the city of Siena. A grain known as *farro* is grown almost exclusively in Tuscany, where it is used to make a nourishing soup.

Umbria

Pork, lamb, game, and freshwater fish, prepared and served simply but deliciously, characterize the excellent cuisine of the region. Fragrant black truffles are a feature and Umbrian cooking makes good use of its high-quality olive oil. Umbria is also famous for *imbrecciata*, a hearty soup made with lentils, garbanzo beans, and navy beans.

Veneto and Friuli

An intensively farmed area in the northeast of Italy, the Veneto and Friuli region produces cereals and almost 20 percent of the country's wine. Polenta and risotto feature in the cuisine, as well as an extensive range of fish and seafood. *Risi e bisi*, rice and peas, is a traditional dish which was served every year at the Doge's banquet in Venice to honor the city's patron saint, Mark.

Basic Recipes

These recipes form the basis of several of the dishes contained throughout this book. Many of these basic recipes can be made in advance and stored in the refrigerator until required.

Basic Tomato Sauce

2 tbsp olive oil

1 small onion, chopped

1 garlic clove, chopped

14-oz can chopped tomatoes

2 tbsp chopped parsley

1 tsp dried oregano

2 bay leaves

2 tbsp tomato paste

1 tsp sugar

salt and pepper

1 Heat the oil in a pan over a medium heat and fry the onion for 2–3 minutes, or until translucent. Add the garlic and fry for 1 minute.

2 Stir in the chopped tomatoes, parsley, oregano, bay leaves, tomato paste, sugar, and salt and pepper to taste.

3 Bring the sauce to a boil, then simmer, uncovered, for 15–20 minutes or until the sauce has reduced by half. Taste the sauce and adjust the seasoning if necessary. Discard the bay leaves just before serving.

Béchamel Sauce

1¼ cups milk

2 bay leaves

3 cloves

1 small onion

4 tbsp butter, plus extra for greasing

6 tbsp all-purpose flour

1¼ cups light cream

large pinch of freshly grated nutmeg

salt and pepper

1 Pour the milk into a small pan and add the bay leaves. Press the cloves into the onion, add to the pan, and bring the milk to a boil. Remove the pan from the heat and set aside to cool.

2 Strain the milk into a jug and rinse the pan. Melt the butter in the pan and stir in the flour. Stir for 1 minute, then gradually pour in the milk, stirring constantly. Cook the sauce for 3 minutes, then pour in the cream and bring it to a boil. Remove from the heat and season with nutmeg and salt and pepper to taste.

Lamb Sauce

2 tbsp olive oil

1 large onion, sliced

2 celery stalks, thinly sliced

1 lb 2 oz lean lamb, ground

3 tbsp tomato paste

5½ oz bottled sun-dried tomatoes, drained and chopped

1 tsp dried oregano

1 tbsp red-wine vinegar

⅔ cup chicken stock

salt and pepper

1 Heat the oil in a skillet over a medium heat and fry the onion and celery until the onion is translucent, about 3 minutes. Add the lamb and fry, stirring frequently, until it browns.

2 Stir in the tomato paste, sun-dried tomatoes, oregano, vinegar, and stock. Season with salt and pepper to taste.

3 Bring to a boil and cook, uncovered, for 20 minutes, or until the meat has absorbed the stock. Taste and adjust the seasoning if necessary.

Cheese Sauce

2 tbsp butter

1 tbsp all-purpose flour

1 cup milk

2 tbsp light cream

pinch of freshly grated nutmeg

⅓ cup grated sharp Cheddar

1 tbsp freshly grated Parmesan

salt and pepper

1 Melt the butter in a pan. Stir in the flour and cook for 1 minute. Gradually pour in the milk, stirring all the time. Stir in the cream and season the sauce with nutmeg and salt and pepper to taste.

2 Simmer the sauce for 5 minutes to reduce, then remove it from the heat and stir in the cheeses. Stir until the cheeses have melted and blended into the sauce.

Espagnole Sauce

2 tbsp butter

¼ cup all-purpose flour

1 tsp tomato paste

1 cup plus 2 tbsp veal stock, hot

1 tbsp Madeira wine

1½ tsp white-wine vinegar

2 tbsp olive oil

2 tbsp diced bacon

2 tbsp diced carrot

2 tbsp diced onion

1 tbsp diced celery

1 tbsp chopped leek

1 tbsp diced fennel

1 fresh thyme sprig

1 bay leaf

1 Melt the butter in a pan. Add the flour and cook, stirring, until lightly colored. Add the tomato paste, then stir in the hot veal stock, Madeira and white-wine vinegar and cook for 2 minutes.

2 Heat the oil in a separate pan. Add the bacon, carrot, onion, celery, leek, fennel, thyme sprig, and bay leaf and fry until the vegetables have softened. Remove the vegetables from the pan with a draining spoon and drain thoroughly. Add the vegetables to the sauce and leave to simmer for 4 hours, stirring occasionally. Strain the sauce before using.

Italian Red-Wine Sauce

⅔ cup Brown Stock (see page 16)

1⅔ cup Espagnole Sauce (see left)

½ cup red wine

2 tbsp red-wine vinegar

4 tbsp chopped shallots

1 bay leaf

1 thyme sprig

pepper

1 First make a demiglace sauce. Put the Brown Stock and Espagnole Sauce in a pan and heat for 10 minutes, stirring occasionally.

2 Meanwhile, put the red wine, red-wine vinegar, shallots, bay leaf, and thyme in a pan, bring to a boil and reduce by three-quarters.

3 Strain the demiglace sauce and add to the pan containing the red-wine sauce and leave to simmer for 20 minutes, stirring occasionally. Season with pepper to taste and strain the sauce before using.

Basic Recipes

Italian Cheese Sauce

2 tbsp butter

¼ cup all-purpose flour

1¼ cups milk, hot

pinch of nutmeg

pinch of dried thyme

2 tbsp white-wine vinegar

3 tbsp heavy cream

½ cup grated mozzarella cheese

½ cup grated Parmesan cheese

1 tsp English mustard

2 tbsp sour cream

salt and pepper

1 Melt the butter in a pan and stir in the flour. Cook, stirring, over a low heat until the roux is light in color and crumbly in texture. Stir in the hot milk and cook, stirring, for 15 minutes until thick and smooth.

2 Add the nutmeg, thyme, and white-wine vinegar, and season to taste. Stir in the cream and mix well.

3 Stir in the cheeses, mustard, and cream and mix until the cheeses have melted and blended into the sauce.

Fish Stock

2 lb non-oily fish pieces, such as
    heads, tails, trimmings, and bones

⅔ cup white wine

1 onion, chopped

1 carrot, sliced

1 celery stalk, sliced

4 black peppercorns

1 bouquet garni

7½ cups water

1 Put the fish pieces, wine, onion, carrot, celery, black peppercorns, bouquet garni, and water in a large pan and leave to simmer for 30 minutes, stirring occasionally. Strain and blot the fat from the surface with paper towels before using.

Garlic Mayonnaise

2 garlic cloves, crushed

8 tbsp mayonnaise

chopped parsley

salt and pepper

1 Put the mayonnaise in a bowl. Add the garlic, parsley, and salt and pepper to taste and mix together well.

Brown Stock

2 lb veal bones and shin of beef

1 leek, sliced

1 onion, chopped

1 celery stalk, sliced

1 carrot, sliced

1 bouquet garni

⅔ cup white-wine vinegar

1 thyme sprig

7½ cups cold water

1 Roast the veal bones and shin of beef in their own juices in the oven for 40 minutes.

2 Transfer the bones to a large pan. Add the leeks, onion, celery, carrots, bouquet garni, white-wine vinegar, and thyme and cover with the cold water. Leave to simmer over a very low heat for about 3 hours. Strain and blot the fat from the surface with paper towels before using.

How to Use This Book

Each recipe contains a wealth of useful information, including a breakdown of nutritional quantities, preparation and cooking times, and level of difficulty. All of this information is explained in detail below.

This amount of time represents the actual cooking time.

The nutritional information provided for each recipe is per serving or per portion. Optional ingredients, variations or serving suggestions have not been included in the calculations.

The number of chef's hats represents the difficulty of each recipe, ranging from easy (1 chef's hat) to difficult (5 chef's hats).

This amount of time represents the preparation of ingredients, including cooling, chilling, and soaking times.

The ingredients for each recipe are listed in the order that they are used.

The method is illustrated with step-by-step photographs, making the recipe easy to follow.

A full-color photograph of the finished dish.

Variations and cook's tips provide useful information regarding ingredients or cooking techniques.

The method is clearly explained with step-by-step directions that are easy to follow.

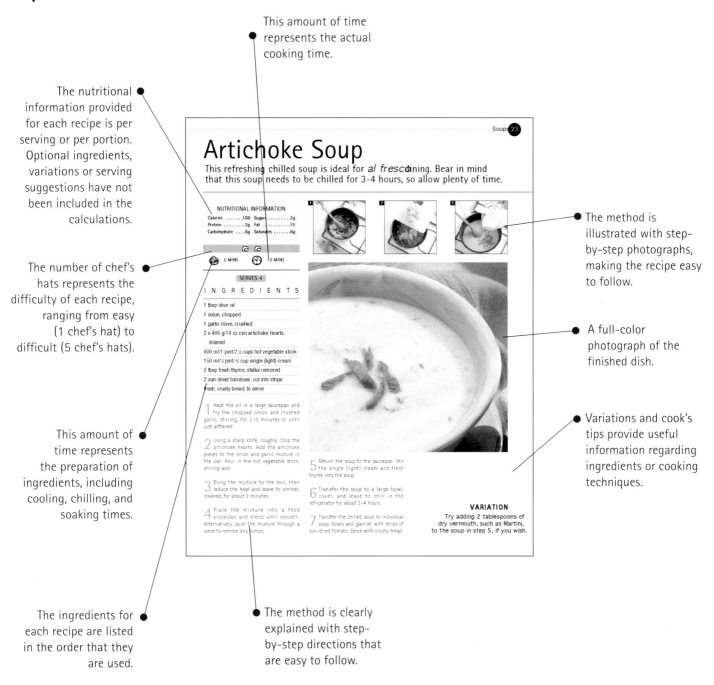

Soups 23

Artichoke Soup

This refreshing chilled soup is ideal for *al fresco* dining. Bear in mind that this soup needs to be chilled for 3-4 hours, so allow plenty of time.

NUTRITIONAL INFORMATION

Calories ....159 Sugar 2g
Protein ....2g Fat 15
Carbohydrate ....5g Saturates 6g

5 MINS   15 MINS

SERVES 4

INGREDIENTS

1 tbsp olive oil

1 onion, chopped

1 garlic clove, crushed

2 x 400 g/14 oz can artichoke hearts, drained

600 ml/1 pint/2½ cups hot vegetable stock

150 ml/¼ pint/⅔ cup single (light) cream

2 tbsp fresh thyme, stalks removed

2 sun-dried tomatoes, cut into strips

fresh, crusty bread, to serve

1 Heat the oil in a large saucepan and fry the chopped onion and crushed garlic, stirring, for 2–3 minutes or until just softened.

2 Using a sharp knife, roughly chop the artichoke hearts. Add the artichoke pieces to the onion and garlic mixture in the pan. Pour in the hot vegetable stock, stirring well.

3 Bring the mixture to the boil, then reduce the heat and leave to simmer, covered, for about 3 minutes.

4 Place the mixture into a food processor and blend until smooth. Alternatively, push the mixture through a sieve to remove any lumps.

5 Return the soup to the saucepan. Stir the single (light) cream and fresh thyme into the soup.

6 Transfer the soup to a large bowl, cover, and leave to chill in the refrigerator for about 3–4 hours.

7 Transfer the chilled soup to individual soup bowls and garnish with strips of sun-dried tomato. Serve with crusty bread.

VARIATION
Try adding 2 tablespoons of dry vermouth, such as Martini, to the soup in step 5, if you wish.

Soups

Soups are an important part of the Italian cuisine. They vary in consistency from light and delicate to hearty main meal soups. Texture is always apparent – Italians rarely serve smooth soups. Some may be partially puréed, but the identity of the ingredients is never entirely obliterated. There are regional characteristics, too. In the north, soups

are often based on rice, while in Tuscany, thick bean- or bread-based soups are popular. Tomato, garlic, and pasta soups are typical of the south. Minestrone is known world-wide, but the best-known version probably comes from Milan. However, all varieties are full of vegetables and are delicious and satisfying. Fish soups also abound in one guise or another, and most of these are village specialties, so the variety is unlimited and always tasty.

Tuscan Onion Soup

This soup is best made with white onions, which have a mild flavor. If you cannot get hold of them, try using large Spanish onions instead.

NUTRITIONAL INFORMATION

Calories	390	Sugars	.........0g
Protein	.........9g	Fat	..........33g
Carbohydrate	...15g	Saturates	......14g

5–10 MINS   40–45 MINS

SERVES 4

INGREDIENTS

2 tbsp diced pancetta ham

1 tbsp olive oil

4 large white onions, thinly sliced into rings

3 garlic cloves, chopped

3½ cups hot chicken or ham stock

4 slices ciabatta or other Italian bread

3 tbsp butter

2¾ oz Gruyère or cheddar cheese

salt and pepper

1 Dry fry the pancetta in a large saucepan for 3–4 minutes until it begins to brown. Remove the pancetta from the pan and set aside until required.

2 Add the oil to the pan and cook the onions and garlic over a high heat for 4 minutes. Reduce the heat, cover, and cook for 15 minutes, or until the onions are lightly caramelized.

3 Add the stock to the saucepan and bring to a boil. Reduce the heat and leave the mixture to simmer, covered, for about 10 minutes.

4 Toast the slices of ciabatta on both sides, under a heated broiler, for 2–3 minutes, or until golden. Spread the ciabatta with butter and top with the Gruyère or cheddar cheese. Cut the bread into bite-size pieces.

5 Add the reserved pancetta to the soup and season with salt and pepper to taste.

6 Pour into 4 soup bowls and top with the toasted bread.

COOK'S TIP

Pancetta is similar to bacon, but it is air- and salt-cured for about 6 months. Pancetta is available from most delicatessens and large supermarkets. If you cannot find pancetta use unsmoked bacon instead.

Tuscan Bean Soup

A thick and creamy soup that is based on a traditional Tuscan recipe. If you use dried beans, the preparation and cooking times will be longer.

NUTRITIONAL INFORMATION

Calories ....250 Sugars 4g
Protein ....13g Fat 10g
Carbohydrate ...29g Saturates 2g

2 MINS   10 MINS

SERVES 4

INGREDIENTS

1⅓ cups dried butter beans, soaked
overnight, or 2 x 14-oz cans butter beans

1 tbsp olive oil

2 garlic cloves, crushed

2 vegetable or chicken bouillon cubes,
  crumbled

⅔ cup milk

2 tbsp chopped fresh oregano

salt and pepper

1 If you are using dried beans that have been soaked overnight, drain them thoroughly. Bring a large pan of water to the boil, add the beans and boil for 10 minutes. Cover the pan and simmer for a further 30 minutes, or until tender. Drain the beans, reserving the cooking liquid. If you are using canned beans, drain them thoroughly and reserve the liquid.

2 Heat the oil in a large skillet and fry the garlic for 2–3 minutes, or until just beginning to brown.

3 Add the beans and 1¾ cups of the reserved liquid to the skillet, stirring. Add a little water if there is insufficient liquid. Stir in the crumbled bouillon cube. Bring the mixture to a boil and then remove the pan from the heat.

4 Place the bean mixture in a food processor and blend to form a smooth purée. Alternatively, mash the bean mixture to a smooth consistency. Season to taste with salt and pepper and stir in the milk.

5 Pour the soup back into the pan and gently heat to just below boiling point. Stir in the chopped oregano just before serving.

Pumpkin Soup

This thick, creamy soup has a wonderful, warming golden color.
It is flavored with orange and thyme.

NUTRITIONAL INFORMATION

Calories	111	Sugars	.........4g
Protein	.........2g	Fat	..........6g
Carbohydrate	....5g	Saturates	.......2g

  10 MINS · 35–40 MINS

SERVES 4

INGREDIENTS

2 tbsp olive oil

2 onions, chopped

2 garlic cloves, chopped

2 lb pumpkin, peeled and cut into
 1-inch chunks

6¼ cups vegetable or chicken stock, boiling

finely grated peel and juice of 1 orange

3 tbsp fresh thyme, stems removed

⅔ cup milk

salt and pepper

crusty bread, to serve

1 Heat the olive oil in a large saucepan. Add the onions to the pan and cook for 3–4 minutes, or until softened. Add the garlic and pumpkin and cook for a further 2 minutes, stirring well.

2 Add the boiling vegetable or chicken stock, orange peel and juice, and 2 tablespoons of the thyme to the pan. Leave to simmer, covered, for 20 minutes, or until the pumpkin is tender.

3 Place the mixture in a food processor and blend until smooth. Alternatively, mash the mixture with a potato masher until smooth. Season to taste.

4 Return the soup to the saucepan and add the milk. Reheat the soup for 3–4 minutes, or until it is piping hot but not boiling.

5 Sprinkle with the remaining fresh thyme just before serving.

6 Divide the soup between 4 warm soup bowls and serve with lots of fresh crusty bread.

COOK'S TIP

Pumpkins are usually large vegetables, so to make things a little easier, ask the greengrocer to cut a chunk off for you. Alternatively, make double the quantity and freeze the soup for up to 3 months.

Artichoke Soup

This refreshing chilled soup is ideal for *al fresco* dining. Bear in mind that this soup needs to be chilled for 3-4 hours, so allow plenty of time.

NUTRITIONAL INFORMATION

Calories	159	Sugars 2g
Protein	.........2g	Fat 15
Carbohydrate	....5g	Saturates 6g

5 MINS   15 MINS

SERVES 4

I N G R E D I E N T S

1 tbsp olive oil

1 onion, chopped

1 garlic clove, crushed

2 x 14-oz cans artichoke hearts, drained

2 ½ cups vegetable stock, hot

⅔ cup light cream

2 tbsp fresh thyme, stems removed

2 sun-dried tomatoes, cut into strips

fresh, crusty bread, to serve

1 Heat the oil in a large saucepan and fry the chopped onion and crushed garlic, stirring, for 2–3 minutes, or until just softened.

2 Using a sharp knife, roughly chop the artichoke hearts. Add the artichoke pieces to the onion and garlic mixture in the pan. Pour in the hot vegetable stock, stirring well.

3 Bring the mixture to a boil, then reduce the heat and leave to simmer, covered, for about 3 minutes.

4 Place the mixture into a food processor and blend until smooth. Alternatively, push the mixture through a strainer to remove any lumps.

5 Return the soup to the saucepan. Stir the light cream and fresh thyme into the soup.

6 Transfer the soup to a large bowl, cover, and leave to chill in the refrigerator for about 3–4 hours.

7 Transfer the chilled soup to individual soup bowls and garnish with strips of sun-dried tomato. Serve with crusty bread.

VARIATION

Add 2 tablespoons of dry vermouth, to the soup in step 5, if you wish.

Cream of Artichoke Soup

A creamy soup with the unique, subtle flavoring of Jerusalem artichokes and a garnish of grated carrots for extra crunch.

NUTRITIONAL INFORMATION

Calories 19   Sugars 0g
Protein ....0.4g   Fat 2g
Carbohydrate ...0.7g   Saturates 0.7g

10–15 MINS   55–60 MINS

SERVES 6

INGREDIENTS

1 lb 10 oz Jerusalem artichokes

1 lemon, thickly sliced

¼ cup butter or margarine

2 onions, chopped

1 garlic clove, crushed

5½ cups chicken or vegetable stock

2 bay leaves

¼ tsp ground mace or nutmeg

1 tbsp lemon juice

⅔ cup light cream or plain fromage blanc

salt and pepper

TO GARNISH

coarsely grated carrot

chopped fresh parsley or cilantro

1 Peel and slice the artichokes. Put into a bowl of water with the lemon slices.

2 Melt the butter or margarine in a large saucepan. Add the onions and garlic and fry gently for 3–4 minutes until soft but not colored.

3 Drain the artichokes (discarding the lemon) and add to the pan. Mix well and cook gently for 2–3 minutes without allowing to color.

4 Add the stock, seasoning, bay leaves, mace or nutmeg, and lemon juice. Bring slowly to a boil, then cover and simmer gently for about 30 minutes until the vegetables are very tender.

5 Discard the bay leaves. Cool the soup slightly then press through a strainer or blend in a food processor until smooth. If liked, a little of the soup may be only partially puréed and added to the rest of the puréed soup, to give extra texture.

6 Pour into a clean pan and bring to a boil. Adjust the seasoning and stir in the cream or fromage blanc. Reheat gently without boiling. Garnish with grated carrot and chopped parsley or cilantro.

Spinach & Mascarpone Soup

Spinach is the basis for this delicious soup, but use sorrel or watercress instead for a pleasant change.

NUTRITIONAL INFORMATION

Calories 537	Sugars 2g	
Protein 6g	Fat 53g	
Carbohydrate 9g	Saturates 29g	

    5 MINS   35 MINS

SERVES 4

INGREDIENTS

¼ cup butter

1 bunch scallions, trimmed and chopped

2 celery stalks, chopped

3 cups spinach or sorrel, or 3 bunches
   watercress

3 ½ cups vegetable stock

mascarpone cheese

1 tbsp olive oil

2 slices thickly cut bread, cut into cubes

½ tsp caraway seeds

salt and pepper

sesame bread sticks, to serve

1 Melt half the butter in a very large saucepan. Add the scallions and celery and cook gently for about 5 minutes, or until softened.

2 Pack the spinach, sorrel, or watercress into the saucepan. Add the vegetable stock and bring to a boil, then reduce the heat and simmer, covered, for 15–20 minutes.

3 Transfer the soup to a blender or food processor and blend until smooth, or pass through a strainer. Return to the saucepan.

4 Add the mascarpone cheese to the soup and heat gently, stirring, until smooth and blended. Taste and season with salt and pepper.

5 Heat the remaining butter with the oil in a skillet. Add the bread cubes and fry in the hot oil until golden brown, adding the caraway seeds toward the end of cooking, so they do not burn.

6 Ladle the soup into 4 warm bowls. Sprinkle with the croûtons and serve at once, accompanied by the sesame bread sticks.

VARIATIONS

Any leafy vegetable can be used to make this soup to give variations to the flavor. For anyone who grows their own vegetables, it is the perfect recipe for experimenting with a glut of produce. Try young beet leaves or surplus lettuces for a change.

Calabrian Mushroom Soup

The Calabrian mountains in southern Italy provide large amounts of wild mushrooms that are rich in flavor and color.

NUTRITIONAL INFORMATION

Calories 452   Sugars 5g
Protein . . . . .15g   Fat 26g
Carbohydrate . . .42g   Saturates 12g

  5 MINS 25–30 MINS

SERVES 4

I N G R E D I E N T S

2 tbsp olive oil

1 onion, chopped

1 lb mixed mushrooms, such as ceps,
   oyster, and button

1¼ cups milk

3¾ cups vegetable stock, hot

8 slices of rustic bread or French bread

2 garlic cloves, crushed

3 tbsp butter, melted

2 ¾ oz finely grated Gruyère cheese

salt and pepper

  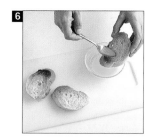

1 Heat the oil in a large skillet and cook the onion for 3–4 minutes, or until soft and golden.

2 Wipe each mushroom with a damp cloth and cut any large mushrooms into smaller, bite-size pieces.

3 Add the mushrooms to the pan, stirring quickly to coat them in the oil.

4 Add the milk to the pan, bring to a boil, cover, and leave to simmer for about 5 minutes. Gradually stir in the hot vegetable stock and season with salt and pepper to taste.

5 Under a preheated broiler, toast the bread on both sides until golden.

6 Mix together the garlic and butter and spoon generously over the toast.

7 Place the toast in the bottom of a large tureen or divide it between 4 individual serving bowls and pour the hot soup over. Top with the grated Gruyère cheese and serve at once.

COOK'S TIP

Mushrooms absorb liquid, which can lessen the flavor and affect cooking properties. Therefore, carefully wipe them with a damp cloth rather than rinsing them in water.

Green Soup

This fresh-tasting soup with green beans, cucumber, and watercress can be served warm or chilled on a hot summer day.

NUTRITIONAL INFORMATION

Calories 121   Sugars 2g
Protein . . . . .2g   Fat 8g
Carbohydrate . . .10g   Saturates 1g

    5 MINS   🕐 25–30 MINS

SERVES 4

I N G R E D I E N T S

1 tbsp olive oil

1 onion, chopped

1 garlic clove, chopped

1½ cups peeled potato, cut into 1-inch
   cubes

scant 3 cups vegetable or chicken stock

1 small cucumber or ½ large cucumber, cut
   into chunks

3 oz bunch watercress

4½ oz green beans, trimmed and halved
   lengthwise

salt and pepper

VARIATION

Use 4½ oz snow peas
instead of the green
beans, if you prefer.

1 Heat the oil in a large pan and fry the onion and garlic for 3–4 minutes, or until softened.

2 Add the cubed potato and fry for a further 2–3 minutes.

3 Stir in the stock, bring to a boil, and leave to simmer for 5 minutes.

4 Add the cucumber to the pan and cook for a further 3 minutes, or until the potatoes are tender. Test by inserting the tip of a knife into the potato cubes – it should pass through easily.

5 Add the watercress and leave it to wilt. Then place the soup in a food processor and blend until smooth. Alternatively, before adding the watercress, mash the soup with a potato masher and push through a strainer, then chop the watercress finely and stir into the soup.

6 Bring a small pan of water to a boil and steam the beans for 3–4 minutes, or until tender.

7 Add the beans to the soup, season, and warm through.

Red Bean Soup

Beans feature widely in Italian soups, making them hearty and tasty. The beans need to be soaked overnight, so begin this well in advance.

NUTRITIONAL INFORMATION

Calories	184	Sugars	.........5g
Protein	.........4g	Fat	...........11g
Carbohydrate	...19g	Saturates	.......2g

5–10 MINS   3¾ HOURS

SERVES 6

INGREDIENTS

scant 1 cup dried red kidney beans, soaked overnight

7½ cups water

1 large ham bone or bacon knuckle

2 carrots, chopped

1 large onion, chopped

2 celery stalks, thinly sliced

1 leek, trimmed, washed, and sliced

1 or 2 bay leaves

2 tbsp olive oil

2–3 tomatoes, peeled and chopped

1 garlic clove, crushed

1 tbsp tomato paste

4½ tbsp arborio or other Italian rice

1½–2 cups finely shredded green cabbage

salt and pepper

1 Drain the beans and place them in a saucepan with enough water to cover. Bring to a boil, and boil for 15 minutes to remove any harmful toxins. Reduce the heat and simmer for 45 minutes.

2 Drain the beans and put into a clean saucepan with the water, ham bone or knuckle, carrots, onion, celery, leek, bay leaves, and olive oil. Bring to a boil, then cover and simmer for 1 hour, or until the beans are very tender.

3 Discard the bay leaves and bone, reserving any ham pieces from the bone. Remove a small cupful of the beans and reserve. Purée the soup in a food processor or blender, or push through a coarse strainer, then return to a clean pan.

4 Add the tomatoes, garlic, tomato paste, rice, and seasonings. Bring back to a boil and simmer for about 15 minutes, or until the rice is tender.

5 Add the cabbage and reserved beans and ham, and continue to simmer for 5 minutes. Adjust the seasoning and serve very hot. If liked, a piece of toasted crusty bread may be put in the base of each soup bowl before ladling in the soup. If the soup is too thick, add a little boiling water or stock.

Vegetable & Bean Soup

This wonderful combination of cannellini beans, vegetables, and vermicelli is made even richer by the addition of pesto and dried mushrooms.

NUTRITIONAL INFORMATION

Calories 294	Sugars 2g
Protein 11g	Fat 16g
Carbohydrate ...30g	Saturates 2g

🍲 30 MINS   🕐 30 MINS

SERVES 4

I N G R E D I E N T S

1 small eggplant

2 large tomatoes

1 potato, peeled

1 carrot, peeled

1 leek

15-oz can cannellini beans

3¾ cups vegetable or chicken stock, hot

2 tsp dried basil

½ oz dried porcini mushrooms, soaked for
   10 minutes in enough warm water to
   cover

1¾ oz vermicelli

3 tbsp pesto (see page 31 or use bought)

freshly grated Parmesan cheese, to serve
   (optional)

1 Slice the eggplant into rings about ½ inch thick, then cut each ring into 4.

2 Cut the tomatoes and potato into small dice. Cut the carrot into sticks, about 1 inch long and cut the leek into rings.

3 Place the cannellini beans and their liquid in a large saucepan. Add the eggplant, tomatoes, potatoes, carrot, and leek, stirring to mix.

4 Add the stock to the pan and bring to a boil. Reduce the heat and leave to simmer for 15 minutes.

5 Add the basil, dried mushrooms and their soaking liquid, and the vermicelli and simmer for 5 minutes, or until all of the vegetables are tender.

6 Remove the pan from the heat and stir in the pesto.

7 Serve with freshly grated Parmesan cheese, if using.

Garbanzo Bean Soup

A thick vegetable soup which is a delicious meal in itself. Serve with Parmesan cheese and warm sun-dried-tomato-flavored ciabatta bread.

NUTRITIONAL INFORMATION

Calories 297	Sugars 0g	
Protein 11g	Fat 18g	
Carbohydrate ...24g	Saturates 2g	

5 MINS · 15 MINS

SERVES 4

INGREDIENTS

2 tbsp olive oil

2 leeks, sliced

2 zucchini, diced

2 garlic cloves, crushed

2 x 14-oz cans chopped tomatoes

1 tbsp tomato paste

1 fresh bay leaf

3¾ cups chicken stock

14-oz can garbanzo beans, drained and rinsed

8 oz spinach

salt and pepper

TO SERVE

Parmesan cheese

sun-dried tomato bread

COOK'S TIP

Garbanzo beans are used extensively in North African cuisine and are also found in Italian, Spanish, Middle Eastern, and Indian cooking. They have a deliciously nutty flavor with a firm texture and are an excellent canned product.

1 Heat the oil in a large saucepan. Add the leeks and zucchini and cook briskly for 5 minutes, stirring constantly.

2 Add the garlic, tomatoes, tomato paste, bay leaf, stock, and garbanzo beans. Bring to a boil and simmer for 5 minutes.

3 Shred the spinach finely, add to the soup, and cook for 2 minutes. Season.

4 Remove the bay leaf from the soup and discard.

5 Serve the soup with freshly grated Parmesan cheese and sun-dried-tomato bread.

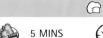

Potato & Pesto Soup

Fresh pesto is a treat to the taste buds and very different in flavor from that available from supermarkets. Store fresh pesto in the refrigerator.

NUTRITIONAL INFORMATION

Calories	548	Sugars	.........0g
Protein	........11g	Fat	..........52g
Carbohydrate	...10g	Saturates	......18g

5–10 MINS   50 MINS

SERVES 4

I N G R E D I E N T S

3 slices smoked, fatty bacon

1 lb floury potatoes

1 lb onions

2 tbsp olive oil

2 tbsp butter

2 ½ cups chicken stock

2 ½ cups milk

¾ cup dried conchigliette

⅔ cup heavy cream

chopped fresh parsley

salt and pepper

freshly grated Parmesan cheese and garlic
    bread, to serve

P E S T O   S A U C E

1 cup finely chopped fresh parsley

2 garlic cloves, crushed

⅔ cup pine kernels, crushed

2 tbsp chopped fresh basil leaves

⅔ cup freshly grated Parmesan cheese

white pepper

⅔ cup olive oil

1 To make the pesto sauce, put all of the ingredients in a blender or food processor and process for 2 minutes, or blend by hand using a mortar and pestle.

2 Finely chop the bacon, potatoes, and onions. Fry the bacon in a large pan over a medium heat for 4 minutes. Add the butter, potatoes, and onions and cook for 12 minutes, stirring constantly.

3 Add the stock and milk to the pan. Bring to the boil and simmer for 10 minutes. Add the conchigliette and simmer for a further 10-12 minutes.

4 Stir in the cream and simmer for 5 minutes. Add the parsley, salt and pepper, and 2 tbsp pesto sauce. Transfer the soup to serving bowls and serve with Parmesan cheese and fresh garlic bread.

Creamy Tomato Soup

This quick-and-easy creamy soup has a fresh tomato flavor. Basil leaves complement tomatoes perfectly.

NUTRITIONAL INFORMATION

Calories . . . . .218 Sugars 10g

Protein . . . . .3g Fat 19g

Carbohydrate . . .10g Saturates 11g

 5 MINS   25–30 MINS

SERVES 4

INGREDIENTS

3 tbsp butter

1 lb 9 oz ripe tomatoes, preferably plum, roughly chopped

3 ¾ hot vegetable stock

¼ cup ground, blanched almonds

⅔ cup milk or light cream

1 tsp sugar

2 tbsp shredded basil leaves

salt and pepper

1 Melt the butter in a large saucepan. Add the tomatoes and cook for 5 minutes until the skins start to wrinkle. Season to taste with salt and pepper.

2 Add the stock to the pan, bring to a boil, cover and simmer for 10 minutes.

3 Meanwhile, under a heated broiler, lightly toast the ground almonds until they are golden brown. This will take only 1-2 minutes, so watch them closely.

4 Remove the soup from the heat and place in a food processor and blend the mixture to form a smooth consistency. Alternatively, mash the soup with a potato masher until smooth.

5 Pass the soup through a strainer to remove any tomato skin or seeds.

6 Place the soup in the pan and return to the heat. Stir in the milk or cream, toasted ground almonds, and sugar. Warm the soup through and add the shredded basil leaves just before serving.

7 Transfer the creamy tomato soup to warm soup bowls and serve hot.

COOK'S TIP

Very fine bread crumbs can be used instead of the ground almonds, if you prefer. Toast them in the same way as the almonds and add with the milk or cream in step 6.

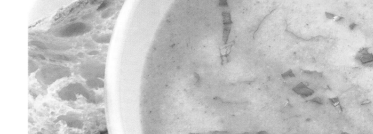

Minestrone Soup

Minestrone translates as "big soup" in Italian. It is made all over Italy, but this version comes from Livorno, a port on the western coast.

NUTRITIONAL INFORMATION

Calories	311	Sugars	.........8g
Protein	........12g	Fat	..........19g
Carbohydrate	...26g	Saturates	.......5g

 10 MINS   30 MINS

SERVES 4

I N G R E D I E N T S

1 tbsp olive oil

¾ cup diced pancetta ham

2 onions, chopped

2 garlic cloves, crushed

1 potato, peeled and cut into ½-inch cubes

1 carrot, peeled and cut into chunks

1 leek, sliced into rings

¼ green cabbage, shredded

1 celery stalk, chopped

1 lb canned chopped tomatoes

7-oz can small navy beans, drained and
    rinsed

2½ cups hot ham or chicken stock, diluted
with 2½ cups boiling water

bouquet garni (2 bay leaves, 2 sprigs
    rosemary, and 2 sprigs thyme, tied
    together)

salt and pepper

freshly grated Parmesan cheese, to serve

1 Heat the olive oil in a large saucepan. Add the diced pancetta, chopped onions, and garlic and fry for about 5 minutes, stirring, or until the onions are soft and golden.

2 Add the prepared potato, carrot, leek, cabbage, and celery to the saucepan. Cook for a further 2 minutes, stirring frequently, to coat all of the vegetables in the oil.

3 Add the tomatoes, small navy beans, hot ham or chicken stock, and bouquet garni to the pan, stirring to mix. Leave the soup to simmer, covered, for 15–20 minutes, or until all of the vegetables are just tender.

4 Remove the bouquet garni, season with salt and pepper to taste, and serve with plenty of freshly grated Parmesan cheese.

Tomato & Pasta Soup

Plum tomatoes are ideal for making soups and sauces because they have denser, less watery flesh than rounder varieties.

NUTRITIONAL INFORMATION

Calories 503	Sugars 16g
Protein 9g	Fat 28g
Carbohydrate ...59g	Saturates 17g

5 MINS   50–55 MINS

SERVES 4

I N G R E D I E N T S

4 tbsp unsalted butter

1 large onion, chopped

2 ½ cups vegetable stock

2 lb Italian plum tomatoes, skinned and
  roughly chopped

pinch of baking soda

2 cups dried fusilli

1 tbsp sugar

⅔ cup heavy cream

salt and pepper

fresh basil leaves, to garnish

1 Melt the butter in a large pan. Add the onion and fry for 3 minutes, stirring. Add 1¼ cups of vegetable stock to the pan, with the chopped tomatoes and

VARIATION

To make orange and tomato soup, simply use half the quantity of vegetable stock, topped up with the same amount of fresh orange juice, and garnish the soup with orange peel.

 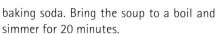 

baking soda. Bring the soup to a boil and simmer for 20 minutes.

2 Remove the pan from the heat and set aside to cool. Purée the soup in a blender or food processor and pour through a fine strainer back into the rinsed saucepan.

3 Add the remaining vegetable stock and the fusilli to the pan, and season to taste with salt and pepper.

4 Add the sugar to the pan, bring to the boil, then lower the heat and simmer for about 15 minutes.

5 Pour the soup into a warm tureen, swirl the heavy cream around the surface of the soup and garnish with fresh basil leaves. Serve immediately.

Brown Lentil & Pasta Soup

In Italy, this soup is called *Minestrade Lentiche*. A *minestra* is a soup cooked with pasta; here, farfalline, a small bow-shaped variety, is used.

NUTRITIONAL INFORMATION

Calories ....225 Sugars 1g
Protein ....13g Fat 8g
Carbohydrate ...27g Saturates 3g

 5 MINS   25 MINS

SERVES 4

INGREDIENTS

4 slices streaky bacon, cut into small
  squares

1 onion, chopped

2 garlic cloves, crushed

2 stalks celery, chopped

2 oz farfalline or spaghetti, broken into
  small pieces

14-oz can brown lentils, drained

5 cups ham or vegetable stock, hot

2 tbsp chopped, fresh mint

1 Place the bacon in a large skillet together with the onions, garlic, and celery. Dry fry for 4–5 minutes, stirring, until the onion is tender and the bacon is just beginning to brown.

COOK'S TIP

If you prefer to use dried lentils, add the stock before the pasta and cook for 1–1¼ hours until the lentils are tender. Add the pasta and cook for a further 12–15 minutes.

2 Add the pasta to the skillet and cook, stirring, for about 1 minute to coat the pasta in the oil.

3 Add the lentils and the stock and bring to a boil. Reduce the heat and leave to simmer for 12–15 minutes, or until the pasta is tender.

4 Remove the skillet from the heat and stir in the chopped fresh mint.

5 Transfer the soup to warm soup bowls and serve immeditely.

Minestrone & Pasta Soup

Italian cooks have created many very heart-warming soups and this is the best known of all.

NUTRITIONAL INFORMATION

Calories 231   Sugars 3g
Protein . . . . .8g   Fat 16g
Carbohydrate . . .14g   Saturates 7g

10 MINS   1¾ HOURS

SERVES 10

I N G R E D I E N T S

3 garlic cloves

3 large onions

2 celery stalks

2 large carrots

2 large potatoes

3 ½ oz green beans

3 ½ oz zucchini

4 tbsp butter

¼ cup olive oil

⅓ cup fatty bacon, finely diced

7 cups vegetable or chicken stock

1 bunch fresh basil, finely chopped

½ cup chopped tomatoes

2 tbsp tomato paste

3 ½ oz Parmesan cheese rind

3 oz dried spaghetti, broken up

salt and pepper

freshly grated Parmesan cheese, to serve

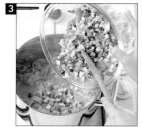

1 Finely chop the garlic, onions, celery, carrots, potatoes, beans, and zucchini.

2 Heat the butter and oil together in a large saucepan. Add the bacon and cook for 2 minutes.

3 Add the garlic and onion and fry for 2 minutes, then stir in the celery, carrots, and potatoes and fry for a further 2 minutes.

4 Add the beans to the pan and fry for 2 minutes. Stir in the zucchini and fry for a further 2 minutes. Cover the pan and cook all the vegetables, stirring frequently, for 15 minutes.

5 Add the stock, basil, tomatoes, tomato paste and cheese rind and season to taste. Bring to a boil, lower the heat and simmer for 1 hour. Remove and discard the cheese rind.

6 Add the spaghetti to the pan and cook for 20 minutes. Serve in large, warm soup bowls; sprinkle with freshly grated Parmesan cheese.

Bean & Pasta Soup

A dish with proud Mediterranean origins, this soup is a winter warmer.
Serve with warm, crusty bread and, if you like, a slice of cheese.

NUTRITIONAL INFORMATION

Calories 463	Sugars 5g
Protein 13g	Fat 33g
Carbohydrate . . .30g	Saturates 7g

5–10 MINS   1¼ HOURS

SERVES 4

I N G R E D I E N T S

1⅓ cup dried navy beans, soaked, drained,
   and rinsed

4 tbsp olive oil

2 large onions, sliced

3 garlic cloves, chopped

14-oz can chopped tomatoes

1 tsp dried oregano

1 tsp tomato paste

3½ cups water

3 oz small pasta shapes, such as fusilli
   or conchigliette

1 cup sun-dried tomatoes, drained and
   sliced thinly

1 tbsp chopped cilantro or flat-leaf parsley

2 tbsp freshly grated Parmesan cheese

salt and pepper

1 Put the soaked beans into a large pan,
cover with cold water, and bring them
to a boil. Boil rapidly for 15 minutes to
remove any harmful toxins; drain in a
colander.

2 Heat the oil in a pan over a medium
heat and fry the onions until they are
just beginning to change color. Stir in the
garlic and cook for 1 further minute. Stir

in the chopped tomatoes, oregano, and
the tomato paste and pour in the water.
Add the beans, bring to a boil and cover
the pan. Simmer for 45 minutes, or until
the beans are almost tender.

3 Add the pasta, season the soup with
salt and pepper to taste, and stir in
the sun-dried tomatoes. Return the soup

to the boil, partly cover the pan, and
continue cooking for 10 minutes, or until
the pasta is nearly tender.

4 Stir in the chopped cilantro or parsley.
Taste the soup and adjust the
seasoning, if necessary. Transfer to a warm
soup tureen to serve. Sprinkle with the
cheese and serve hot.

Ravioli alla Parmigiana

This soup is traditionally served at Easter and Christmas in the province of Parma.

NUTRITIONAL INFORMATION

Calories	554	Sugars	.........3g
Protein	........26g	Fat	..........24g
Carbohydrate	...64g	Saturates	.......9g

4½–5 HOURS | 25 MINS

SERVES 4

INGREDIENTS

10 oz basic pasta dough

5 cups veal stock

freshly grated Parmesan cheese, to serve

FILLING

½ cup Espagnole Sauce (see page 15)

1 cup freshly grated Parmesan cheese

1⅔ cup fine white bread crumbs

2 eggs

1 small onion, finely chopped

1 tsp freshly grated nutmeg

1 Make the basic pasta dough and the Espagnole Sauce (see page 15).

2 Carefully roll out 2 sheets of the pasta dough and cover with a damp dish cloth while you make the filling for the ravioli.

3 To make the filling, place the freshly grated Parmesan cheese, fine white bread crumbs, eggs, Espagnole Sauce, finely chopped onion, and the freshly grated nutmeg in a large mixing bowl, and mix together well.

4 Place spoonfuls of the filling at regular intervals on 1 sheet of pasta dough. Cover with the second sheet of pasta dough, then cut into squares and seal the edges.

5 Bring the veal stock to the boil in a large saucepan.

6 Add the ravioli to the pan and cook for about 15 minutes.

7 Transfer the soup and ravioli to warm serving bowls and serve, generously sprinkled with Parmesan cheese.

COOK'S TIP

It is advisable to prepare the basic pasta dough and the Espagnole Sauce (see page 15) well in advance, or buy them if you are short of time.

Lemon & Chicken Soup

This delicately flavored summer soup is surprisingly easy to make, and tastes delicious.

NUTRITIONAL INFORMATION

Calories	506	Sugars	.........4g
Protein	........19g	Fat	..........31g
Carbohydrate	...41g	Saturates	......19g

5–10 MINS   1¼ HOURS

SERVES 4

I N G R E D I E N T S

4 tbsp butter

8 shallots, thinly sliced

2 carrots, thinly sliced

2 celery stalks, thinly sliced

8 oz boned chicken breasts, finely chopped

3 lemons

5 cups chicken stock

8 oz dried spaghetti, broken into small
   pieces

⅔ cup heavy cream

salt and white pepper

T O   G A R N I S H

fresh parsley sprig

3 lemon slices, halved

COOK'S TIP

You can prepare this soup up to the end of step 3 in advance, so all you need do before serving is heat it through before adding the pasta and the finishing touches.

1 Melt the butter in a large saucepan. Add the shallots, carrots, celery, and chicken and cook over a low heat, stirring occasionally, for 8 minutes.

2 Thinly pare the lemons and blanch the lemon peel in boiling water for 3 minutes. Squeeze the juice from the lemons.

3 Add the lemon peel and juice to the pan, together with the chicken stock. Bring slowly to a boil over a low heat and simmer for 40 minutes, stirring occasionally.

4 Add the spaghetti to the pan and cook for 15 minutes. Season to taste with salt and white pepper and add the cream. Heat through, but do not allow the soup to boil or it will curdle.

5 Pour the soup into a tureen or individual bowls, garnish with the parsley and half slices of lemon and serve immediately.

Chicken & Pasta Broth

This satisfying soup makes a good lunch or supper dish and you can use any vegetables you like. Children will love the tiny pasta shapes.

NUTRITIONAL INFORMATION

Calories	185	Sugars	.........5g
Protein	........17g	Fat	...........5g
Carbohydrate	...20g	Saturates	.......1g

🍲 5 MINS   🕐 15-20 MINS

SERVES 6

INGREDIENTS

12 oz boneless chicken breast meat

2 tbsp sunflower oil

1 onion, diced

1½ cups diced carrots

9 oz cauliflower flowerets

3¾ cups chicken stock

2 tsp Italian seasoning

4 oz small pasta shapes

salt and pepper

Parmesan cheese (optional) and crusty
   bread, to serve

1 Using a sharp knife, finely dice the chicken, discarding any skin.

2 Heat the oil in a large saucepan and quickly sauté the chicken, onion, carrots, and cauliflower until they are lightly colored.

3 Stir in the chicken stock and Italian seasoning and bring to a boil.

4 Add the pasta shapes to the pan and return to a boil. Cover the pan and leave the broth to simmer for 10 minutes, stirring occasionally to prevent the pasta shapes from sticking together.

5 Season the broth with salt and pepper to taste and sprinkle with Parmesan cheese, if using. Serve the broth with fresh crusty bread.

COOK'S TIP

You can use any small pasta shapes for this soup – try conchigliette or ditalini, or even spaghetti broken up into small pieces. To make a fun soup for children add animal-shaped or alphabet pasta.

Chicken & Bean Soup

This hearty and nourishing soup, combining garbanzo beans and chicken, is an ideal first course for a family supper.

NUTRITIONAL INFORMATION

Calories	347	Sugars	.........2g
Protein	........28g	Fat	...........11g
Carbohydrate	...37g	Saturates	.......4g

5 MINS   1¾ HOURS

SERVES 4

INGREDIENTS

2 tbsp butter

3 scallions, chopped

2 garlic cloves, crushed

1 fresh marjoram sprig, finely chopped

2 cups diced, boned chicken breasts

5 cups chicken stock

12-oz can garbanzo beans, drained

1 bouquet garni

1 red bell pepper, diced

1 green bell pepper, diced

1 cup small dried pasta shapes, such as
  elbow macaroni

salt and white pepper

croûtons, to serve

COOK'S TIP

If you prefer, use dried garbanzo beans. Cover with cold water and set aside to soak for 5–8 hours. Drain and add the beans to the soup, according to the recipe, and allow an additional 30 minutes–1 hour cooking time.

1 Melt the butter in a large saucepan. Add the scallions, garlic, sprig of fresh marjoram, and the diced chicken and cook, stirring frequently, over a medium heat for 5 minutes.

2 Add the chicken stock, garbanzo beans, and bouquet garni and season with salt and white pepper.

3 Bring the soup to a boil, lower the heat, and simmer for about 2 hours.

4 Add the diced bell peppers and pasta to the pan, then simmer for a further 20 minutes.

5 Transfer the soup to a warm tureen. To serve, ladle the soup into individual serving bowls and serve immediately, garnished with the croûtons.

Tuscan Veal Broth

Veal plays an important role in Italian cuisine and there are dozens of recipes for all cuts of this meat.

NUTRITIONAL INFORMATION

Calories	420	Sugars	.........5g
Protein	........54g	Fat	...........7g
Carbohydrate	...37g	Saturates	.......2g

 2¼ HOURS 4¾ HOURS

SERVES 4

INGREDIENTS

⅓ cup dried peas, soaked for 2 hours and
   drained

2 lb boned neck of veal, diced

5 cups beef or brown stock (see Cook's Tip)

2½ cups water

⅓ cup barley, washed

1 large carrot, diced

1 cup diced turnip

1 large leek, thinly sliced

1 red onion, finely chopped

¾ cup chopped tomatoes

1 fresh basil sprig

3½ oz dried vermicelli

salt and white pepper

1 Put the peas, veal, stock, and water into a large pan and bring to a boil over a low heat. Using a draining spoon, skim off any scum that rises to the surface.

2 When all of the scum has been removed, add the barley and a pinch of salt to the mixture. Simmer gently over a low heat for 25 minutes.

3 Add the carrot, turnip, leek, onion, tomatoes, and basil to the pan, and season with salt and pepper to taste. Leave to simmer for about 2 hours, skimming the surface from time to time to remove any scum. Remove the pan from the heat and set aside for 2 hours.

4 Set the pan over a medium heat and bring to a boil. Add the vermicelli and cook for 12 minutes. Season with salt and pepper to taste; remove and discard the basil. Ladle into soup bowls and serve immediately.

COOK'S TIP

The best brown stock is made with veal bones and shin of beef roasted with drippings in the oven for 40 minutes. Transfer the bones to a pan and add sliced leeks, onion, celery, and carrots, a bouquet garni, white wine vinegar, and a thyme sprig and cover with cold water. Simmer over a very low heat for 3 hours; strain before use.

Veal & Wild Mushroom Soup

Wild mushrooms are available commercially and an increasing range of cultivated varieties is now sold in many supermarkets.

NUTRITIONAL INFORMATION

Calories 413   Sugars 3g
Protein . . . . .28g   Fat 22g
Carbohydrate . . .28g   Saturates 12g

5 MINS   3¼ HOURS

SERVES 4

I N G R E D I E N T S

1 lb veal, thinly sliced

1 lb veal bones

5 cups water

1 small onion

6 peppercorns

1 tsp cloves

pinch of mace

2 cups roughly chopped oyster and shiitake
  mushrooms

⅔ cup heavy cream

3½ oz dried vermicelli

1 tbsp cornstarch

3 tbsp milk

salt and pepper

1 Put the veal, bones, and water into a large saucepan. Bring to a boil and lower the heat. Add the onion, peppercorns, cloves, and mace and simmer for about 3 hours, until the veal stock is reduced by one-third.

2 Strain the stock, skim off any fat on the surface with a draining spoon, and pour the stock into a clean saucepan. Add the veal meat to the pan.

3 Add the mushrooms and cream, bring to a boil over a low heat and then leave to simmer for 12 minutes, stirring occasionally.

4 Meanwhile, cook the vermicelli in lightly salted boiling water for 10 minutes, or until tender, but still firm to the bite. Drain and keep warm.

5 Mix the cornstarch and milk to form a smooth paste. Stir into the soup to thicken. Season to taste with salt and pepper and just before serving, add the vermicelli. Transfer the soup to a warm tureen and serve immediately.

COOK'S TIP

Make this soup with the more inexpensive cuts of veal, such as breast or neck slices. These are lean and the long cooking time insures that the meat is really tender.

Veal & Ham Soup

Veal and ham is a classic combination, complemented here with the addition of sherry to create a richly flavored Italian soup.

NUTRITIONAL INFORMATION

Calories 501   Sugars 10g
Protein . . . . .38g   Fat 18g
Carbohydrate . . .28g   Saturates 10g

 5 MINS   3¼ HOURS

SERVES 4

INGREDIENTS

4 tbsp butter

1 onion, diced

1 carrot, diced

1 celery stalk, diced

1 lb veal, very thinly sliced

1 lb ham, thinly sliced

½ cup all-purpose flour

4½ cups beef stock

1 bay leaf

8 black peppercorns

pinch of salt

3 tbsp red-currant jelly

⅔ cup cream sherry

3 ½ oz dried vermicelli

garlic croutons (see Cook's Tip), to serve

1 Melt the butter in a large pan. Add the onions, carrot, celery, veal, and ham and cook over a low heat for 6 minutes.

2 Sprinkle over the flour and cook, stirring constantly, for a further 2 minutes. Gradually stir in the stock, then add the bay leaf, peppercorns, and salt. Bring to a boil and simmer for 1 hour.

3 Remove the pan from the heat and add the red-currant jelly and cream sherry, stirring to combine. Set aside for about 4 hours.

4 Remove the bay leaf from the pan and discard. Reheat the soup over a very low heat until warmed through.

5 Meanwhile, cook the vermicelli in a saucepan of lightly salted boiling water for 10-12 minutes. Stir the vermicelli into the soup and transfer to soup bowls. Serve with garlic croûtons.

COOK'S TIP

To make garlic croûtons, remove the crusts from 3 slices of day-old white bread. Cut the bread into ¼-inch cubes. Heat 3 tbsp oil over a low heat and stir-fry 1–2 chopped garlic cloves for 1–2 minutes. Remove the garlic and add the bread. Cook, stirring frequently, until golden. Remove with a draining spoon.

Fish Soup

There are many varieties of fish soup in Italy, some including shellfish. This one, from Tuscany, is more like a chowder.

NUTRITIONAL INFORMATION

Calories	305	Sugars	.........3g
Protein	........47g	Fat	...........7g
Carbohydrate	....11g	Saturates	.......1g

5–10 MINS   1 HOUR

SERVES 6

INGREDIENTS

2 lb 4 oz assorted prepared fish (including
   mixed fish fillets, squid, and so on.)

2 onions, thinly sliced

2 celery stalks, thinly sliced

a few sprigs of parsley

2 bay leaves

⅔ cup white wine

4½ cups water

2 tbsp olive oil

1 garlic clove, crushed

1 carrot, finely chopped

14-oz can peeled tomatoes, puréed

2 potatoes, chopped

1 tbsp tomato paste

1 tsp chopped fresh oregano, or ½ tsp
   dried oregano

12 oz fresh mussels

6 oz peeled shrimp

2 tbsp chopped fresh parsley

salt and pepper

crusty bread, to serve

1 Cut the fish into slices and put into a pan with half the onion and celery, the parsley, bay leaves, wine, and water. Bring to a boil, cover and simmer for 25 minutes.

2 Strain the fish stock and discard the vegetables. Skin the fish, remove any bones and reserve.

3 Heat the oil in a pan. Fry the remaining onion and celery with the garlic and carrot until soft but not colored, stirring occasionally. Add the puréed canned tomatoes, potatoes, tomato paste, oregano, reserved stock and seasoning. Bring to a boil and simmer for about 15 minutes, or until the potato is almost tender.

4 Meanwhile, thoroughly scrub the mussels. Add the mussels to the pan with the shrimp and leave to simmer for about 5 minutes, or until the mussels have opened; discard any that remain closed.

5 Return the fish to the soup with the chopped parsley, bring back to a boil, and simmer for 5 minutes. Adjust the seasoning.

6 Serve the soup in warmed bowls with chunks of fresh crusty bread, or put a toasted slice of crusty bread in the bottom of each bowl before adding the soup. If possible, remove a few half shells from the mussels before serving.

Mussel & Potato Soup

This quick-and-easy soup makes a delicious summer lunch, especially when served with fresh crusty bread.

NUTRITIONAL INFORMATION

Calories	804	Sugars	.........3g
Protein	........17g	Fat	..........68g
Carbohydrate	...32g	Saturates	......38g

10 MINS   35 MINS

SERVES 4

INGREDIENTS

1 lb 10 oz mussels

2 tbsp olive oil

7 tbsp unsalted butter

2 slices fatty bacon, chopped

1 onion, chopped

2 garlic cloves, crushed

½ cup all-purpose flour

3 cups thinly sliced potatoes

3½ oz dried conchigliette

1¼ cups heavy cream

1 tbsp lemon juice

2 egg yolks

salt and pepper

TO GARNISH

2 tbsp finely chopped fresh parsley

lemon wedges

1 Debeard the mussels and scrub them under cold water for 5 minutes. Discard any mussels that do not close immediately when sharply tapped.

2 Bring a large pan of water to a boil, add the mussels, oil, and a little pepper. Cook until the mussels open. Discard any mussels that remain closed.

3 Drain the mussels, reserving the cooking liquid. Remove the mussels from their shells.

4 Melt the butter in a large saucepan, add the bacon, onion, and garlic and cook for 4 minutes. Carefully stir in the flour. Measure 5 cups of the reserved cooking liquid and stir it into the pan.

5 Add the potatoes to the pan and simmer for 5 minutes. Add the conchigliette and simmer for a further 10 minutes.

6 Add the cream and lemon juice and season to taste with salt and pepper. Add the mussels to the pan.

7 Blend the egg yolks with 1-2 tbsp of the remaining cooking liquid, stir into the pan, and cook for 4 minutes.

8 Ladle the soup into 4 warm individual soup bowls, garnish with the chopped fresh parsley and lemon wedges. Serve immediately.

Italian Fish Stew

This robust stew is full of Mediterranean flavors. If you do not want to prepare the fish yourself, ask your local fishmonger to do it for you.

NUTRITIONAL INFORMATION

Calories . . . . . . .236 Sugars 4g
Protein . . . . .20g Fat 7g
Carbohydrate . . .25g Saturates 1g

5–10 MINS   25 MINS

SERVES 4

I N G R E D I E N T S

2 tbsp olive oil

2 red onions, finely chopped

1 garlic clove, crushed

2 zucchini, sliced

14-oz can chopped tomatoes

3½ cups fish or vegetable stock

3 oz dried pasta shapes

12 oz firm white fish, such as cod, haddock,
    or hake

1 tbsp chopped fresh basil or oregano, or
    1 tsp dried oregano

1 tsp grated lemon peel

1 tbsp cornstarch

1 tbsp water

salt and pepper

sprigs of fresh basil or oregano, to garnish

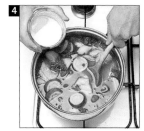

1 Heat the oil in a large saucepan and fry the onions and garlic for 5 minutes. Add the zucchini and cook for 2–3 minutes, stirring often.

2 Add the tomatoes and stock to the saucepan and bring to a boil. Add the pasta, cover, and reduce the heat. Simmer for 5 minutes.

3 Skin and bone the fish, then cut it into chunks. Add to the saucepan with the basil or oregano and lemon peel and cook gently for 5 minutes until the fish is opaque and flakes easily; take care not to overcook it.

4 Blend the cornstarch with the water and stir into the stew. Cook gently for 2 minutes, stirring, until thickened. Season with salt and pepper to taste and ladle into 4 warmed soup bowls. Garnish with basil or oregano and serve.

Appetisers & Snacks

Appetisers are known as antipasto in Italy, which is translated as meaning 'before the main course'. Antipasti usually come in three categories: meat, fish, and vegetables. There are many varieties of cold meats, including ham, invariably sliced paper-thin. All varieties of fish are popular

in Italy, including inkfish, octopus, and cuttlefish. Seafood is also highly prized, especially jumbo shrimp, mussels, and fresh sardines. Numerous vegetables feature in Italian cuisine and are an important part of the daily diet. They are served as an appetiser, as an accompaniment to main dishes, or as a course on their own. In Italy, vegetables are cooked only until "al dente" and still slightly crisp.
This ensures that they retain more nutrients and the colors remain bright and appealing.

Spinach & Ricotta Patties

Nudo or naked is the word used to describe this mixture, which can also be wrapped in thin crepes or used as a filling for tortelloni.

NUTRITIONAL INFORMATION

Calories 374	Sugars 4g	
Protein 16g	Fat 31g	
Carbohydrate 9g	Saturates 19g	

🥖 5 MINS   🕐 30 MINS

SERVES 4

INGREDIENTS

1 lb fresh spinach

generous 1 cup ricotta cheese

1 egg, beaten

2 tsp fennel seeds, lightly crushed

½ cup finely grated pecorino or Parmesan cheese, plus extra to garnish

2 tbsp all-purpose flour, mixed with 1 tsp dried thyme

5 tbsp butter

2 garlic cloves, crushed

salt and pepper

tomato wedges, to serve

1 Wash the spinach and trim off any long stems. Place in a pan, cover, and cook for 4–5 minutes until wilted. This will probably have to be done in batches because the volume of spinach is very large. Place in a colander and leave to drain and cool.

2 Mash the ricotta and beat in the egg and the fennel seeds. Season with plenty of salt and pepper, then stir in the pecorino or Parmesan cheese.

3 Squeeze as much excess water as possible from the spinach and finely chop the leaves. Stir the spinach into the cheese mixture.

4 Taking about 1 tablespoon of the spinach and cheese mixture, shape it into a ball, and flatten it slightly to form a patty. Gently roll in the seasoned flour. Continue this process until all of the mixture has been used.

5 Half-fill a large skillet with water and bring to a boil. Carefully add the patties and poach for 3–4 minutes, or until they rise to the surface. Remove with a draining spoon.

6 Melt the butter in a pan. Add the garlic and cook for 2–3 minutes. Pour the garlic butter over the patties, season with freshly ground black pepper, and serve at once.

Bell Pepper Salad

Colourful marinated Mediterranean vegetables make a tasty starter.
Serve with fresh bread or Tomato Toasts (see below).

NUTRITIONAL INFORMATION

Calories	234	Sugars	........4g
Protein	.........6g	Fat	..........17g
Carbohydrate	...15g	Saturates	.......2g

  5–10 MINS   35 MINS

SERVES 4

INGREDIENTS

1 onion

2 red bell peppers

2 yellow bell peppers

3 tbsp olive oil

2 large zucchini, sliced

2 garlic cloves, sliced

1 tbsp balsamic vinegar

1¾ oz anchovy fillets, chopped

¼ cup black olives, halved and pitted

1 tbsp chopped fresh basil

salt and pepper

TOMATO TOASTS

small stick of French bread

1 garlic clove, crushed

1 tomato, peeled and chopped

2 tbsp olive oil

1 Cut the onion into wedges. Core and deseed the bell peppers and cut into thick slices.

2 Heat the oil in a large heavy-based skillet. Add the onion, bell peppers, zucchini and garlic and fry gently for 20 minutes, stirring occasionally.

3 Add the vinegar, anchovies, olives, and seasoning to taste, mix thoroughly and leave to cool.

4 Spoon on to individual plates and sprinkle with the basil.

5 To make the tomato toasts, cut the French bread diagonally into ½-inch slices.

6 Mix the garlic, tomato, oil, and seasoning together, and spread thinly over each slice of bread.

7 Place the bread on a cookie sheet, drizzle with the olive oil and bake in a heated oven, 425°F, for 5–10 minutes until crisp. Serve the Tomato Toasts with the Bell Pepper Salad.

Eggplant Rolls

Thin slices of eggplant are fried in olive oil and garlic, and then topped with pesto sauce and finely sliced mozzarella cheese.

NUTRITIONAL INFORMATION

Calories 278   Sugars 2g
Protein ....4g   Fat 28g
Carbohydrate ....2g   Saturates 7g

15–20 MINS   20 MINS

SERVES 4

INGREDIENTS

2 eggplants, thinly sliced lengthwise

5 tbsp olive oil

1 garlic clove, crushed

4 tbsp pesto

1½ cups grated mozzarella cheese

basil leaves, torn into pieces

salt and pepper

fresh basil leaves, to garnish

1 Sprinkle the eggplant slices liberally with salt and leave for 10–15 minutes to extract the bitter juices. Turn the slices over and repeat. Rinse well with cold water and drain on paper towels.

2 Heat the olive oil in a large skillet and add the garlic. Fry the eggplant slices lightly on both sides, a few at a time. Drain them on paper towels.

3 Spread the pesto on to one side of the eggplant slices. Top with the grated Mozzarella and sprinkle with the torn basil leaves. Season with a little salt and pepper. Roll up the slices and secure with wooden toothpicks.

4 Arrange the eggplant rolls in a greased baking dish. Place in a

preheated oven, 350°F, and bake for 8–10 minutes.

5 Transfer the eggplant rolls to a warmed serving plate. Scatter with fresh basil leaves and serve at once.

Stewed Artichokes

This is a traditional Roman dish. The artichokes are stewed in olive oil with fresh herbs.

NUTRITIONAL INFORMATION

Calories	129	Sugars	.........0g
Protein	.........4g	Fat	...........8g
Carbohydrate	...10g	Saturates	.......1g

5 MINS　　50 MINS

SERVES 4

INGREDIENTS

4 small globe artichokes

olive oil

4 garlic cloves, peeled

2 bay leaves

finely grated peel and juice of 1 lemon

2 tbsp fresh marjoram

lemon wedges, to serve

1 Using a sharp knife, carefully peel away the tough outer leaves surrounding the artichokes. Trim the stems to about 1 inch.

2 Using a knife, cut each artichoke in half and scoop out the heart.

3 Place the artichokes in a large heavy-based pan. Pour over enough olive oil to half cover the artichokes in the pan.

4 Add the garlic cloves, bay leaves, and half of the grated lemon peel.

5 Start to heat the artichokes gently, cover the pan, and continue to cook over a low heat for about 40 minutes. It is important that the artichokes should be stewed in the oil, not fried.

6 Once the artichokes are tender, remove them with a draining spoon

and drain thoroughly. Remove the bay leaves and discard.

7 Transfer the artichokes to warm serving plates. Garnish the artichokes with the remaining grated lemon peel, fresh marjoram, and a little lemon juice. Serve with lemon wedges.

COOK'S TIP

To prevent the artichokes from oxidizing and turning brown before cooking, brush them with a little lemon juice. In addition, use the oil used for cooking the artichokes for salad dressings – it will impart a lovely lemon-and-herb flavor.

Baked Fennel Gratinati

Fennel is a common ingredient in Italian cooking. In this dish its distinctive flavor is offset by the smooth béchamel sauce.

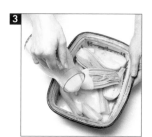

NUTRITIONAL INFORMATION

Calories 426   Sugars 9g
Protein ....13g   Fat 35g
Carbohydrate ...16g   Saturates 19g

5–10 MINS   45 MINS

SERVES 4

I N G R E D I E N T S

4 heads fennel

2 tbsp butter

⅔ cup dry white wine

Béchamel Sauce (see page 14),
    enriched with 2 egg yolks

½ cup fresh white bread crumbs

3 tbsp freshly grated Parmesan

salt and pepper

fennel fronds, to garnish

1 Remove any bruised or tough outer stems of fennel and cut each head in half. Put into a saucepan of boiling salted water and simmer for 20 minutes until tender; drain.

2 Butter a baking dish liberally and arrange the drained fennel in it.

3 Mix the wine into the Béchamel Sauce and season with salt and pepper to taste. Pour over the fennel.

4 Sprinkle evenly with the bread crumbs and then the Parmesan.

5 Place in a preheated oven, 400°F, and bake for 20 minutes until the top is golden. Serve garnished with fennel fronds.

Crepes with Smoked Fish

These are delicious as a first course or light supper dish and you can vary the filling with whichever fish you prefer.

NUTRITIONAL INFORMATION

Calories	399	Sugars 6g
Protein	........36g	Fat 18g
Carbohydrate	...25g	Saturates 10g

🍲 15 MINS ⏱ 1 HR 20 MINS

Makes 12 pancakes

INGREDIENTS

PANCAKES

⅔ cup all-purpose flour

½ tsp salt

1 egg, beaten

1 ¼ cups milk

1 tbsp oil, for frying

SAUCE

1 lb smoked haddock, skinned

1 ¼ cups milk

3 tbsp butter or margarine

3 tbsp all-purpose flour

1¼ cups fish stock

¾ cup grated Parmesan cheese

3 ½ oz frozen peas, defrosted

½ cup shrimp, cooked and peeled

3 tbsp grated Gruyère cheese

salt and pepper

1 To make the crepe batter, sift the flour and salt into a large bowl and make a well in the center. Add the egg and, using a wooden spoon, begin to draw in the flour. Slowly add the milk and beat together to form a smooth batter. Set aside until required.

2 Place the fish in a large skillet, add the milk and bring to the boil. Simmer for 10 minutes, or until the fish begins to flake. Drain thoroughly, reserving the milk.

3 Melt the butter in a saucepan. Add the flour, mix to a paste, and cook for 2–3 minutes. Remove the pan from the heat and add the reserved milk a little at a time, stirring to make a smooth sauce. Repeat with the fish stock. Return to the heat and bring to a boil, stirring. Stir in the Parmesan and season with salt and pepper to taste.

4 Grease a skillet with oil. Add 2 tablespoons of the crepe batter, swirling it around the pan and cook for 2–3 minutes. Loosen the sides with a spatula and flip over the crepe. Cook for 2–3 minutes until golden; repeat. Stack the crepes with sheets of waxed paper between them and keep warm in the oven.

5 Stir the flaked fish, peas, and shrimp into half of the sauce and use to fill each crepe. Pour the remaining sauce over, top with the Gruyere, and bake for 20 minutes until golden.

Mozzarella Snacks

These deep-fried mozzarella sandwiches are a tasty snack at any time of the day, or serve cut into smaller triangles as an antipasto with drinks.

NUTRITIONAL INFORMATION

Calories	379	Sugars	.........4g
Protein	........20g	Fat	..........22g
Carbohydrate	...28g	Saturates	.......5g

 20 MINS   5–10 MINS

SERVES 4

INGREDIENTS

8 slices bread, preferably slightly stale,
   crusts removed

3 ½ oz mozzarella cheese, thickly sliced

⅓ cup black olives, chopped

8 canned anchovy fillets, drained and
   chopped

16 fresh basil leaves

4 eggs, beaten

⅔ cup milk

oil, for deep-frying

salt and pepper

1 Cut each slice of bread into 2 triangles. Top 8 of the bread triangles with the mozzarella slices, olives, and chopped anchovies.

2 Place the basil leaves on top and season with salt and pepper to taste.

3 Lay the other 8 triangles of bread over the top and press down, round the edges to seal.

4 Mix the eggs and milk and pour into a baking dish. Add the sandwiches and leave to soak for about 5 minutes.

5 Heat the oil in a large saucepan to 350°–375°F, or until a cube of bread browns in 30 seconds.

6 Before cooking the sandwiches, squeeze the edges together again.

7 Carefully place the sandwiches in the oil and deep-fry for 2 minutes, or until golden, turning once. Remove the sandwiches with a draining spoon and drain on paper towels. Serve immediately while still hot.

Garlic & Pine Kernel Tarts

A crisp lining of bread is filled with garlic butter and pine kernels to make a delightful light meal.

NUTRITIONAL INFORMATION

Calories 435	Sugars 1g
Protein 6g	Fat 39g
Carbohydrate . . .17g	Saturates 20g

🍳 20 MINS   🕐 15 MINS

SERVES 4

I N G R E D I E N T S

4 slices wholewheat bread

½ cup pine kernels

⅔ cup butter

5 garlic cloves, halved

2 tbsp chopped fresh oregano, plus extra
   for garnish

4 black olives, halved

oregano leaves, to garnish

1 Using a rolling pin, flatten the bread slightly. Using a pastry cutter, cut out 4 circles of bread to fit your individual tart pans: they should measure about 4 inches across. Reserve the offcuts of bread and leave them in the refrigerator for 10 minutes or until required.

VARIATION

Puff pastry dough can be used for the tarts. Use 7oz dough to line 4 tart pans. Leave the dough to chill for 20 minutes. Line the pans with the dough and foil and bake blind for 10 minutes. Remove the foil and bake for 3–4 minutes, or until the dough is set. Cool, then continue from step 2, adding 2 tbsp bread crumbs to the mixture.

2 Meanwhile, place the pine kernels on a cookie sheet. Toast the pine kernels under a heated broiler for 2–3 minutes or until golden.

3 Put the bread offcuts, pine kernels, butter, garlic, and oregano into a food processor and blend for about 20 seconds. Alternatively, pound the ingredients by hand in a mortar and pestle. The mixture should have a rough texture.

4 Spoon the pine kernel butter mixture into the lined pan and top with the olives. Bake in a preheated oven at 400°F for 10–15 minutes or until golden.

5 Transfer the tarts to serving plates and serve warm, garnished with the fresh oregano leaves.

Onion & Mozzarella Tarts

These individual tarts are delicious served hot or cold and are great for packing in lunchboxes or for picnics.

NUTRITIONAL INFORMATION

Calories ....327 Sugars 3g
Protein ....5g Fat 23g
Carbohydrate ...25g Saturates 9g

 45 MINS   45 MINS

SERVES 4

INGREDIENTS

9 oz puff pastry dough, defrosted if frozen

2 red onions

1 red bell pepper

8 cherry tomatoes, halved

¾ cup chopped mozzarella cheese

8 sprigs thyme

1 Roll out the dough to make 4 x 3-inch squares. Using a sharp knife, trim the edges of the dough, reserving the trimmings. Leave the dough to chill in the refrigerator for 30 minutes.

2 Place the dough squares on a cookie sheet. Brush a little water along each edge of the dough squares and use the reserved dough trimmings to make a rim around each tart.

3 Cut the red onions into thin wedges and halve and deseed the bell peppers.

4 Place the onions and bell pepper in a roasting pan. Cook under a heated broiler for 15 minutes or until charred.

5 Place the roasted bell pepper halves in a plastic bag and leave to sweat for 10 minutes. Peel off the skin from the bell peppers and cut the flesh into strips.

6 Line the dough squares with squares of foil. Bake in a preheated oven at 400°F for 10 minutes. Remove the foil squares and bake for a further 5 minutes.

7 Place the onions, bell pepper strips, tomatoes, and cheese in each tart and sprinkle with the fresh thyme.

8 Return to the oven for 15 minutes or until the dough is golden. Serve hot.

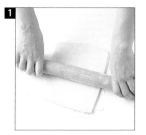

Bruschetta with Tomatoes

Using ripe tomatoes and the best olive oil will make this traditional Tuscan dish absolutely delicious.

NUTRITIONAL INFORMATION

Calories 330   Sugars 4g
Protein . . . . .8g   Fat 14g
Carbohydrate . . .45g   Saturates 2g

    15 MINS   🕐 5 MINS

SERVES 4

INGREDIENTS

10½ oz cherry tomatoes

4 sun-dried tomatoes

4 tbsp extra virgin olive oil

16 fresh basil leaves, shredded

2 garlic cloves, peeled

8 slices ciabatta

salt and pepper

1 Using a sharp knife, cut the cherry tomatoes in half.

2 Using a sharp knife, slice the sun-dried tomatoes into strips.

3 Place the cherry tomatoes and sun-dried tomatoes in a bowl. Add the olive oil and the shredded basil leaves and toss to mix well. Season to taste with a little salt and pepper.

4 Using a sharp knife, cut the garlic cloves in half. Lightly toast the ciabatta bread.

5 Rub the garlic, cut-side down, over both sides of the lightly toasted ciabatta bread.

6 Top the ciabatta bread with the tomato mixture and serve immediately.

Baked Fennel

Fennel is used extensively in northern Italy. It is a very versatile vegetable, good cooked or used raw in salads.

NUTRITIONAL INFORMATION

Calories 111	Sugars 6g
Protein 7g	Fat 7g
Carbohydrate 7g	Saturates 3g

10 MINS   35 MINS

SERVES 4

I N G R E D I E N T S

2 fennel bulbs

2 celery sticks, cut into 3-inch sticks

6 sun-dried tomatoes, halved

1 cup strained puréed tomatoes

2 tsp dried oregano

½ cup grated Parmesan cheese

1 Using a sharp knife, trim the fennel, discarding any tough outer leaves. Cut the bulb into quarters.

2 Bring a large pan of water to a boil, add the fennel and celery, and cook for 8–10 minutes, or until just tender. Remove with a draining spoon.

3 Place the fennel pieces, celery and sun-dried tomatoes in a large baking dish.

4 Mix the strained tomato and oregano together and pour the mixture over the fennel.

5 Sprinkle with the Parmesan cheese and bake in a preheated oven at 375°F for 20 minutes or until hot. Serve as an appetiser with bread or as a vegetable side dish.

Bean & Tomato Casserole

This quick-and-easy casserole can be served as a hearty first course or as a side dish to accompany sausages or broiled fish.

NUTRITIONAL INFORMATION

Calories	273	Sugars	.........8g
Protein	........15g	Fat	...........7g
Carbohydrate	...40g	Saturates	.......1g

 10 MINS   15 MINS

SERVES 4

INGREDIENTS

14-oz can cannellini beans

14-oz can borlotti beans

2 tbsp olive oil

1 stalk celery

2 garlic cloves, chopped

1 cup pearl onions, halved

1 lb tomatoes

2¾ oz arugula

1 Drain both cans of beans and reserve 6 tablespoons of the liquid.

2 Heat the oil in a large pan. Add the celery, garlic, and onions and sauté for 5 minutes, or until the onions are golden.

3 Cut a cross in the bottom of each tomato and plunge them into a bowl of boiling water for 30 seconds until the skins split. Remove the tomatoes with a draining spoon and leave until cool enough to handle. Peel off the skin and chop the flesh.

4 Add the tomato flesh and the reserved bean liquid to the pan and cook for 5 minutes.

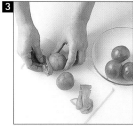

5 Add the beans to the pan and cook for a further 3–4 minutes, or until the beans are hot.

6 Stir in the arugula and allow to wilt slightly before serving. Serve hot.

VARIATION

For a spicier tasting dish, add 1–2 teaspoons of hot-pepper sauce with the cannellini and borlotti beans in step 5.

Antipasto Platter

This is a typical *antipasto* dish with the cold cured meats, stuffed olives and fresh tomatoes, dressed with basil and balsamic vinegar.

NUTRITIONAL INFORMATION

Calories . . . . .312 Sugars 1g
Protein . . . . .12g Fat 28g
Carbohydrate . . . .2g Saturates 1g

 10 MINS   5 MINS

SERVES 4

I N G R E D I E N T S

4 plum tomatoes

1 tbsp balsamic vinegar

6 canned anchovy fillets, drained and rinsed

2 tbsp capers, drained and rinsed

1 cup pitted green olives

6 oz mixed, cured meats, sliced

8 fresh basil leaves

1 tbsp extra virgin olive oil

salt and pepper

crusty bread, to serve

1 Using a sharp knife, cut the tomatoes into even slices. Sprinkle the tomato slices with the balsamic vinegar and a little salt and pepper to taste; set aside.

2 Chop the anchovy fillets into pieces measuring about the same length as the olives.

3 Push a piece of anchovy and a caper into each olive.

4 Arrange the sliced meat on 4 individual serving plates together with the tomatoes, filled olives and basil leaves.

5 Lightly drizzle the olive oil over the sliced meat, tomatoes and olives.

6 Serve the cured meats, olives and tomatoes with plenty of fresh crusty bread.

COOK'S TIP

The cured meats for this recipe are up to your individual taste. They can include a selection of prosciutto, pancetta, dried salt beef and *salame di Milano*, pork and beef sausage.

Figs & Prosciutto

This colorful fresh salad is delicious at any time of the year. *Prosciutto di Parma* is considered by many to be the best ham in the world.

NUTRITIONAL INFORMATION

Calories	121	Sugars	........6g
Protein	.........1g	Fat	...........11g
Carbohydrate	....6g	Saturates	.......2g

 15 MINS   5 MINS

SERVES 4

I N G R E D I E N T S

1½ oz arugula

4 fresh figs

4 large slices prosciutto

4 tbsp olive oil

1 tbsp fresh orange juice

1 tbsp honey

1 small red chili

1 Tear the arugula into more manageable pieces and arrange on 4 serving plates.

2 Using a sharp knife, cut each of the figs into quarters and place them on top of the arugula leaves.

3 Using a sharp knife, cut the prosciutto into strips and arrange around the arugula and figs.

4 Place the oil, orange juice, and honey in a screw-top jar. Shake the jar until the mixture emulsifies and forms a thick dressing. Transfer to a bowl.

5 Using a sharp knife, dice the chili, remembering not to touch your face before you have washed your hands (see Cook's Tip, below). Add the chopped chili to the dressing and mix well.

6 Drizzle the dressing over the prosciutto, arugula, and figs. Serve at once.

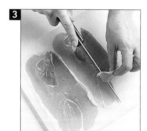

COOK'S TIP

Chilies can burn the skin for several hours after chopping, so it is advisable to wear gloves when you are handling the very hot varieties.

Crostini alla Fiorentina

Serve as a first course, or simply spread on small pieces of crusty fried bread (*crostini*) to enjoy as an appetizer with drinks.

NUTRITIONAL INFORMATION

Calories . . . . . . .393 Sugars 2g
Protein . . . . .17g Fat 25g
Carbohydrate . . .19g Saturates 9g

 10 MINS   40-45 MINS

SERVES 4

I N G R E D I E N T S

3 tbsp olive oil

1 onion, chopped

1 celery stalk, chopped

1 carrot, chopped

1–2 garlic cloves, crushed

4½ oz chicken livers

4½ oz calf, lamb, or pig's liver

⅔ cup red wine

1 tbsp tomato paste

2 tbsp chopped fresh parsley

3–4 canned anchovy fillets, finely chopped

2 tbsp stock or water

2–3 tbsp butter

1 tbsp capers

salt and pepper

small pieces of fried crusty bread, to serve

chopped fresh parsley, to garnish

1 Heat the oil in a pan. Add the onion, celery, carrot, and garlic, and cook gently for 4–5 minutes or until the onion is soft, but not colored.

2 Meanwhile, rinse and dry the chicken livers. Dry the calf or other liver, and slice into strips. Add the liver to the pan and fry gently for a few minutes until the strips are well sealed on all sides.

3 Add half of the wine and cook until it has mostly evaporated. Then add the rest of the wine, tomato paste, half of the parsley, the anchovy fillets, stock or water, a little salt and plenty of black pepper.

4 Cover the pan and leave to simmer, stirring occasionally, for 15–20 minutes, or until tender and most of the liquid has been absorbed.

5 Leave the mixture to cool a little, then either coarsely grind or put into a food processor and process to a chunky purée.

6 Return to the pan and add the butter, capers, and remaining parsley. Heat through gently until the butter melts. Adjust the seasoning and turn out into a bowl. Serve warm or cold spread on the slices of crusty bread and sprinkled with chopped parsley.

Mussels in White Wine

This soup of mussels, cooked in white wine with onions and cream, can be served as an appetizer or a main dish with plenty of crusty bread.

NUTRITIONAL INFORMATION

Calories	396	Sugars	.........2g
Protein	........23g	Fat	..........24g
Carbohydrate	....8g	Saturates	......15g

 5–10 MINS   25 MINS

SERVES 4

I N G R E D I E N T S

about 3 quarts fresh mussels

¼ cup butter

1 large onion, very finely chopped

2–3 garlic cloves, crushed

1 ½ cups dry white wine

⅔ cup water

2 tbsp lemon juice

good pinch of finely grated lemon peel

1 bouquet garni

1 tbsp all-purpose flour

4 tbsp light or heavy cream

2–3 tbsp chopped fresh parsley

salt and pepper

warm crusty bread, to serve

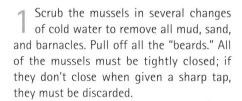   

1 Scrub the mussels in several changes of cold water to remove all mud, sand, and barnacles. Pull off all the "beards." All of the mussels must be tightly closed; if they don't close when given a sharp tap, they must be discarded.

2 Melt half the butter in a large saucepan. Add the onion and garlic, and fry gently until soft but not colored.

3 Add the wine, water, lemon juice and peel, bouquet garni, and plenty of seasoning. Bring to a boil, then cover and simmer for 4–5 minutes.

4 Add the mussels to the pan, cover tightly, and simmer for 5 minutes, shaking the pan frequently, until all the mussels have opened. Discard any mussels which have not opened. Remove the bouquet garni.

5 Remove the empty half shell from each mussel. Blend the remaining butter with the flour and whisk into the soup, a little at a time. Simmer gently for 2–3 minutes until slightly thickened.

6 Add the cream and half the parsley to the soup and reheat gently. Adjust the seasoning. Ladle the mussels and soup into warmed large soup bowls, sprinkle with the remaining parsley and serve with plenty of warm crusty bread.

Deep-Fried Seafood

Deep-fried seafood is popular all around the Mediterranean, where fish of all kinds is fresh and abundant.

NUTRITIONAL INFORMATION

Calories	393	Sugars	.......0.2g
Protein	........27g	Fat	..........26g
Carbohydrate	...12g	Saturates	.......3g

5 MINS   15 MINS

SERVES 4

INGREDIENTS

7 oz prepared squid

7 oz raw tiger prawns or jumbo shrimp, peeled

5½ oz whitebait

vegetable oil, for deep-frying

3 tbsp all-purpose flour

1 tsp dried basil

salt and pepper

TO SERVE

garlic mayonnaise

lemon wedges

1 Carefully rinse the squid, prawns or shrimp, and whitebait under cold running water, removing any dirt or grit.

2 Using a sharp knife, slice the squid into rings, leaving the tentacles whole.

3 Heat the oil in a large saucepan to 350°–375°F, or until a cube of bread browns in 30 seconds.

4 Place the flour in a bowl, add the basil, and season with salt and pepper to taste. Mix together well.

5 Roll the squid, prawns or shrimp, and whitebait in the seasoned flour until coated all over. Carefully shake off any excess flour.

6 Cook the seafood in the heated oil, in batches, for 2–3 minutes, or until crispy and golden all over. Remove all the seafood with a draining spoon and leave to drain thoroughly on paper towels.

7 Transfer the deep-fried seafood to serving plates and serve with garlic mayonnaise and a few lemon wedges.

  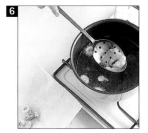

Pasta with Bacon & Tomatoes

As this dish cooks, the mouth-watering aroma of bacon, sweet tomatoes and oregano is a feast in itself.

NUTRITIONAL INFORMATION

Calories	431	Sugars	.........8g
Protein	........10g	Fat	..........29g
Carbohydrate	...34g	Saturates	......14g

 10 MINS   35 MINS

SERVES 4

I N G R E D I E N T S

2 lb small, sweet tomatoes

6 slices smoked bacon

4 tbsp butter

1 onion, chopped

1 garlic clove, crushed

4 fresh oregano sprigs, finely chopped

1 lb dried orecchiette

1 tbsp olive oil

salt and pepper

freshly grated Pecorino cheese, to serve

1 Blanch the tomatoes in boiling water. Drain, skin, and seed the tomatoes, then roughly chop the flesh.

2 Using a sharp knife, chop the bacon into small dice.

3 Melt the butter in a saucepan. Add the bacon and fry until it is golden.

4 Add the onion and garlic and fry over a medium heat for 5-7 minutes until just softened.

5 Add the tomatoes and oregano to the pan and then season to taste with salt and pepper. Lower the heat and simmer for 10-12 minutes.

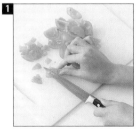  

6 Bring a large pan of lightly salted water to a boil. Add the orecchiette and oil and cook for 12 minutes, until just tender, but still firm to the bite. Drain the pasta and transfer to a warm serving dish or bowl.

7 Spoon the bacon and tomato sauce over the pasta, toss to coat, and serve with the cheese.

COOK'S TIP

For an authentic Italian flavor use pancetta, rather than ordinary bacon. This kind of bacon is streaked with fat and adds flavor to traditional dishes. It is available smoked and unsmoked from supermarkets and delicatessens.

Chorizo & Mushroom Pasta

Simple and quick to make, this spicy dish is sure to set the taste buds tingling.

NUTRITIONAL INFORMATION

Calories	495	Sugars	.........1g
Protein	........15g	Fat	..........35g
Carbohydrate	...33g	Saturates	.......5g

 5 MINS 🕐 20 MINS

SERVES 6

INGREDIENTS

1½ lb dried vermicelli

½ cup olive oil

2 garlic cloves

4½ oz chorizo or other spicy sausage, sliced

8 oz wild mushrooms

3 fresh red chilies, chopped

2 tbsp freshly grated Parmesan cheese

salt and pepper

10 anchovy fillets, to garnish

1 Bring a large saucepan of lightly salted water to a boil. Add the vermicelli and 1 tablespoon of the oil and cook for 8–10 minutes, or until just tender, but still firm to the bite.

2 Drain the pasta thoroughly, place on a large, warm serving plate, and keep warm.

3 Meanwhile, heat the remaining oil in a large skillet. Add the garlic and fry for 1 minute.

4 Add the chorizo and wild mushrooms and cook for 4 minutes,

5 Add the chopped chilies and cook for 1 further minute.

6 Pour the chorizo and wild mushroom mixture over the vermicelli and season with a little salt and pepper.

7 Sprinkle with freshly grated Parmesan cheese, garnish with a lattice of anchovy fillets, and serve immediately.

COOK'S TIP

Many varieties of mushrooms are cultivated and indistinguishable from the wild varieties. Mixed color oyster mushrooms are used here, but you can also use chanterelles. Chanterelles shrink during cooking, so start with more.

Smoked Ham Linguini

Served with freshly made Italian bread or tossed with pesto, this makes a mouth-watering light lunch.

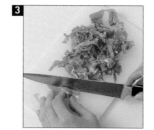

NUTRITIONAL INFORMATION

Calories 537	Sugars 4g
Protein 22g	Fat 29g
Carbohydrate 71g	Saturates 8g

 25 MINS   15 MINS

SERVES 4

I N G R E D I E N T S

1 lb dried linguini

1 lb green broccoli flowerets

8 oz Italian smoked ham

⅔ cup Italian Cheese Sauce (see page 16)

salt and pepper

Italian bread, such as ciabatta or focaccia,
   to serve

1 Bring a large saucepan pan of lightly salted water to a boil. Add the linguini and broccoli flowerets and cook for about 10 minutes, or until the linguini is tender, but still firm to the bite.

2 Drain the linguini and broccoli thoroughly set aside and keep warm until required.

3 Cut the Italian smoked ham into thin strips.

4 Toss the linguini, broccoli, and ham into the Italian Cheese Sauce and gently warm through over a very low heat.

5 Transfer the pasta mixture to a warm serving dish. Sprinkle with pepper and serve with Italian bread.

COOK'S TIP

There are many types of Italian bread which are suitable to serve with this dish. Ciabatta is made with olive oil and is available plain and with different ingredients, such as olives or sun-dried tomatoes.

Pancetta & Pecorino Cakes

These make an excellent first course when served with a topping of pesto or anchovy sauce.

NUTRITIONAL INFORMATION

Calories	619	Sugars	4g
Protein	22g	Fat	29g
Carbohydrate	71g	Saturates	8g

20 MINS   25 MINS

SERVES 4

INGREDIENTS

2 tbsp butter, plus extra for greasing

3½ oz pancetta, rind removed

2 cups self-rising flour

¾ cup grated pecorino cheese

⅔ cup milk, plus extra for glazing

1 tbsp tomato catsup

1 tsp Worcestershire sauce

3½ cups dried farfalle

1 tbsp olive oil

salt and pepper

3 tbsp Pesto or anchovy sauce (optional)

green salad, to serve

1 Grease a cookie sheet with butter. Broil the pancetta until it is cooked through. Allow the pancetta to cool, then chop finely.

2 Sift together the flour and a pinch of salt into a mixing bowl. Add the butter and rub in with your fingertips. When the butter and flour have been thoroughly incorporated, add the pancetta and one-third of the grated cheese.

3 Mix together the milk, tomato catsup and Worcestershire sauce and add to the dry ingredients, mixing to make a soft dough.

4 Roll out the dough on a lightly floured board to make an 7-inch round. Brush with a little milk to glaze and cut into 8 wedges.

5 Arrange the dough wedges on the prepared cookie sheet and sprinkle the

remaining cheese over. Bake in a preheated oven at 400°F for 20 minutes.

6 Meanwhile, bring a saucepan of lightly salted water to a boil. Add the farfalle and the oil and cook for 8–10 minutes until just tender, but still firm to the bite. Drain and transfer to a large serving dish. Top with the pancetta and pecorino cakes. Serve with the sauce of your choice and a green salad.

Eggplant & Pasta

Prepare the marinated eggplant well in advance so all you have to do is cook the pasta.

NUTRITIONAL INFORMATION

Calories .... .378	Sugars 3g	
Protein 12g	Fat .... .30g	
Carbohydrate ...16g	Saturates 3g	

12¼ HOURS   15 MINS

SERVES 4

INGREDIENTS

⅔ cup vegetable stock

⅔ cup white wine vinegar

2 tsp balsamic vinegar

3 tbsp olive oil

fresh oregano sprig

3½ cups peeled and sliced thinly eggplant

14 oz dried linguine

MARINADE

2 tbsp extra virgin oil

2 garlic cloves, crushed

2 tbsp chopped fresh oregano

2 tbsp finely chopped roasted almonds

2 tbsp diced red bell pepper

2 tbsp lime juice

grated peel and juice of 1 orange

salt and pepper

1 Put the vegetable stock, wine vinegar, and balsamic vinegar into a saucepan and bring to a boil over a low heat. Add 2 tsp of the olive oil and the sprig of oregano and simmer gently for about 1 minute.

2 Add the eggplant slices to the pan, remove from the heat, and set aside for 10 minutes.

3 Meanwhile make the marinade. Combine the oil, garlic, fresh oregano, almonds, bell pepper, lime juice, orange peel, and juice together in a large bowl and season to taste.

4 Carefully remove the eggplant from the saucepan with a draining spoon, and drain well. Add the eggplant slices to the marinade, mixing well, and set aside in the refrigerator for about 12 hours.

5 Bring a large pan of lightly salted water to a boil. Add half of the remaining oil and the linguine and cook for 8–10 minutes until just tender. Drain the pasta thoroughly and toss with the remaining oil while still warm.

6 Arrange the pasta on a serving plate with the eggplant slices and the marinade and serve.

Spinach & Ricotta Shells

This is a classic Italian combination in which the smooth, creamy cheese balances the sharper taste of the spinach.

NUTRITIONAL INFORMATION

Calories	672	Sugars	........10g
Protein	........23g	Fat	..........26g
Carbohydrate	...93g	Saturates	.......8g

5 MINS   40 MINS

SERVES 4

I N G R E D I E N T S

14 oz dried large ridged pasta shells

5 tbsp olive oil

1 cup fresh white bread crumbs

½ cup milk

10 oz frozen spinach, thawed and drained

1 cup ricotta cheese

pinch of freshly grated nutmeg

14 oz-can chopped tomatoes, drained

1 garlic clove, crushed

salt and pepper

1 Bring a large saucepan of lightly salted water to a boil. Add the pasta shells and 1 tbsp of the olive oil and cook for 8–10 minutes until just tender, but still firm to the bite. Drain the pasta, refresh under cold water, and set aside until required.

2 Put the bread crumbs, milk, and 3 tbsp of the remaining olive oil in a food processor and work to combine.

3 Add the spinach and ricotta cheese to the food processor and work to a smooth mixture. Transfer to a bowl, stir in the nutmeg, and season with salt and pepper to taste.

4 Mix together the tomatoes, garlic, and remaining oil and spoon the mixture into the base of a large baking dish.

5 Using a teaspoon, fill the lumache with the spinach and ricotta mixture and arrange on top of the tomato mixture in the dish. Cover and bake in a preheated oven at 350°F for 20 minutes. Serve hot.

COOK'S TIP

Ricotta is a creamy Italian cheese traditionally made from ewe-milk whey. It is soft and white, with a smooth texture and a slightly sweet flavor. It should be used within 2 or 3 days of purchase.

Spinach & Anchovy Pasta

This colorful first course can be made with a variety of different pasta, including spaghetti, linguine, and fettucine.

NUTRITIONAL INFORMATION

Calories 619   Sugars 5g
Protein . . . . .21g   Fat 31g
Carbohydrate . . .67g   Saturates 3g

10 MINS   25 MINS

SERVES 4

INGREDIENTS

2 lb fresh, young spinach leaves

14 oz dried fettuccine

6 tbsp olive oil

3 tbsp pine kernels

3 garlic cloves, crushed

8 canned anchovy fillets, drained and
  chopped

salt

1 Trim off any tough spinach stems. Rinse the spinach leaves and place them in a large saucepan with only the water that is clinging to them. Cover and cook over a high heat, shaking the pan from time, until the spinach has wilted, but retains its color. Drain well, set aside, and keep warm.

COOK'S TIP

If you are in a hurry, you can use frozen spinach. Thaw and drain it thoroughly, pressing out as much moisture as possible. Cut the leaves into strips and add to the dish with the anchovies in step 4.

2 Bring a large saucepan of lightly salted water to a boil. Add the fettuccine and 1 tablespoon of the oil and cook for 8–10 minutes until it is just tender, but still firm to the bite.

3 Heat 4 tablespoons of the remaining oil in a saucepan. Add the pine kernels and fry until golden. Remove the pine kernels from the pan and set aside until required.

4 Add the garlic to the pan and fry until golden. Add the anchovies and stir in the spinach. Cook, stirring, for 2–3 minutes, until heated through. Return the pine kernels to the pan.

5 Drain the fettuccine, toss in the remaining olive oil, and transfer to a warm serving dish. Spoon the anchovy and spinach sauce over the fettuccine, toss lightly, and serve immediately.

Tagliarini with Gorgonzola

This simple, creamy pasta sauce is a classic Italian recipe. You can use Danish blue cheese instead of the gorgonzola, if you prefer.

NUTRITIONAL INFORMATION

Calories ....904 Sugars 4g
Protein ....27g Fat 53g
Carbohydrate ...83g Saturates 36g

 5 MINS   🕐 20 MINS

SERVES 4

INGREDIENTS

2 tbsp butter

1½ cups roughly crumbled gorgonzola
  cheese

⅔ cup heavy cream

2 tbsp dry white wine

1 tsp cornstarch

4 fresh sage sprigs, finely chopped

14 oz dried tagliarini

2 tbsp olive oil

salt and white pepper

1 Melt the butter in a heavy-bottomed pan. Stir in 1 cup of the cheese and melt, over a low heat, for about 2 minutes.

2 Add the cream, wine, and cornstarch and beat with a whisk until fully incorporated.

COOK'S TIP

Gorgonzola is one of the world's oldest veined cheeses and, arguably, its finest. When buying, always check that it is creamy yellow with delicate green veining. Avoid hard or discolored cheese. It should have a rich, piquant aroma, not a bitter smell.

3 Stir in the sage and season to taste with salt and white pepper. Bring to a boil over a low heat, whisking constantly, until the sauce thickens. Remove from the heat and set aside while you cook the pasta.

4 Bring a large saucepan of lightly salted water to a boil. Add the tagliarini and 1 tbsp of the olive oil. Cook the pasta for 8–10 minutes, or until just tender. Drain thoroughly and toss in the remaining olive oil. Transfer the pasta to a serving dish and keep warm.

5 Reheat the sauce over a low heat, whisking constantly. Spoon the gorgonzola sauce over the tagliarini, generously sprinkle over the remaining cheese, and serve immediately.

Spaghetti with Ricotta

This light pasta dish has a delicate flavor ideally suited for a summer lunch.

NUTRITIONAL INFORMATION

Calories	701	Sugars	........12g
Protein	........17g	Fat	..........40g
Carbohydrate	...73g	Saturates	......15g

 5 MINS   25 MINS

SERVES 4

I N G R E D I E N T S

12 oz dried spaghetti

3 tbsp olive oil

3 tbsp butter

2 tbsp chopped fresh flat-leaf parsley

1 cup freshly ground almonds

½ cup ricotta cheese

pinch of grated nutmeg

pinch of ground cinnamon

¾ cup crème fraîche or sour cream

½ cup hot chicken stock

1 tbsp pine kernels

salt and pepper

fresh flat leaf parsley sprigs, to garnish

1 Bring a pan of lightly salted water to a boil. Add the spaghetti and 1 tbsp of the oil and cook for 8–10 minutes until tender, but still firm to the bite.

2 Drain the pasta, return it to the pan, and toss with the butter and chopped parsley. Set aside and keep warm.

3 To make the sauce, mix together the ground almonds, ricotta cheese, nutmeg, cinnamon, and crème fraîche over a low heat to form a thick paste. Gradually stir in the remaining oil. When the oil has been fully incorporated, gradually stir in the hot chicken stock, until smooth. Season to taste with black pepper.

4 Transfer the spaghetti to a warm serving dish, pour the sauce over and toss together well (see Cook's Tip, right). Sprinkle the pine kernels over, garnish with the sprigs of flat-leaf parsley and serve warm.

COOK'S TIP

Use two large forks to toss spaghetti or other long pasta, so it is thoroughly coated with the sauce. Special spaghetti forks are available from some cookware departments and kitchen stores.

Three-Cheese Bake

Serve this dish while the cheese is still hot and melted, because cooked cheese can become very rubbery if it is left to cool.

NUTRITIONAL INFORMATION

Calories 710   Sugars 6g
Protein . . . . .34g   Fat 30g
Carbohydrate . . .80g   Saturates 16g

5 MINS   1 HOUR

SERVES 4

INGREDIENTS

butter, for greasing

14 oz dried penne

1 tbsp olive oil

2 eggs, beaten

1 ½ cups ricotta cheese

4 fresh basil sprigs

1 cup grated mozzarella or halloumi cheese

4 tbsp freshly grated Parmesan cheese

salt and pepper

fresh basil leaves (optional), to garnish

1 Lightly grease a large baking dish with butter.

2 Bring a large pan of lightly salted water to a boil. Add the penne and olive oil and cook for 8–10 minutes until just tender, but still firm to the bite. Drain the pasta, set aside and keep warm.

3 Beat the eggs into the ricotta cheese and season to taste.

4 Spoon half of the penne into the base of the dish and cover with half of the basil leaves.

5 Spoon half of the ricotta cheese mixture over. Sprinkle the mozzarella or halloumi cheese over and top with the remaining basil leaves. Cover with the remaining penne and then spoon the remaining ricotta cheese mixture over. Lightly sprinkle with the freshly grated Parmesan cheese.

6 Bake in a preheated oven at 375°F for 30–40 minutes, until golden brown and the cheese topping is hot and bubbling. Garnish with fresh basil leaves, if liked, and serve hot.

VARIATION

Try substituting smoked Bavarian cheese for the Mozzarella or halloumi and grated Cheddar cheese for the Parmesan, for a slightly different but just as delicious flavour.

Penne with Fried Mussels

This is quick and simple, but one of the nicest of Italian fried fish dishes, served with penne.

NUTRITIONAL INFORMATION

Calories . . . . .537 Sugars 2g
Protein . . . . .22g Fat 24g
Carbohydrate . . .62g Saturates 3g

10 MINS   25 MINS

SERVES 6

I N G R E D I E N T S

14 oz cups dried penne

½ cup olive oil

1 lb mussels, cooked and shelled

1 tsp sea salt

⅔ cup all-purpose flour

¾ cup sliced sun-dried tomatoes

2 tbsp chopped fresh basil leaves

salt and pepper

1 lemon, thinly sliced, to garnish

1 Bring a large saucepan of lightly salted water to a boil. Add the penne and 1 tbsp of the olive oil and cook for 8–10 minutes, or until the pasta is just tender, but still firm to the bite.

2 Drain the pasta thoroughly and place in a large, warm serving dish. Set aside and keep warm while you cook the mussels.

3 Lightly sprinkle the mussels with the sea salt. Season the flour with salt and pepper to taste, sprinkle into a bowl and toss the mussels in the flour until well coated.

4 Heat the remaining oil in a large skillet. Add the mussels and fry, stirring frequently, until a golden brown color.

5 Toss the mussels with the penne and sprinkle with the sun-dried tomatoes and basil leaves. Garnish with slices of lemon and serve immediately.

COOK'S TIP

Sun-dried tomatoes are dried and preserved in oil. They have a concentrated, roasted flavor and a dense texture. They should be drained and chopped or sliced before using.

Baked Tuna & Ricotta Rigatoni

Ribbed tubes of pasta are filled with tuna and ricotta cheese and then baked in a creamy sauce for a filling first course.

NUTRITIONAL INFORMATION

Calories	949	Sugars	.........5g
Protein	........51g	Fat	..........48g
Carbohydrate	...85g	Saturates	......26g

 10 MINS   45 MINS

SERVES 4

I N G R E D I E N T S

butter, for greasing

1 lb dried rigatoni

1 tbsp olive oil

7-oz can flaked tuna, drained

1 cup ricotta cheese

½ cup heavy cream

2⅔ cups grated Parmesan cheese

1 cup drained and sliced sun-dried
   tomatoes

salt and pepper

1 Lightly grease a large baking dish with butter.

2 Bring a large saucepan of lightly salted water to a boil. Add the rigatoni and olive oil and cook for 8–10 minutes until just tender, but still firm to the bite. Drain the pasta and set aside until cool enough to handle.

3 Meanwhile, in a bowl, mix together the tuna and ricotta cheese to form a soft paste. Spoon the mixture into a pastry bag and use to fill the rigatoni. Arrange the filled pasta tubes side by side in the prepared baking dish.

4 To make the sauce, mix the cream and Parmesan cheese and season with salt and pepper to taste. Spoon the sauce over the rigatoni and top with the sun-dried tomatoes, arranged in a crisscross pattern. Bake in a preheated oven at 400°F for 20 minutes. Serve hot straight from the dish.

VARIATION

For a vegetarian alternative of this recipe, simply substitute a mixture of pitted and chopped black olives and chopped walnuts for the tuna. Follow exactly the same cooking method.

Rotelle with Spicy Sauce

Prepare the sauce well in advance — it is a good idea to freeze batches of the sauce so you always have some to hand.

NUTRITIONAL INFORMATION

Calories 530	Sugars 4g	
Protein 13g	Fat 18g	
Carbohydrate ...78g	Saturates 3g	

🐻 🐻 🐻

🍲 8¼ HOURS   🕐 40 MINS

SERVES 4

I N G R E D I E N T S

1 cup Italian Red Wine Sauce (see page 15)

5 tbsp olive oil

3 garlic cloves, crushed

2 fresh red chilies, chopped

1 green chili, chopped

3½ cups dried rotelle

salt and pepper

warm Italian bread, to serve

1 Make the Italian Red Wine Sauce (see page 15).

2 Heat 4 tbsp of the oil in a saucepan. Add the garlic and chilies and fry for 3 minutes.

3 Stir in the Italian Red Wine Sauce, season with salt and pepper to taste, and simmer gently over a low heat for 20 minutes.

4 Bring a large saucepan of lightly salted water to a boil. Add the rotelle and the remaining oil and cook for 8 minutes, until just tender, but still firm to the bite. Drain the pasta.

5 Pour the Italian Red Wine Sauce over the rotelle and toss to mix.

6 Transfer to a warm serving dish and serve with warm Italian bread.

COOK'S TIP

Remove chili seeds before chopping the chilies, because they are the hottest part, and shouldn't be allowed to slip into the food.

Tuna-Stuffed Tomatoes

Deliciously sweet roasted tomatoes are filled with a homemade lemon mayonnaise and tuna mixture.

NUTRITIONAL INFORMATION

Calories ....196 Sugars 2g
Protein ....9g Fat 17g
Carbohydrate ....2g Saturates 3g

5–10 MINS   25 MINS

SERVES 4

INGREDIENTS

4 plum tomatoes

2 tbsp sun-dried tomato paste

2 egg yolks

2 tsp lemon juice

finely grated peel of 1 lemon

4 tbsp olive oil

4-oz can tuna, drained

2 tbsp capers, rinsed

salt and pepper

TO GARNISH

2 sun-dried tomatoes, cut into strips

fresh basil leaves

1 Halve the tomatoes and scoop out the seeds. Divide the sun-dried tomato paste among the tomato halves and spread around the inside of the skin.

2 Place on a cookie sheet and roast in a preheated oven at 400°F for 12–15 minutes. Leave to cool slightly.

3 Meanwhile, make the mayonnaise. In a food processor, blend the egg yolks and lemon juice with the lemon peel until smooth. Once mixed and with the motor still running slowly, add the olive oil. Stop the processor as soon as the mayonnaise has thickened. Alternatively, use a hand whisk, beating the mixture continuously until it thickens.

4 Add the tuna and capers to the mayonnaise and season.

5 Spoon the tuna mayonnaise mixture into the tomato shells and garnish with sun-dried tomato strips and basil leaves. Return to the oven for a few minutes or serve chilled.

COOK'S TIP

For a picnic, do not roast the tomatoes, just scoop out the seeds and drain, cut-side down on paper towels for 1 hour. Then fill with the mayonnaise mixture. They are firmer and easier to handle this way. If you prefer, commercial mayonnaise may be used instead – just stir in the lemon peel.

Ciabatta Rolls

Sandwiches are always a welcome snack, but can be mundane. These crisp rolls filled with roast bell peppers and cheese are irresistible.

NUTRITIONAL INFORMATION

Calories	328	Sugars 6g
Protein	.........8g	Fat 19g
Carbohydrate	...34g	Saturates 9g

15 MINS   10 MINS

SERVES 4

INGREDIENTS

4 ciabatta rolls

2 tbsp olive oil

1 garlic clove, crushed

FILLING

1 red bell pepper

1 green bell pepper

1 yellow bell pepper

4 radishes, sliced

1 bunch watercress

½ cup cream cheese

1 Slice the ciabatta rolls in half. Heat the olive oil and crushed garlic in a saucepan. Pour the garlic and oil mixture over the cut surfaces of the rolls and leave to stand.

2 Halve the bell peppers and place, skin side uppermost, on a broiler rack. Toast under a hot broiler for 8–10 minutes, until just beginning to char. Remove the bell peppers from the broiler, peel, and slice thinly.

3 Arrange the radish slices on one half of each roll with a few watercress leaves. Spoon the cream cheese on top. Pile the bell peppers on top of the cream cheese and top with the other half of the roll. Serve immediately.

Fish & Seafood

Italians eat everything that comes out of the sea, from the smallest whitebait to the massive tuna. Fish markets in Italy are fascinating, with a huge variety of fish on display,

but as most of the fish comes from the Mediterranean it is not always easy to find an equivalent elsewhere. However, fresh or frozen imported fish of all kinds is increasingly appearing in supermarkets and fishmerchants. After pasta, fish is probably the most important source of food in Italy, and in many recipes fish or seafood are served with one type of pasta or another — a winning combination!

Orange Mackerel

Mackerel can be very rich, but when it is stuffed with oranges and toasted ground almonds it is tangy and light.

NUTRITIONAL INFORMATION

Calories 623	Sugars 7g	
Protein 42g	Fat 47g	
Carbohydrate 8g	Saturates 8g	

15 MINS   35 MINS

SERVES 4

INGREDIENTS

2 tbsp oil

4 scallions, chopped

2 oranges

¾ cup blanched and chopped almonds

1 tbsp oats

⅓ cup mixed green and black olives, pitted and chopped

8 mackerel fillets

salt and pepper

crisp salad, to serve

1 Heat the oil in a skille). Add the scallions and cook for 2 minutes.

2 Finely grate the peel of the oranges. Using a sharp knife, cut away the remaining skin and white pith.

3 Using a sharp knife, segment the oranges by cutting down each side of the lines of pith to loosen the segments. (Do this over a plate so that you can reserve any juices). Cut each orange segment in half.

4 Lightly toast the almonds, under a preheated broiler, for 2–3 minutes or until golden; watch them carefully because they brown very quickly.

5 Mix the scallions, oranges, ground almonds, oats, and olives together in a bowl and season to taste with salt and pepper.

6 Spoon the orange mixture along the center of each fillet. Roll up each fillet, securing it in place with a wooden toothpick or skewer.

7 Bake in a preheated oven at 375°F for 25 minutes until the fish is tender.

8 Transfer to serving plates and serve warm with a salad.

Sea Bass with Olive Sauce

A favorite fish for chefs, the delicious sea bass is now becoming increasingly common in supermarkets and fish stores for family meals.

NUTRITIONAL INFORMATION

Calories	877	Sugars	.........3g
Protein	........50g	Fat	..........47g
Carbohydrate	...67g	Saturates	......26g

🧊 10 MINS   🕐 30 MINS

SERVES 4

I N G R E D I E N T S

1 lb dried macaroni

1 tbsp olive oil

8 x 4-oz sea bass medallions

S A U C E

2 tbsp butter

4 shallots, chopped

2 tbsp capers

1½ cups chopped, pitted green olives

4 tbsp balsamic vinegar

1¼ cups fish stock

1¼ cups heavy cream

juice of 1 lemon

salt and pepper

TO GARNISH

lemon slices

shredded leek

shredded carrot

1 To make the sauce, melt the butter in a skillet. Add the shallots and cook over a low heat for 4 minutes. Add the capers and olives and cook for a further 3 minutes.

2 Stir in the balsamic vinegar and fish stock. Bring to a boil and reduce by half. Add the cream, stirring, and reduce again by half. Season to taste with salt and pepper and stir in the lemon juice. Remove the pan from the heat; set aside and keep warm.

3 Bring a large pan of lightly salted water to the boil. Add the pasta and olive oil and cook for about 12 minutes, until tender but still firm to the bite.

4 Meanwhile, lightly broil the sea bass medallions for 3–4 minutes on each side, until cooked through, but still moist and delicate.

5 Drain the pasta thoroughly and transfer to large individual serving dishes. Top the pasta with the fish medallions and pour the olive sauce over. Garnish with lemon slices, shredded leek and carrot, and serve immediately.

Baked Sea Bass

Sea bass is a delicious white-fleshed fish. If cooking two small fish, they can be broiled; if cooking one large fish, bake it in the oven.

NUTRITIONAL INFORMATION

Calories	378	Sugars	.........0g
Protein	........62g	Fat	.........14g
Carbohydrate	....0g	Saturates	.......2g

 15–20 MINS   20–55 MINS

SERVES 4

INGREDIENTS

3 lb fresh sea bass, or

  2 x 1 lb 10 oz sea bass, dressed

2–4 sprigs fresh rosemary

½ lemon, thinly sliced

2 tbsp olive oil

bay leaves and lemon wedges, to garnish

GARLIC SAUCE

2 tsp coarse sea salt

2 tsp capers

2 garlic cloves, crushed

4 tbsp water

2 fresh bay leaves

1 tsp lemon juice or wine vinegar

2 tbsp olive oil

pepper

1 Scrape off the scales from the fish and cut off the sharp fins. Make diagonal cuts along both sides. Wash and dry thoroughly. Place a sprig of rosemary in the cavity of each of the smaller fish with half the lemon slices; or 2 sprigs and all the lemon in the large fish.

2 To broil, place in a foil-lined pan, brush with 1–2 tbsp oil and broil under a moderate heat for 5 minutes each side, or until cooked through.

3 To bake: place the fish in a foil-lined dish or roasting pan brushed with oil, and brush the fish with the rest of the oil. Cook in a preheated oven, 375°F, for 30 minutes for the small fish or 45–50 minutes for the large fish, until the thickest part of the fish is opaque.

4 To make the sauce: crush the salt and capers with the garlic in a mortar and pestle and then work in the water. Or, work in a food processor or blender until smooth.

5 Bruise the bay leaves and remaining sprigs of rosemary and put in a bowl. Add the garlic mixture, lemon juice or vinegar, and oil and pound together until the flavors are released. Season with pepper to taste.

6 Place the fish on a serving dish and, if liked, remove the skin. Spoon some of the sauce over the fish and serve the rest separately. Garnish with fresh bay leaves and lemon wedges.

Celery & Salt Cod Casserole

Salt cod is dried and salted to preserve it. It has a unique flavor, which goes particularly well with celery in this dish.

NUTRITIONAL INFORMATION

Calories 173	Sugars 3g	
Protein 14g	Fat 12g	
Carbohydrate 3g	Saturates 1g	

25 MINS   25 MINS

SERVES 4

INGREDIENTS

9 oz salt cod, soaked overnight

1 tbsp oil

4 shallots, finely chopped

2 garlic cloves, chopped

3 celery stalks, chopped

14-oz can tomatoes, chopped

⅔ cup fish stock

¼ cup pine kernels

2 tbsp roughly chopped tarragon

2 tbsp capers

crusty bread or mashed potato, to serve

1 Drain the salt cod, rinse it under plenty of running water, and drain again thoroughly. Remove and discard any skin and bones. Pat the fish dry with paper towels and cut it into chunks.

2 Heat the oil in a large skillet. Add the shallots and garlic and cook for 2–3 minutes. Add the celery and cook for a further 2 minutes, then add the tomatoes and stock.

3 Bring the mixture to a boil, reduce the heat, and leave to simmer for about 5 minutes.

4 Add the fish and cook for 10 minutes, or until tender.

5 Meanwhile, place the pine kernels on a cookie sheet. Place under a preheated broiler and toast for 2–3 minutes, or until golden.

6 Stir the tarragon, capers, and pine kernels into the fish casserole and heat gently to warm through.

7 Transfer to serving plates and serve with lots of fresh crusty bread or mashed potato.

COOK'S TIP

Salt cod is a useful ingredient to keep in the pantry and, once soaked, can be used in the same way as any other fish. It does, however, have a stronger, salty flavor than normal. It can be found at fishmerchants, larger supermarkets, and delicatessens.

Spaghetti alla Bucaniera

Brill, popular throughout the Mediterranean, is a flat fish, favored for its delicate flavor. If you can't find any, use sole.

NUTRITIONAL INFORMATION

Calories 588   Sugars 5g
Protein . . . . .36g   Fat 18g
Carbohydrate . . .68g   Saturates 9g

 25 MINS   50 MINS

SERVES 4

INGREDIENTS

¾ cup all-purpose flour

1 lb brill or sole fillets, skinned and chopped

1 lb hake or cod fillets, skinned and
   chopped

6 tbsp butter

4 shallots, finely chopped

2 garlic cloves, crushed

1 carrot, diced

1 leek, finely chopped

1¼ cups hard cider

1¼ cups medium-sweet cider

2 tsp anchovy extract

1 tbsp tarragon vinegar

1 lb dried spaghetti

1 tbsp olive oil

salt and pepper

chopped fresh parsley, to garnish

crusty brown bread, to serve

1 Season the flour with salt and pepper. Sprinkle ¼ cup of the seasoned flour onto a shallow plate. Press the fish pieces into the seasoned flour to coat thoroughly.

2 Melt the butter in a flameproof casserole. Add the fish fillets, shallots, garlic, carrot and leek and cook over a low heat, stirring frequently, for about 10 minutes.

3 Sprinkle over the remaining seasoned flour and cook, stirring constantly, for 2 minutes. Gradually stir in the cider, anchovy extract, and tarragon vinegar. Bring to a boil and simmer over a low heat for 35 minutes. Alternatively, bake in a preheated oven at 350°F for 30 minutes.

4 About 15 minutes before the end of the cooking time, bring a large pan of lightly salted water to a boil. Add the spaghetti and olive oil and cook for about 12 minutes, until tender, but still firm to the bite. Drain the pasta thoroughly and transfer to a large serving dish.

5 Arrange the fish on top of the spaghetti and pour the sauce over. Garnish with chopped parsley and serve immediately with warm, crusty brown bread.

Sole Fillets in Marsala

A rich wine and cream sauce makes this an excellent dinner-party dish.
Make the stock the day before to cut down on the preparation time.

NUTRITIONAL INFORMATION

Calories 474   Sugars 3g
Protein . . . . .47g   Fat 28g
Carbohydrate . . . .3g   Saturates 14g

1¼ HOURS   1½ HOURS

SERVES 4

I N G R E D I E N T S

1 tbsp black peppercorns, lightly crushed

8 sole fillets

⅓ cup Marsala wine

⅔ cup heavy cream

S T O C K

2½ cups water

bones and skin from the sole fillets

1 onion, peeled and halved

1 carrot, peeled and halved

3 fresh bay leaves

S A U C E

1 tbsp olive oil

1 tbsp butter

4 shallots, finely chopped

13½ cups wiped and halved baby button
        mushrooms

1 To make the stock, place the water, fish bones and skin, onion, carrot, and bay leaves in a large saucepan and bring to a boil.

2 Reduce the heat and leave the mixture to simmer for 1 hour or until the stock has reduced to about ⅔ cup. Drain the stock through a fine strainer, discarding the bones and vegetables; set aside.

3 To make the sauce, heat the oil and butter in a skillet. Add the shallots and cook, stirring, for 2–3 minutes, or until just softened.

4 Add the mushrooms to the skillet and cook, stirring, for a further 2–3 minutes, or until they are just beginning to brown.

5 Add the peppercorns and sole fillets to the skillet in batches. Fry the sole fillets for 3–4 minutes on each side, or until golden brown. Remove the fish with

a draining spoon, set aside and keep warm while you cook the remainder.

6 When all the fillets have been cooked and removed from the pan, pour the wine and stock into the pan and leave to simmer for 3 minutes. Increase the heat and boil the mixture in the pan for about 5 minutes, or until the sauce has reduced and thickened.

7 Pour in the cream and heat through. Pour the sauce over the fish and serve with the cooked vegetables of your choice.

Broiled Stuffed Sole

A delicious stuffing of sun-dried tomatoes and fresh lemon thyme are used to stuff whole sole.

NUTRITIONAL INFORMATION

Calories 207   Sugars 0.2g
Protein . . . . .24g   Fat 10g
Carbohydrate . . . .8g   Saturates 4g

 25 MINS   20 MINS

SERVES 4

I N G R E D I E N T S

1 tbsp olive oil

2 tbsp butter

1 small onion, finely chopped

1 garlic clove, chopped

3 sun-dried tomatoes, chopped

2 tbsp lemon thyme

¾ cup fresh white bread crumbs

1 tbsp lemon juice

4 small whole sole, gutted and cleaned

salt and pepper

lemon wedges, to garnish

fresh green salad leaves, to serve

1 Heat the oil and butter in a skillet until it just begins to froth.

2 Add the onion and garlic to the skillet and cook, stirring, for 5 minutes until just softened.

3 To make the stuffing, mix the tomatoes, thyme, bread crumbs and lemon juice in a bowl, and season to taste.

4 Add the stuffing mixture to the pan, and stir to mix.

5 Using a sharp knife, pare the skin from the bone inside the gut hole of the fish to make a pocket. Spoon the tomato-and-herb stuffing into the pocket.

6 Cook the fish, under a heated broiler, for 6 minutes on each side or until golden brown.

7 Transfer the stuffed fish to serving plates and garnish with lemon wedges. Serve immediately with fresh green salad leaves.

COOK'S TIP

Lemon thyme (*Thymus* x *citriodorus*) has a delicate lemon scent and flavor. Ordinary thyme can be used instead, but mix it with 1 teaspoon of lemon peel to add extra flavor.

Lemon Sole & Haddock Ravioli

This delicate-tasting dish is surprisingly satisfying for even the hungriest appetites. Prepare the Italian Red Wine Sauce well in advance.

NUTRITIONAL INFORMATION

Calories 977	Sugars 7g	
Protein 67g	Fat 40g	
Carbohydrate ...93g	Saturates 17g	

9¾ HOURS   25 MINS

SERVES 4

INGREDIENTS

1 lb lemon sole fillets, skinned

1 lb haddock fillets, skinned

3 eggs beaten

1 lb cooked potato gnocchi

3 cups fresh white bread crumbs

¼ cup heavy cream

1 lb basic pasta dough

1¼ cups Italian Red Wine Sauce (see page 15)

½ cup freshly grated Parmesan cheese

salt and pepper

1 Flake the lemon sole and haddock fillets with a fork and transfer the flesh to a large mixing bowl.

2 Mix the eggs, cooked potato gnocchi, bread crumbs and cream in a bowl until thoroughly combined. Add the fish to the bowl containing the gnocchi and season the mixture with salt and pepper to taste.

3 Roll out the pasta dough on to a lightly floured surface and cut out 3-inch rounds using a plain cutter.

4 Place a spoonful of the fish stuffing on each circle. Dampen the edges slightly and fold the pasta rounds over, pressing together to seal.

5 Bring a large saucepan of lightly salted water to a boil. Add the ravioli and cook for 15 minutes.

6 Drain the ravioli, using a draining spoon, and transfer to a large serving dish. Pour the Italian Red Wine Sauce over, sprinkle the Parmesan cheese over, and serve immediately.

COOK'S TIP

For square ravioli, divide the dough in half. Wrap half in plastic wrap; thinly roll out the other half. Cover; roll out the remaining dough. Pipe the filling at regular intervals and brush the spaces in between with water or beaten egg. Lift the second sheet of dough into position with a rolling pin and press between the filling to seal.

Trout in Red Wine

This recipe from Trentino is best when the fish are freshly caught, but it is a good way to cook any trout, giving it an interesting flavor.

NUTRITIONAL INFORMATION

Calories	489	Sugars	.......0.6g
Protein	........48g	Fat	..........27g
Carbohydrate	...0.6g	Saturates	......14g

 20 MINS   45 MINS

SERVES 4

I N G R E D I E N T S

4 fresh trout, about 10 oz each

1 cup red or white wine vinegar

1¼ cups red or dry white wine

⅔ cup water

1 carrot, sliced

2–4 bay leaves

thinly pared peel of 1 lemon

1 small onion, very thinly sliced

4 sprigs fresh parsley

4 sprigs fresh thyme

1 tsp black peppercorns

6–8 whole cloves

6 tbsp butter

1 tbsp chopped fresh mixed herbs

salt and pepper

TO GARNISH

sprigs of herbs

lemon slices

1 Draw the trout, leaving their heads on. Dry on paper towels and lay the fish head to tail in a shallow container or baking pan large enough to hold them.

2 Bring the wine vinegar to a boil and slowly pour all over the fish. Leave the fish to marinate in the refrigerator for about 20 minutes.

3 Meanwhile, put the wine, water, carrot, bay leaves, lemon peel, onion, herbs, peppercorns, and cloves into a pan with a good pinch of sea salt and heat gently.

4 Drain the fish thoroughly, discarding the vinegar. Place the fish in a fish kettle or large skillet so they touch. When the wine mixture boils, strain gently over the fish so they are about half covered. Cover the pan and simmer very gently for 15 minutes.

5 Carefully remove the fish from the pan, draining off as much of the liquid as possible, and arrange on a serving dish; keep warm.

6 Boil the cooking liquid until reduced to 4–6 tbsp. Melt the butter in a pan and strain in the cooking liquor. Season and spoon the sauce over the fish. Garnish and serve.

Trout with Smoked Bacon

Most trout available nowadays is farmed, however, if you can, buy wild brown trout for this recipe, for its natural flavor.

NUTRITIONAL INFORMATION

Calories 802   Sugars 8g
Protein ....68g   Fat 36g
Carbohydrate ...54g   Saturates 10g

35 MINS   25 MINS

SERVES 4

INGREDIENTS

butter, for greasing

4 x 9½-oz trout, drawn and rinsed

12 anchovies in oil, drained and chopped

2 apples, peeled, cored, and sliced

4 fresh mint sprigs

juice of 1 lemon

12 slices smoked fatty bacon

1 lb dried tagliatelle

1 tbsp olive oil

salt and pepper

TO GARNISH

2 apples, cored and sliced

4 fresh mint sprigs

1 Grease a deep baking tray with butter.

2 Open the cavities of each trout and rinse with warm saltwater.

3 Season each cavity with salt and pepper. Divide the anchovies, sliced apples, and mint sprigs between each of the cavities. Sprinkle the lemon juice into each cavity.

4 Carefully cover the whole of each trout, except the head and tail, with three slices of smoked bacon in a spiral.

5 Arrange the trout on the baking tray with the loose ends of bacon tucked underneath. Season with pepper and bake in a preheated oven at 400°F for 20 minutes, turning the trout over after 10 minutes.

6 Meanwhile, bring a large pan of lightly salted water to a boil. Add the tagliatelle and olive oil and cook for about 12 minutes, until tender but still firm to the bite. Drain the pasta and transfer to a large, warm serving dish.

7 Remove the trout from the oven and arrange on the tagliatelle. Garnish with sliced apples and fresh mint sprigs and serve immediately.

Fillets of Red Mullet & Pasta

This simple recipe complements the sweet flavor and delicate texture of the fish, which is popular in Italy. Use goatfish as an alternative.

NUTRITIONAL INFORMATION

Calories	457	Sugars	.........3g
Protein	........39g	Fat	..........12g
Carbohydrate	...44g	Saturates	.......5g

15 MINS   1 HOUR

SERVES 4

I N G R E D I E N T S

2 lb 4 oz red mullet, or goatfish, fillets

1¼ cups dry white wine

4 shallots, finely chopped

1 garlic clove, crushed

3 tbsp finely chopped mixed fresh herbs

finely grated peel and juice of 1 lemon

pinch of freshly grated nutmeg

3 anchovy fillets, roughly chopped

2 tbsp heavy cream

1 tsp cornstarch

1 lb dried vermicelli

1 tbsp olive oil

salt and pepper

T O   G A R N I S H

1 fresh mint sprig

lemon slices

lemon rind

1 Put the fish fillets in a large casserole. Pour the wine over and add the shallots, garlic, herbs, lemon peel and juice, nutmeg, and anchovies. Season. Cover and bake in a preheated oven at 350°F for 35 minutes.

2 Transfer the fish to a warm dish. Set aside and keep warm.

3 Pour the cooking liquid into a pan and bring to a boil. Simmer for 25 minutes, until reduced by half. Mix the cream and cornstarch and stir into the sauce to thicken.

4 Meanwhile, bring a pan of lightly salted water to a boil. Add the vermicelli and oil and cook for 8–10 minutes, until tender but still firm to the bite. Drain the pasta and transfer to a warm serving dish.

5 Arrange the fillets on top of the vermicelli and pour the sauce over. Garnish with a fresh mint sprig, slices of lemon and strips of lemon peel. Serve immediately.

Sardinian Red Mullet

Red mullet has a beautiful pink skin, which is enhanced in this dish by being cooked in red wine and orange juice.

NUTRITIONAL INFORMATION

Calories	287	Sugars	........15g
Protein	........31g	Fat	...........9g
Carbohydrate	...15g	Saturates	.......1g

2½ HOURS   25 MINS

SERVES 4

INGREDIENTS

1¾ oz sultanas

⅔ cup red wine

2 tbsp olive oil

2 medium onions, sliced

1 zucchini, cut into 2-inch sticks

2 oranges

2 tsp coriander seeds, lightly crushed

4 red mullet, boned and filleted

1¾-oz can anchovy fillets, drained

2 tbsp chopped, fresh oregano

1 Place the sultanas in a bowl. Pour the red wine over and leave to soak for about 10 minutes.

COOK'S TIP

Red mullet is usually available all year round – frozen, if not fresh – from your fishmerchant or supermarket. If you cannot get hold of it try using telapia. This dish can also be served warm, if you prefer.

2 Heat the oil in a large skillet. Add the onions and sauté for 2 minutes.

3 Add the zucchini to the skillet and fry for a further 3 minutes, or until tender.

4 Using a zester, pare long, thin strips from one of the oranges. Using a sharp knife, remove the skin from both of the oranges, then segment the oranges by slicing between the lines of pith.

5 Add the orange zest to the skillet with the coriander seeds, red wine, sultanas, red mullet, and anchovies. Leave to simmer for 10–15 minutes, or until the fish is cooked through.

6 Stir in the oregano, set aside, and leave to cool. Place the mixture in a large bowl and leave to chill, covered, in the refrigerator for at least 2 hours to allow the flavors to mingle. Transfer to serving plates and serve.

Charred Tuna Steaks

Tuna has a firm flesh, which is ideal for barbecuing, but it can be a little dry unless it is marinated first.

NUTRITIONAL INFORMATION

Calories	 153	Sugars	.... 1g	
Protein	.... 29g	Fat	.... 3g	
Carbohydrate	.... 1g	Saturates	...... 1g	

2 HOURS   15 MINS

SERVES 4

INGREDIENTS

4 tuna steaks

3 tbsp soy sauce

1 tbsp Worcestershire sauce

1 tsp wholegrain mustard

1 tsp sugar

1 tbsp sunflower oil

green salad, to serve

TO GARNISH

flat-leaf parsley

lemon wedges

1 Place the tuna steaks in a shallow, non-metallic dish.

2 Mix together the soy sauce, Worcestershire sauce, mustard, sugar, and oil in a small bowl.

3 Pour the marinade over the tuna steaks.

4 Gently turn over the tuna steaks, using your fingers or a fork. Make sure the fish steaks are well coated with the marinade.

5 Cover and place the tuna steaks in the refrigerator. Leave to chill for between 30 minutes and 2 hours.

6 Barbecue the marinated fish over hot coals for 10–15 minutes, turning once. Alternatively, broil on high for about 5 minutes on each side

7 Baste frequently with any of the marinade that is left in the dish.

8 Garnish with flat-leaf parsley and lemon wedges. Serve with a fresh green salad.

COOK'S TIP

If a marinade contains soy sauce, the marinating time should be limited, usually to 2 hours. If allowed to marinate for too long, the fish will dry out and become tough.

Poached Salmon with Penne

Fresh salmon and pasta in a mouthwatering lemon and watercress sauce — a wonderful summer evening treat.

NUTRITIONAL INFORMATION

Calories 968	Sugars 3g	
Protein 59g	Fat 58g	
Carbohydrate ...49g	Saturates 19g	

 10 MINS   30 MINS

SERVES 4

I N G R E D I E N T S

9½-oz fresh salmon steaks

4 tbsp butter

¾ cup dry white wine

sea salt

8 black peppercorns

fresh dill sprig

fresh tarragon sprig

1 lemon, sliced

1 lb dried penne

2 tbsp olive oil

lemon slices and fresh watercress,
   to garnish

LEMON &
WATERCRESS SAUCE

2 tbsp butter

2 tbsp all-purpose flour

⅔ cup warm milk

juice and finely grated peel of 2 lemons

1 cup chopped watercress

salt and pepper

1 Put the salmon in a large, nonstick pan. Add the butter, wine, a pinch of sea salt, the peppercorns, dill, tarragon, and lemon. Cover, bring to a boil, and simmer for 10 minutes.

2 Using a pancake turner, carefully remove the salmon. Strain and reserve the cooking liquid. Remove and discard the salmon skin and center bones. Place on a warm dish, cover, and keep warm.

3 Meanwhile, bring a saucepan of salted water to the boil. Add the penne and 1 tbsp of the oil and cook for 8–10 minutes, until tender but still firm to the bite. Drain and sprinkle the remaining olive oil over. Place on a warm serving dish, top with the salmon steaks, and keep warm.

4 To make the sauce, melt the butter and stir in the flour for 2 minutes. Stir in the milk and about 7 tbsp of the reserved cooking liquid. Add the lemon juice and peel and cook, stirring, for a further 10 minutes.

5 Add the watercress to the sauce, stir gently, and season to taste with salt and pepper.

6 Pour the sauce over the salmon and penne, garnish with slices of lemon and fresh watercress and serve.

Salmon Lasagne Rolls

Sheets of green lasagne are filled with a mixture of fresh salmon and oyster mushrooms. This recipe has been adapted for the microwave.

NUTRITIONAL INFORMATION

Calories 352	Sugars 5g	
Protein 19g	Fat 19g	
Carbohydrate ...25g	Saturates 9g	

  20 MINS · 35 MINS

SERVES 4

INGREDIENTS

8 sheets green lasagne

1 onion, sliced

1 tbsp butter

½ red bell pepper, chopped

1 zucchini, diced

1 tsp chopped gingerroot

1½ cups chopped oyster mushrooms,
　preferably yellow

8 oz fresh salmon fillet, skinned, and
　cut into chunks

2 tbsp dry sherry

2 tsp cornstarch

3 tbsp all-purpose flour

1½ tbsp butter

1¼ cups milk

¼ cup grated Cheddar cheese

¼ cup fresh white bread crumbs

salt and pepper

salad leaves, to serve

1 Place the lasagne sheets in a large shallow dish. Cover with plenty of boiling water. Cook on HIGH power for 5 minutes. Leave to stand, covered, for a few minutes before draining. Rinse in cold water and lay the sheets out on a clean work surface.

2 Put the onion and butter into a bowl. Cover and cook on HIGH power for 2 minutes. Add the bell pepper, zucchini and gingerroot. Cover and cook on HIGH power for 3 minutes.

3 Add the mushrooms and salmon to the bowl. Mix the sherry into the cornstarch, then stir into the bowl. Cover and cook on HIGH power for 4 minutes until the fish flakes when tested with a fork. Season to taste.

4 Whisk the flour, butter, and milk in a bowl. Cook on HIGH power for 3–4 minutes, whisking every minute, to give a sauce of coating consistency. Stir in half the cheese and season with salt and pepper to taste.

5 Spoon the salmon filling in equal quantities along the shorter side of each lasagne sheet. Roll up to enclose the filling. Arrange in a lightly oiled large rectangular dish. Pour the sauce over and sprinkle the remaining cheese and the bread crumbs over.

6 Cook on HIGH power for 3 minutes until heated through. If possible, lightly brown under a preheated broiler before serving. Serve with a salad.

Tuna with Roasted Peppers

Fresh tuna will be either a small bonito fish or steaks from a skipjack.
The more delicately flavored fish have a paler flesh.

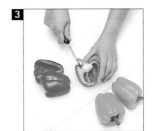

NUTRITIONAL INFORMATION

Calories 428   Sugars 5g
Protein ....60g   Fat 19g
Carbohydrate ....5g   Saturates 3g

 20 MINS   30 MINS

SERVES 4

INGREDIENTS

4 tuna steaks, about 9 oz each

3 tbsp lemon juice

4 cups water

6 tbsp olive oil

2 orange bell peppers

2 red bell peppers

12 black olives

1 tsp balsamic vinegar

salt and pepper

1 Put the tuna steaks into a bowl with the lemon juice and water. Leave for 15 minutes.

2 Drain and brush the steaks all over with olive oil and season well with salt and pepper.

3 Halve, core, and seed the bell peppers. Put them over a hot barbecue and cook for 12 minutes until they are charred all over. Put them into a plastic bag and seal it.

4 Meanwhile, cook the tuna over a hot barbecue for 12–15 minutes, turning once.

5 When the bell peppers are cool enough to handle, peel them and cut each piece into 4 strips. Toss them with the remaining olive oil, olives, and balsamic vinegar.

6 Serve the tuna steaks piping hot, with the roasted bell pepper salad.

COOK'S TIP

Red, orange, and yellow bell peppers can also be peeled by cooking them in a hot oven for 30 minutes, turning them frequently, or roasting them straight over a gas flame, again turning them frequently. In both methods, seed the bell peppers after peeling.

Spaghetti al Tonno

The classic Italian combination of pasta and tuna is enhanced in this recipe with a delicious parsley sauce.

NUTRITIONAL INFORMATION

Calories 1065	Sugars 3g
Protein 27g	Fat 85g
Carbohydrate . . .52g	Saturates 18g

10 MINS   15 MINS

SERVES 4

INGREDIENTS

7-oz can tuna, drained

2-oz can anchovies, drained

1 cup olive oil, plus 2 tbsp

1 cup roughly chopped flat-leaf parsley

⅔ cup crème fraîche or sour cream

1 lb dried spaghetti

2 tbsp butter

salt and pepper

black olives, to garnish

crusty bread, to serve

1 Remove any bones from the tuna. Put the tuna into a food processor or blender, together with the anchovies, olive oil, and the flat-leaf parsley. Process until the sauce is very smooth.

VARIATION

You can also add 1 or 2 garlic cloves to the sauce, substitute ½ cup chopped fresh basil for half the parsley, and garnish with capers instead of black olives.

2 Spoon the crème fraîche into the food processor or blender and process again for a few seconds to blend thoroughly. Season with salt and pepper to taste.

3 Bring a large pan of lightly salted water to a boil. Add the spaghetti and the remaining olive oil and cook for 8–10 minutes until tender, but still firm to the bite.

4 Drain the spaghetti, return to the pan and place over a medium heat. Add the butter and toss well to coat. Spoon in the sauce and quickly toss into the spaghetti.

5 Remove the pan from the heat and divide the spaghetti between 4 warm individual serving plates. Garnish with the olives and serve immediately with warm, crusty bread.

Baked Red Snapper

You can substitute other whole fish for the snapper, or use cutlets of cod or halibut.

NUTRITIONAL INFORMATION

Calories 519	Sugars 12g	
Protein 61g	Fat 23g	
Carbohydrate ...18g	Saturates 3g	

 20 MINS 50 MINS

SERVES 4

INGREDIENTS

1 red snapper, about 2 lb 12 oz, drawn

juice of 2 limes, or 1 lemon

4-5 sprigs of thyme or parsley

3 tbsp olive oil

1 large onion, chopped

2 garlic cloves, finely chopped

1 x 15-oz can chopped tomatoes

2 tbsp tomato paste

2 tbsp red-wine vinegar

5 tbsp low-fat plain yogurt

2 tbsp chopped parsley

2 tsp dried oregano

6 tbsp dry bread crumbs

¼ cup low-fat feta cheese, crumbled

salt and pepper

SALAD

1 small lettuce, thickly sliced

10-12 young spinach leaves, torn

½ small cucumber, sliced and quartered

4 scallions, thickly sliced

3 tbsp chopped parsley

2 tbsp olive oil

2 tbsp plain low-fat yogurt

1 tbsp red-wine vinegar

 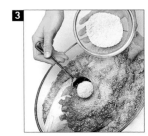

1 Sprinkle the lime or lemon juice inside and over the fish and season. Place the herbs inside the fish.

2 Heat the oil in a pan and fry the onion until translucent. Stir in the garlic and cook for 1 minute, then add the chopped tomatoes, tomato paste, and vinegar. Simmer, uncovered, for 5 minutes. Allow the sauce to cool, then stir in the yogurt, parsley, and oregano.

3 Pour half of the sauce into a baking dish just large enough for the fish. Add the fish and then pour the remainder of the sauce over it, and sprinkle with bread crumbs. Bake, uncovered, for 30-35 minutes. Sprinkle the cheese over the fish and serve with lime wedges and dill sprigs.

4 Arrange the salad ingredients in a bowl. Whisk the oil, yogurt, and vinegar and pour over the salad.

Salmon with Caper Sauce

The richness of salmon is perfectly balanced by the tangy capers in this creamy herb sauce.

NUTRITIONAL INFORMATION

Calories . . . . . . .302 Sugars 0g
Protein . . . . .21g Fat 24g
Carbohydrate . . . .1g Saturates 9g

5 MINS   25 MINS

SERVES 4

INGREDIENTS

4 salmon fillets, skinned

1 fresh bay leaf

few black peppercorns

1 tsp white-wine vinegar

⅔ cup fish stock

3 tbsp heavy cream

1 tbsp capers

1 tbsp chopped fresh dill

1 tbsp chopped fresh chives

1 tsp cornstarch

2 tbsp skim milk

salt and pepper

new potatoes, to serve

TO GARNISH

fresh dill sprigs

chive flowers

1 Lay the salmon fillets in a shallow baking dish. Add the bay leaf, peppercorns, vinegar, and stock.

2 Cover with foil and bake in a preheated oven at 350°F for 15–20 minutes until the flesh is opaque and flakes easily when tested with a fork.

3 Transfer the fish to warmed serving plates, cover, and keep warm.

4 Strain the cooking liquid into a saucepan. Stir in the cream, capers, dill, and chives and seasoning to taste.

5 Blend the cornstarch with the milk. Add to the saucepan and heat, stirring, until thickened slightly. Boil for 1 minute.

6 Spoon the sauce over the salmon and garnish with dill sprigs and chive flowers.

7 Serve with boiled new potatoes.

COOK'S TIP

Ask the fishmerchant to skin the fillets for you. The cooking time for the salmon will depend on the thickness of the fish: the thin tail end of the salmon takes the least time to cook.

Marinated Fish

Marinating fish, for even a short period, adds a subtle flavor to the flesh and makes even simply broiled or fried fish delicious.

NUTRITIONAL INFORMATION

Calories 361   Sugars 0g

Protein . . . . .26g   Fat 29g

Carbohydrate . . . .0g   Saturates 5g

45 MINS   🕐 15 MINS

SERVES 4

I N G R E D I E N T S

4 whole mackerel, cleaned

4 tbsp chopped marjoram

2 tbsp extra-virgin olive oil

finely grated peel and juice of 1 lime

2 garlic cloves, crushed

salt and pepper

1 Under gently running water, scrape the mackerel with the blunt side of a knife to remove any scales.

2 Using a sharp knife, make a slit in the stomach of the fish and cut horizontally along until the knife will go no farther very easily. Gut the fish and rinse under water. You may prefer to remove the heads before cooking, but it is not necessary.

3 Using a sharp knife, cut 4–5 diagonal slashes on each side of the fish. Place the fish in a shallow, nonmetallic dish.

4 To make the marinade, mix together the marjoram, olive oil, lime peel and juice, garlic, and salt and pepper in a bowl.

5 Pour the marinade over the fish. Leave to marinate in the refrigerator for about 30 minutes.

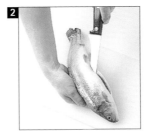 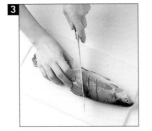 

6 Cook the mackerel, under a heated broiler, for 5–6 minutes on each side, brushing occasionally with the reserved marinade, until golden.

7 Transfer the fish to serving plates. Pour any remaining marinade over before serving.

COOK'S TIP

If the lime is too firm to squeeze, microwave on high power for 30 seconds to release the juice. This dish is also excellent cooked on the barbecue.

Macaroni & Seafood Bake

This adaptation of an eighteenth-century Italian dish is baked until it is golden brown and sizzling, then cut into wedges like a cake.

NUTRITIONAL INFORMATION

Calories ....478 Sugars 6g
Protein ....27g Fat 17g
Carbohydrate ...57g Saturates 7g

 30 MINS   50 MINS

SERVES 4

I N G R E D I E N T S

3 cups dried short-cut macaroni

1 tbsp olive oil, plus extra for brushing

6 tbsp butter, plus extra for greasing

2 small fennel bulbs, thinly sliced and
    fronds reserved

⅔ cup mushrooms, thinly sliced

6 oz peeled, cooked shrimp

pinch of cayenne pepper

1 ¼ cups Béchamel Sauce (see page 14)

⅔ cup freshly grated Parmesan cheese

2 large tomatoes, sliced

1 tsp dried oregano

salt and pepper

1 Bring a saucepan of salted water to a boil. Add the pasta and oil and cook for 8–10 minutes until tender, but still firm to the bite. Drain the pasta and return to the pan.

2 Add 2 tbsp of the butter to the pasta, cover, and shake the pan; keep warm.

3 Melt the remaining butter in a saucepan. Fry the fennel for 3–4 minutes. Stir in the mushrooms and fry for a further 2 minutes.

4 Stir in the shrimp, then remove the pan from the heat.

5 Stir the cayenne pepper and shrimp mixture into the Béchamel Sauce.

6 Pour into a greased baking dish and spread evenly. Sprinkle the Parmesan cheese over and arrange the tomato slices in a ring around the edge. Brush the tomatoes with olive oil and then sprinkle the oregano over.

7 Bake in a preheated oven at 350°F for 25 minutes, until golden brown. Serve immediately.

Seafood Pizza

Make a change from the standard pizza toppings – this dish is piled high with seafood baked with a red bell pepper and tomato sauce.

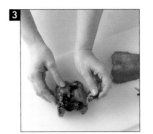

NUTRITIONAL INFORMATION

Calories	248	Sugars	.........7g
Protein	........27g	Fat	............6g
Carbohydrate	...22g	Saturates	......2g

🍲 25 MINS   🕐 55 MINS

SERVES 4

INGREDIENTS

5 oz standard pizza crust mix

4 tbsp chopped fresh dill, or 2 tbsp dried dill

fresh dill, to garnish

SAUCE

1 large red bell pepper

14-oz can chopped tomatoes with onion and herbs

3 tbsp tomato paste

salt and pepper

TOPPING

12 oz assorted cooked seafood, thawed if frozen

1 tbsp capers in brine, drained

¼ cup pitted black olives in brine, drained

¼ cup low-fat grated mozzarella cheese

1 tbsp grated Parmesan cheese

1 Preheat the oven to 400°F. Place the pizza crust mix in a bowl and stir in the dill. Make the dough according to the directions on the packet.

2 Press the dough into a circle measuring 10 inches across on a cookie sheet lined with waxed paper. Set aside to rise.

3 Preheat the broiler to hot. To start making the sauce, halve and seed the bell pepper and arrange on a broiler rack. Broil for 8–10 minutes until softened and charred. Leave the peppers to cool slightly, then peel off the skin and chop the flesh.

4 Place the tomatoes and bell pepper in a saucepan. Bring to a boil and simmer for 10 minutes. Stir in the tomato paste and season to taste.

5 Spread the sauce over the pizza crust and top with the seafood. Sprinkle the capers and olives over, top with the cheeses, and bake for 25–30 minutes.

6 Garnish with sprigs of dill and serve hot.

Mediterranean Fish Stew

Popular in fishing ports around Europe, gentle stewing is an excellent way to maintain the flavour and succulent texture of fish and shellfish.

NUTRITIONAL INFORMATION

Calories . . . . . . .533 Sugars 11g
Protein . . . . .71g Fat 10g
Carbohydrate . . .30g Saturates 2g

  1¼ HOURS   25 MINS

SERVES 4

INGREDIENTS

2 tsp olive oil

2 red onions, sliced

2 garlic cloves, crushed

2 tbsp red-wine vinegar

2 tsp sugar

1¼ cups Fish Stock (see page 16)

1¼ cups dry red wine

2 × 14-oz cans chopped tomatoes

8 oz baby eggplant, quartered

8 oz yellow zucchini, quartered or sliced

1 green bell pepper, sliced

1 tbsp chopped fresh rosemary

1 lb 2 oz halibut fillet, skinned and cut into
    1-inch cubes

1 lb 10 oz fresh mussels, prepared

8 oz baby squid, cleaned, trimmed, and
    sliced into rings

8 oz fresh jumbo shrimp, peeled and
    deveined

salt and pepper

4 slices toasted French bread rubbed with a
    cut garlic clove

lemon wedges, to serve

1 Heat the oil in a large nonstick saucepan and fry the onions and garlic gently for 3 minutes.

2 Stir in the vinegar and sugar and cook for a further 2 minutes.

3 Stir in the stock, wine, canned tomatoes, eggplant, zucchini, bell pepper, and rosemary. Bring to a boil and simmer, uncovered, for 10 minutes.

4 Add the halibut, mussels, and squid. Mix well and simmer, covered, for 5 minutes until the fish is opaque.

5 Stir in the shrimp and continue to simmer, covered, for a further 2–3 minutes until the shrimp are pink and cooked through.

6 Discard any mussels which haven't opened and season to taste.

7 To serve, put a slice of the prepared garlic bread in the bottom of each warm serving bowl and ladle the stew over the top. Serve with lemon wedges.

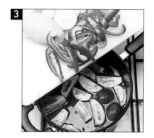

Smoky Fish Pie

This flavorsome and colorful fish pie is perfect for a light supper. The addition of smoked salmon gives it a touch of luxury.

NUTRITIONAL INFORMATION

Calories	523	Sugars	........15g
Protein	........58g	Fat	...........6g
Carbohydrate	...63g	Saturates	......2g

  15 MINS   1 HOUR

SERVES 4

INGREDIENTS

2 lb smoked haddock or cod fillets

2½ cups skim milk

2 bay leaves

1½ cups quartered button mushrooms

1 cup frozen peas

1 cup frozen corn kernels

4 cups diced potatoes

5 tbsp low-fat plain yogurt

4 tbsp chopped fresh parsley

2 oz smoked salmon, sliced into thin strips

3 tbsp cornstarch

¼ cup grated smoked cheese

salt and pepper

COOK'S TIP

Use smoked haddock or cod that has not been dyed bright yellow or artificially flavored to give the illusion of having been smoked.

1 Preheat the oven to 400°F. Place the fish in a pan and add the milk and bay leaves. Bring to a boil, cover, and then simmer for 5 minutes.

2 Add the mushrooms, peas, and corn, bring back to a simmer, cover, and cook for 5–7 minutes. Leave to cool.

3 Place the potatoes in a saucepan, cover with water, boil, and cook for 8 minutes. Drain well and mash with a fork or a potato masher. Stir in the yogurt, parsley, and seasoning. Set aside.

4 Using a draining spoon, remove the fish from the pan. Flake the cooked fish away from the skin and place in a gratin dish. Reserve the cooking liquid.

5 Drain the vegetables, reserving the cooking liquid. Gently stir into the fish with the salmon strips.

6 Blend a little cooking liquid into the cornstarch to make a paste. Transfer the rest of the liquid to a saucepan and add the paste. Heat through, stirring, until thickened. Discard the bay leaves and season to taste. Pour the sauce over the fish and vegetables and stir. Spoon the mashed potato over so the fish is covered, sprinkle with cheese, and bake for 25–30 minutes.

Smoked Fish Lasagne

Use smoked cod or haddock in this delicious lasagne. It's a great way to make a small amount of fish go a long way.

NUTRITIONAL INFORMATION

Calories	483	Sugars	.........8g
Protein	........36g	Fat	..........24g
Carbohydrate	...32g	Saturates	......12g

🍲 20 MINS   🕐 1¼ HOURS

SERVES 4

I N G R E D I E N T S

2 tsp olive or vegetable oil

1 garlic clove, crushed

1 small onion, finely chopped

1½ cups sliced mushrooms,

14-oz can chopped tomatoes

1 small zucchini, sliced

⅔ cup vegetable stock or water

2 tbsp butter or margarine

1¼ cups skim milk

2 tbsp all-purpose flour

1 cup grated sharp Cheddar cheese

1 tbsp chopped fresh parsley

6 sheets precooked lasagne

12 oz skinned and boned smoked cod or
   haddock, cut into chunks

salt and pepper

fresh parsley sprigs to garnish

1 Heat the oil in a saucepan and fry the garlic and onion for about 5 minutes. Add the mushrooms and cook for 3 minutes, stirring.

2 Add the tomatoes, zucchini, and stock or water and simmer, uncovered, for 15–20 minutes until the vegetables are soft. Season.

3 Put the butter or margarine, milk, and flour into a small saucepan and heat, whisking constantly, until the sauce boils and thickens. Remove from the heat and add half of the cheese and all of the parsley. Stir gently to melt the cheese and season to taste.

4 Spoon the tomato sauce mixture into a large, shallow baking dish and top with half of the lasagne sheets. Scatter the chunks of fish evenly over the top, then pour half of the cheese sauce over. Top with the remaining lasagne sheets and then spread the rest of the cheese sauce on top. Sprinkle with the remaining cheese.

5 Bake in a preheated oven at 375°F for 40 minutes, until the top is golden brown and bubbling. Garnish with parsley sprigs and serve hot.

Stuffed Squid

Whole squid are stuffed with a mixture of fresh herbs and sun-dried tomatoes and then cooked in a wine sauce.

NUTRITIONAL INFORMATION

Calories 276   Sugars 1g
Protein ....23g   Fat 8g
Carbohydrate ...20g   Saturates 1g

 25 MINS   35 MINS

SERVES 4

INGREDIENTS

8 squid, cleaned and drawn but left whole
   (ask your fishmerchant to do this)

6 canned anchovies, chopped

2 garlic cloves, chopped

2 tbsp rosemary, stalks removed and
   leaves chopped

2 sun-dried tomatoes, chopped

1½ cups bread crumbs

1 tbsp olive oil

1 onion, finely chopped

¾ cup white wine

¾ cup fish stock

cooked rice, to serve

1 Remove the tentacles from the body of the squid and chop the flesh finely.

2 Grind the anchovies, garlic, rosemary, and tomatoes to a paste in a mortar and pestle.

3 Add the bread crumbs and the chopped squid tentacles and mix. If the mixture is too dry to form a thick paste at this point, add 1 teaspoon of water.

4 Spoon the paste into the body sacs of the squid then tie a piece of thread around the end of each sac to fasten them; do not overfill the sacs, because they will expand during cooking.

5 Heat the oil in a skillet. Add the onion and cook, stirring, for 3–4 minutes, or until golden.

6 Add the stuffed squid to the pan and cook for 3–4 minutes, or until brown all over.

7 Add the wine and stock and bring to a boil. Reduce the heat, cover, and then leave to simmer for 15 minutes.

8 Remove the lid and cook for a further 5 minutes, or until the squid is tender and the juices reduced. Serve with plenty of cooked rice.

Pasta & Shrimp Packages

This is the ideal dish for an after-work dinner party because the packages can be prepared in advance, then put in the oven when you are ready to eat.

NUTRITIONAL INFORMATION

Calories 640	Sugars 1g
Protein 50g	Fat 29g
Carbohydrate ...42g	Saturates 4g

15 MINS   30 MINS

SERVES 4

I N G R E D I E N T S

1 lb dried fettuccine

⅔ cup pesto sauce

4 tsp extra-virgin olive oil

1 lb 10 oz large raw shrimp, peeled and deveined

2 garlic cloves, crushed

½ cup dry white wine

salt and pepper

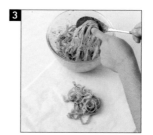  

1 Cut out four 12-inch squares of waxed paper or baking parchment.

2 Bring a large saucepan of lightly salted water to a boil. Add the fettuccine and cook for 2–3 minutes, until just softened; drain and set aside.

3 Mix together the fettuccine and half of the pesto sauce. Spread out the paper squares and put 1 tsp olive oil in the middle of each. Divide the fettuccine between the the squares, then divide the shrimp and place on top of the fettuccine.

4 Mix together the remaining pesto sauce and the garlic and spoon it over the shrimp. Season each package with salt and black pepper and sprinkle with the white wine.

5 Dampen the edges of the paper and wrap the pakcages loosely, twisting the edges to seal.

6 Place the packages on a cookie sheet and bake in a preheated oven at 400°F for 10–15 minutes. Transfer the parcels to 4 individual serving plates and serve.

COOK'S TIP

Traditionally, these packages are designed to look like money bags.

Pan-Fried Shrimp

A luxurious dish which makes an impressive first course or light meal. Shrimp and garlic are a winning combination.

NUTRITIONAL INFORMATION

Calories	455	Sugars	.........0g
Protein	.........6g	Fat	..........37g
Carbohydrate	....0g	Saturates	......18g

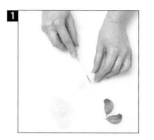

10 MINS   5 MINS

SERVES 4

I N G R E D I E N T S

4 garlic cloves

20–24 unshelled large raw shrimp

½ cup butter

4 tbsp olive oil

6 tbsp brandy

salt and pepper

2 tbsp chopped fresh parsley

T O   S E R V E

lemon wedges

ciabatta bread

1 Using a sharp knife, peel and slice the garlic.

2 Wash the shrimp and pat dry using paper towels.

3 Melt the butter with the oil in a large skillet. Add the garlic and shrimp, and fry over a high heat, stirring, for 3–4 minutes until the shrimp are pink.

4 Sprinkle with brandy and season with salt and pepper to taste. Sprinkle with parsley and serve immediately with lemon wedges and ciabatta bread, if desired.

Pasta Shells with Mussels

Serve this aromatic seafood dish to family and friends who have a love of garlic.

NUTRITIONAL INFORMATION

Calories 686	Sugars 2g
Protein 30g	Fat 45g
Carbohydrate ...36g	Saturates 27g

15 MINS　　25 MINS

SERVES 6

I N G R E D I E N T S

2 lb 12 oz mussels

1 cup dry white wine

2 large onions, chopped

½ cup unsalted butter

6 large garlic cloves, finely chopped

5 tbsp chopped fresh parsley

1¼ cups heavy cream

14 oz dried pasta shells

1 tbsp olive oil

salt and pepper

crusty bread, to serve

1 Scrub and debeard the mussels under cold running water: discard any mussels that do not close immediately when sharply tapped. Put the mussels into a large saucepan, together with the wine and half of the onions. Cover and cook over a medium heat, shaking the pan frequently, for 2–3 minutes, or until the shells open. Remove the pan from the heat.

2 Drain the mussels and reserve the cooking liquid: discard any mussels that have not opened. Strain the cooking liquid through a clean cloth into a glass pitcher or bowl and reserve.

3 Melt the butter in a pan over a medium heat. Add the remaining onion and fry until translucent. Stir in the garlic and cook for 1 minute. Gradually stir in the reserved cooking liquid. Stir in the parsley and cream and season to taste with salt and pepper. Bring to simmering point over a low heat.

4 Meanwhile, bring a large pan of lightly salted water to the boil. Add the pasta and oil and cook for 8–10 minutes until just tender, but still firm to the bite. Drain the pasta, return to the pan, cover, and keep warm.

5 Reserve a few mussels for the garnish and remove the remainder from their shells. Stir the shelled mussels into the cream sauce and warm briefly.

6 Transfer the pasta to a serving dish. Pour the sauce over and toss to coat. Garnish with the reserved mussels.

Farfallini Buttered Lobster

This is one of those dishes that looks almost too lovely to eat – but you should!

NUTRITIONAL INFORMATION

Calories . . . . . . .686 Sugars 1g
Protein . . . . .45g Fat 36g
Carbohydrate . . .44g Saturates 19g

30 MINS   25 MINS

SERVES 4

I N G R E D I E N T S

2 x 1 lb 9 oz lobsters, split into halves

juice and grated peel of 1 lemon

½ cup butter

4 tbsp fresh white bread crumbs

2 tbsp brandy

5 tbsp heavy cream or crème fraîche

1 lb dried farfallini

1 tbsp olive oil

½ cup freshly grated Parmesan cheese

salt and pepper

TO GARNISH

1 kiwi fruit, sliced

4 unpeeled, cooked jumbo shrimp

fresh dill sprigs

1 Carefully discard the stomach sac, vein, and gills from each lobster. Remove all the meat from the tail and chop. Crack the claws and legs, remove the meat, and chop. Transfer the meat to a bowl and add the lemon juice and grated lemon peel.

2 Clean the shells thoroughly and place in a warm oven at 325°F to dry out.

3 Melt 2 tbsp of the butter in a skillet. Add the bread crumbs and fry for about 3 minutes, until crisp and golden brown.

4 Melt the remaining butter in a saucepan. Add the lobster meat and heat through gently. Add the brandy and cook for a further 3 minutes, then add the cream or crème fraîche and season to taste with salt and pepper.

5 Meanwhile, bring a large pan of lightly salted water to a boil. Add the farfallini and olive oil and cook for 8–10 minutes, until tender but still firm to the bite. Drain and spoon the pasta into the clean lobster shells.

6 Top with the buttered lobster and sprinkle with a little grated Parmesan cheese and the bread crumbs. Broil for 2–3 minutes, until golden brown.

7 Transfer the lobster shells to a warm serving dish, garnish with the lemon slices, kiwi fruit, jumbo shrimp, and dill sprigs. Serve immediately.

Vermicelli with Clams

A quickly cooked recipe that transforms pantry ingredients into a dish with style.

NUTRITIONAL INFORMATION

Calories	520	Sugars	.........2g
Protein	........26g	Fat	..........13g
Carbohydrate	....71g	Saturates	.......4g

10 MINS   25 MINS

SERVES 4

INGREDIENTS

14 oz dried vermicelli, spaghetti, or other
    long pasta

2 tbsp olive oil

2 tbsp butter

2 onions, chopped

2 garlic cloves, chopped

7 oz jars clams in brine

½ cup white wine

4 tbsp chopped fresh parsley

½ tsp dried oregano

pinch of freshly grated nutmeg

salt and pepper

TO GARNISH

2 tbsp Parmesan cheese shavings

fresh basil sprigs

1 Bring a large pan of lightly salted water to a boil. Add the pasta and half of the olive oil and cook for 8–10 minutes until tender, but still firm to the bite. Drain, return to the pan, and add the butter. Cover the pan, shake well, and keep warm.

2 Heat the remaining oil in a pan over a medium heat. Add the onions and fry until they are translucent. Stir in the garlic and cook for 1 minute.

3 Strain the liquid from 1 jar of clams and add the liquid to the pan, with the wine. Stir, bring to simmering point, and simmer for 3 minutes. Drain the second jar of clams and discard the liquid.

4 Add the clams, parsley, and oregano to the pan and season with pepper and nutmeg. Lower the heat and cook until the sauce is heated through.

5 Transfer the pasta to a warm serving dish and pour the sauce over. Sprinkle with the Parmesan cheese, garnish with the basil, and serve immediately.

COOK'S TIP

There are many different types of clams found along almost every coast in the world. Those traditionally used in this dish are the tiny ones – only 1 to 2 inches across – known in Italy as *vongole*.

Baked Scallops & Pasta

This is another tempting seafood dish where the eye is delighted as much as the taste buds.

NUTRITIONAL INFORMATION

Calories 725	Sugars 2g
Protein 38g	Fat 48g
Carbohydrate ...38g	Saturates 25g

20 MINS   30 MINS

SERVES 4

INGREDIENTS

12 scallops

3 tbsp olive oil

12 oz small, dried whole wheat pasta shells

⅔ cup fish stock

1 onion, chopped

juice and finely grated peel of 2 lemons

⅔ cup heavy cream

2 cups grated cheddar cheese

salt and pepper

crusty brown bread, to serve

1 Remove the scallops from their shells. Scrape off the skirt and the black intestinal thread: reserve the white flesh and the orange coral, or roe. Very carefully ease the flesh and coral from the shell with a short, but very strong knife.

2 Wash the shells thoroughly and dry them well. Put the shells on a cookie sheet, sprinkle lightly with two-thirds of the olive oil, and set aside.

3 Meanwhile, bring a large saucepan of lightly salted water to a boil. Add the pasta shells and remaining olive oil and cook for 8–10 minutes or until tender, but still firm to the bite. Drain well and spoon an equal amount of pasta into each scallop shell.

4 Put the scallops, fish stock, lemon peel and onion in a baking dish and season to taste with pepper. Cover with foil and bake in a preheated oven at 350°F for 8 minutes.

5 Remove the dish from the oven. Remove the foil and, using a draining spoon, transfer the scallops to the shells. Add 1 tablespoon of the cooking liquid to each shell, together with a drizzle of lemon juice and a little cream, and top with the grated cheese.

6 Increase the oven temperature to 450°F and return the scallops to the oven for 4 minutes.

7 Serve the scallops in their shells with crusty brown bread and butter.

Meat

Italians have their very own special way of butchering meat, producing different cuts. Most meat is sold boned and often cut straight across the grain. Veal is a great favorite and widely available. Pork is also popular, with roasted pig being the traditional dish of Umbria. Suckling pig is roasted with lots of fresh herbs, especially rosemary,

until the skin is crisp and brown. Lamb is often served for special occasions, cooked on a spit or roasted in the oven with wine, garlic, and herbs; and the very small chops from young lambs feature widely, especially in Rome. Variety meats play an important role, too, with liver, brains, sweetbreads, tongue, heart, tripe, and kidneys always available. Whatever your favorite Italian meat dish is, it's sure to be included in this chapter.

Beef in Barolo

Barolo is a well-known wine from the Piedmont area of Italy. Its mellow flavor is the key to this dish, so don't stint on the quality.

NUTRITIONAL INFORMATION

Calories	744	Sugars	.........1g
Protein	........66g	Fat	..........43g
Carbohydrate	....1g	Saturates	......16g

 15 MINS 2¼ HOURS

SERVES 4

INGREDIENTS

4 tbsp oil

2 lb 4 oz piece boned rolled rib of beef

2 garlic cloves, crushed

4 shallots, sliced

1 tsp chopped fresh rosemary

1 tsp chopped fresh oregano

2 celery stalks, sliced

1 large carrot, diced

2 cloves

1 bottle Barolo wine

freshly grated nutmeg

salt and pepper

cooked vegetables, such as broccoli, carrots, and new potatoes, to serve

1 Heat the oil in a flameproof casserole and brown the meat all over. Remove the meat from the casserole.

2 Add the garlic, shallots, herbs, celery, carrot, and cloves. Fry for 5 minutes.

3 Replace the meat on top of the vegetables. Pour in the wine, cover the casserole, and simmer gently for about 2 hours until tender. Remove the meat from the casserole, slice, and keep warm.

4 Rub the contents of the pan through a strainer or purée in a blender, adding a little hot beef stock if necessary. Season with nutmeg and salt and pepper.

5 Serve the meat with the sauce and accompanied by cooked vegetables, such as broccoli, carrots, and new potatoes, if wished.

Rich Beef Stew

This slow-cooked beef stew is flavored with oranges, red wine, and porcini mushrooms.

NUTRITIONAL INFORMATION

Calories	388	Sugars	........15g
Protein	........30g	Fat	..........21g
Carbohydrate	...16g	Saturates	.......9g

45 MINS   1¾ HOURS

SERVES 4

I N G R E D I E N T S

1 tbsp oil

1 tbsp butter

1½ cups peeled and halved baby onions

1 lb 5 oz stewing steak, diced into 1½-inch chunks

1¼ cup beef stock

⅔ cup red wine

4 tbsp chopped oregano

1 tbsp sugar

1 orange

1 oz porcini or other dried mushrooms

8 oz fresh plum tomatoes

cooked rice or potatoes, to serve

1 Heat the oil and butter in a large skillet. Add the onions and sauté for 5 minutes or until golden. Remove the onions with a draining spoon, set aside, and keep warm.

2 Add the beef to the pan and cook, stirring, for 5 minutes, or until browned all over.

3 Return the onions to the skillet and add the stock, wine, oregano, and sugar, stirring to mix well. Transfer the mixture to a casserole dish.

4 Pare the peel from the orange and cut it into strips. Slice the orange flesh into rings. Add the rings and the peel to the casserole. Cook in a preheated oven, at 350°F, for 1¼ hours.

5 Soak the porcini mushrooms for 30 minutes in a small bowl containing 4 tablespoons of warm water.

6 Peel and halve the tomatoes. Add the tomatoes, porcini mushrooms, and their soaking liquid to the casserole. Cook for a further 20 minutes until the beef is tender and the juices thickened. Serve with cooked rice or potatoes.

Beef Rolls in Rich Gravy

Wafer-thin slices of tender beef with a rich garlic and bacon stuffing, flavored with the tang of orange.

NUTRITIONAL INFORMATION

Calories 379   Sugars 4g
Protein . . . . .26g   Fat 24g
Carbohydrate . . . .4g   Saturates 8g

20 MINS   20 MINS

SERVES 4

I N G R E D I E N T S

8 thin-sliced beef, topside cut into thin strips

4 tbsp chopped fresh parsley

4 garlic cloves, finely chopped

1 cup minced smoked bacon

grated peel of ½ small orange

2 tbsp olive oil

1¼ cups dry red wine

1 bay leaf

1 tsp sugar

½ cup drained pitted black olives

salt and pepper

TO GARNISH

orange slices

chopped fresh parsley

1 Flatten the beef slices as thinly as possible using a meat tenderizer or mallet; trim the edges to neaten them.

2 Mix together the parsley, garlic, bacon, orange peel, and salt and pepper to taste. Spread this mixture evenly over each beef slice.

3 Roll up each beef slice tightly, then secure with a wooden toothpick. Heat

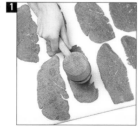

the oil in a skillet and fry the beef on all sides for 10 minutes.

4 Drain the beef rolls, reserving the pan juices; keep warm. Pour the wine into the juices, add the bay leaf, sugar, and seasoning. Bring to a boil and boil rapidly for 5 minutes to reduce slightly, stirring.

5 Return the cooked beef to the pan along with the black olives and heat through for a further 2 minutes. Discard the bay leaf and toothpicks.

6 Transfer the beef rolls and gravy to a serving dish. Serve garnished with orange slices and parsley.

Creamed Strips of Sirloin

This quick-and-easy dish tastes superb and makes a delicious treat for a special occasion.

NUTRITIONAL INFORMATION

Calories	796	Sugars	.........2g
Protein	........29g	Fat	..........63g
Carbohydrate	...26g	Saturates	......39g

15 MINS   30 MINS

SERVES 4

INGREDIENTS

6 tbsp butter

1 lb boneless sirloin steak, trimmed
    and cut into thin strips

2½ cups sliced button mushrooms

1 tsp mustard

pinch of freshly grated gingerroot

2 tbsp dry sherry

⅔ cup heavy cream

salt and pepper

4 slices hot toast, cut into triangles,
    to serve

PASTA

1 lb dried rigatoni

2 tbsp olive oil

2 fresh basil sprigs

½ cup butter

1 Melt the butter in a large skillet and gently fry the steak over a low heat, stirring frequently, for 6 minutes. Using a draining spoon, transfer the steak to a dish and keep warm.

2 Add the sliced mushrooms to the skillet and cook for 2–3 minutes in the juices remaining in the pan. Add the mustard, ginger, and salt and pepper. Cook for 2 minutes, then add the sherry and cream. Cook for a further 3 minutes, then pour the cream sauce over the steak.

3 Bake the steak and cream mixture in a heated oven at 375°F, for 10 minutes.

4 Meanwhile, cook the pasta. Bring a large saucepan of lightly salted water to a boil. Add the rigatoni, olive oil, and 1 of the basil sprigs and boil rapidly for 10 minutes, until tender but still firm to the bite. Drain the pasta and transfer to a warm serving plate. Toss the pasta with the butter and garnish with a sprig of basil.

5 Serve the creamed steak strips with the pasta and triangles of warm toast.

COOK'S TIP

Dried pasta will keep for up to 6 months. Keep it in the package and reseal it once you have opened it, or transfer the pasta to an airtight jar.

Beef & Spaghetti Surprise

This delicious Sicilian recipe originated as a handy way of using up leftover cooked pasta.

NUTRITIONAL INFORMATION

Calories . . . . . . .797 Sugars 7g
Protein . . . . .31g Fat 60g
Carbohydrate . . .35g Saturates 16g

30 MINS   1½ HOURS

SERVES 4

INGREDIENTS

⅔ cup olive oil, plus extra for brushing

2 eggplants

12 oz ground beef

1 onion, chopped

2 garlic cloves, minced

2 tbsp tomato paste

14-oz can chopped tomatoes

1 tsp Worcestershire sauce

1 tsp chopped fresh marjoram or oregano
    or ½ tsp dried marjoram or oregano

½ cup pitted black olives, sliced

1 green, red, or yellow bell pepper, cored,
    seeded, and chopped

6 oz dried spaghetti

1 cup freshly grated Parmesan cheese

salt and pepper

fresh oregano or parsley sprigs,
    to garnish

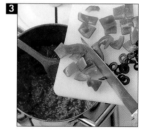

1 Brush a 8 inch loose-bottomed round cake pan with oil, line the base with baking parchment, and brush with oil.

2 Slice the eggplants. Heat a little oil in a pan and fry the eggplant, in batches, for 3–4 minutes or until browned on both sides. Add more oil, as necessary. Drain on paper towels.

3 Put the ground beef, onion, and garlic in a saucepan and cook over a medium heat, stirring occasionally, until browned. Add the tomato paste, tomatoes, Worcestershire sauce, marjoram or oregano, and salt and pepper to taste. Leave to simmer, stirring occasionally, for 10 minutes. Add the olives and bell pepper and cook for a further 10 minutes.

4 Bring a pan of salted water to the boil. Add the spaghetti and 1 tbsp oil and cook for 8–10 minutes until tender, but still firm to the bite. Drain and turn the spaghetti into a bowl. Add the meat mixture and cheese and toss with 2 forks.

5 Arrange eggplant slices over the base and up the sides of the pan. Add the spaghetti, pressing down firmly, then cover with the rest of the eggplant slices. Bake in a preheated oven at 400°F for 40 minutes. Leave to stand for 5 minutes, then invert onto a serving dish. Discard the baking parchment. Garnish with the fresh herbs and serve.

Beef & Potato Ravioli

In this recipe the "pasta" dough is made with potatoes instead of flour. The small round ravioli are filled with a rich spaghetti sauce.

NUTRITIONAL INFORMATION

Calories	618	Sugars	.........4g
Protein	........16g	Fat	..........31g
Carbohydrate	...74g	Saturates	......12g

30 MINS   50 MINS

SERVES 4

INGREDIENTS

FILLING

1 tbsp vegetable oil

4½ oz ground beef

1 shallot, diced

1 garlic clove, minced

1 tbsp all-purpose flour

1 tbsp tomato paste

⅔ cup beef stock

1 celery stalk, chopped

2 tomatoes, peeled and diced

2 tsp chopped fresh basil

salt and pepper

RAVIOLI

1 lb mealy potatoes, diced

3 small egg yolks

3 tbsp olive oil

1½ cups all-purpose flour

¼ cup butter, for frying

shredded basil leaves, to garnish

1 To make the filling, heat the vegetable oil in a pan and fry the beef for 3-4 minutes, breaking it up with a spoon.

2 Add the shallots and garlic to the pan and cook for 2-3 minutes, or until the shallots have softened.

3 Stir in the flour and tomato paste and cook for 1 minute. Stir in the beef stock, celery, tomatoes, and chopped fresh basil. Season to taste with salt and pepper.

4 Cook the mixture over a low heat for 20 minutes. Remove and leave to cool.

5 To make the ravioli, cook the potatoes in a pan of boiling water for 10 minutes until tender.

6 Mash the potatoes and place them in a mixing bowl. Blend in the egg yolks and oil. Season with salt and pepper, then stir in the flour and mix to form a dough.

7 On a lightly floured surface, divide the dough into 24 pieces and shape into flat circles. Spoon the filling on to one half of each circle and fold the dough to cover the filling, pressing down to seal the edges.

8 Melt the butter in a skillet and cook the ravioli for 6-8 minutes, turning once, until golden. Serve hot, garnished with shredded basil leaves.

Beef & Pasta Bake

The combination of Italian and Indian ingredients makes a surprisingly delicious recipe. Marinate the steak in advance to save time.

NUTRITIONAL INFORMATION

Calories 1050	Sugars 4g	
Protein 47g	Fat 81g	
Carbohydrate . . .37g	Saturates 34g	

6¼ HOURS   1¼ HOURS

SERVES 4

I N G R E D I E N T S

2 lb steak, cut into cubes

⅔ cup beef stock

1 lb dried macaroni

1¼ cups heavy cream

½ tsp garam masala

salt

fresh cilantro and slivered almonds, to
    garnish

K O R M A   P A S T E

½ cup blanched almonds

6 garlic cloves

1 inch piece fresh gingerroot,
    coarsely chopped

6 tbsp beef stock

1 tsp ground cardamom

4 cloves, minced

1 tsp cinnamon

2 large onions, chopped

1 tsp coriander seeds

2 tsp ground cumin seeds

pinch of cayenne pepper

6 tbsp of sunflower oil

1 To make the korma paste, grind the almonds finely using a mortar and pestle. Put the ground almonds and the rest of the korma paste ingredients into a food processor or blender and process to make a very smooth paste.

2 Put the steak in a shallow dish and spoon over the korma paste, turning to coat the steak well. Leave in the refrigerator to marinate for 6 hours.

3 Transfer the steak and korma paste to a large saucepan, and simmer over a low heat, adding a little beef stock if required, for 35 minutes.

4 Meanwhile, bring a large saucepan of lightly salted water to a boil. Add the macaroni and cook for 10 minutes until tender, but still firm to the bite. Drain the pasta thoroughly and transfer to a deep casserole. Add the steak, heavy cream, and garam masala.

5 Bake in a preheated oven at 400°F for 30 minutes. Remove the casserole from the oven and allow to stand for about 10 minutes. Garnish the bake with fresh cilantro and serve.

Fresh Spaghetti & Meatballs

This well-loved Italian dish is popular around the world. Make the most of it by using high-quality steak for the meatballs.

NUTRITIONAL INFORMATION

Calories	665	Sugars	.........9g
Protein	........39g	Fat	..........24g
Carbohydrate	...77g	Saturates	.......8g

45 MINS   1¼ HOURS

SERVES 4

I N G R E D I E N T S

2½ cups brown breadcrumbs

⅔ cup milk

2 tbsp butter

¼ cup whole-wheat flour

⅞ cup beef stock

14 oz can chopped tomatoes

2 tbsp tomato paste

1 tsp sugar

1 tbsp finely chopped fresh tarragon

1 large onion, chopped

4 cups ground steak

1 tsp paprika

4 tbsp olive oil

1 lb fresh spaghetti

salt and pepper

fresh tarragon sprigs, to garnish

1 Place the bread crumbs in a bowl, add the milk and set aside to soak for about 30 minutes.

2 Melt half of the butter in a pan. Add the flour and cook, stirring constantly, for 2 minutes. Gradually stir in the beef stock and cook, stirring constantly, for a further 5 minutes. Add the tomatoes, tomato paste, sugar, and tarragon. Season well and simmer for 25 minutes.

3 Mix the onion, steak, and paprika into the bread crumbs and season to taste. Shape the mixture into 16 meatballs.

4 Heat the oil and remaining butter in a skillet and fry the meatballs, turning, until brown all over. Place in a deep casserole, pour the tomato sauce over, cover and bake in a preheated oven, at 350°F for 25 minutes.

5 Bring a large saucepan of lightly salted water to a boil. Add the fresh spaghetti, bring back to the boil, and cook for about 2–3 minutes, or until tender, but still firm to the bite.

6 Meanwhile, remove the meatballs from the oven and allow them to cool for 3 minutes. Serve the meatballs and their sauce with the spaghetti, garnished with tarragon sprigs.

Meatballs in Red Wine Sauce

A different twist is given to this traditional pasta dish with a rich, but subtle sauce.

NUTRITIONAL INFORMATION

Calories 811	Sugars 7g
Protein 30g	Fat 43g
Carbohydrate ...76g	Saturates 12g

45 MINS   1½ HOURS

SERVES 4

INGREDIENTS

⅔ cup milk

2 cups white bread crumbs

2 tbsp butter

9 tbsp olive oil

3 cups sliced oyster mushrooms

¼ cup whole-wheat flour

⅞ cup beef stock

⅔ cup red wine

4 tomatoes, skinned and chopped

1 tbsp tomato paste

1 tsp brown sugar

1 tbsp finely chopped fresh basil

12 shallots, chopped

4 cups ground steak

1 tsp paprika

1 lb dried egg tagliarini

salt and pepper

fresh basil sprigs, to garnish

1 Pour the milk into a bowl and soak the bread crumbs in the milk for 30 minutes.

2 Heat half of the butter and 4 tbsp of the oil in a pan. Fry the mushrooms for 4 minutes, then stir in the flour and cook for 2 minutes. Add the stock and wine and simmer for 15 minutes. Add the tomatoes, tomato paste, sugar, and basil. Season and simmer for 30 minutes.

3 Mix the shallots, steak, and paprika with the bread crumbs and season to taste. Shape the mixture into 16 meatballs.

4 Heat 4 tbsp of the remaining oil and the remaining butter in a large skillet. Fry the meatballs, turning frequently, until brown all over. Transfer to a deep casserole, pour the red wine and the mushroom sauce over, cover, and bake in a preheated oven, at 350°F, for 30 minutes.

5 Bring a pan of salted water to a boil. Add the pasta and the remaining oil, and cook for 8–10 minutes, or until tender. Drain and transfer to a serving dish. Remove the casserole from the oven and cool for 3 minutes. Pour the meatballs and sauce on to the pasta, garnish, and serve.

Pork Chops with Sage

The fresh taste of sage is the perfect ingredient to counteract the richness of pork.

NUTRITIONAL INFORMATION

Calories	364	Sugars	.........5g
Protein	........34g	Fat	..........19g
Carbohydrate	...14g	Saturates	.......7g

10 MINS   15 MINS

SERVES 4

INGREDIENTS

2 tbsp all-purpose flour

1 tbsp chopped fresh sage or 1 tsp dried

4 lean boneless pork chops, trimmed of excess fat

2 tbsp olive oil

1 tbsp butter

2 red onions, sliced into rings

1 tbsp lemon juice

2 tsp superfine sugar

4 plum tomatoes, quartered

salt and pepper

1 Mix the flour, sage, and salt and pepper to taste on a plate. Lightly dust the pork chops on both sides with the seasoned flour.

2 Heat the oil and butter in a skillet. Add the chops and cook them for 6–7 minutes on each side until cooked through. Drain the chops, reserving the pan juices, and keep warm.

3 Toss the onion in the lemon juice and fry along with the sugar and tomatoes for 5 minutes until tender.

4 Serve the pork with the tomato and onion mixture and a green salad.

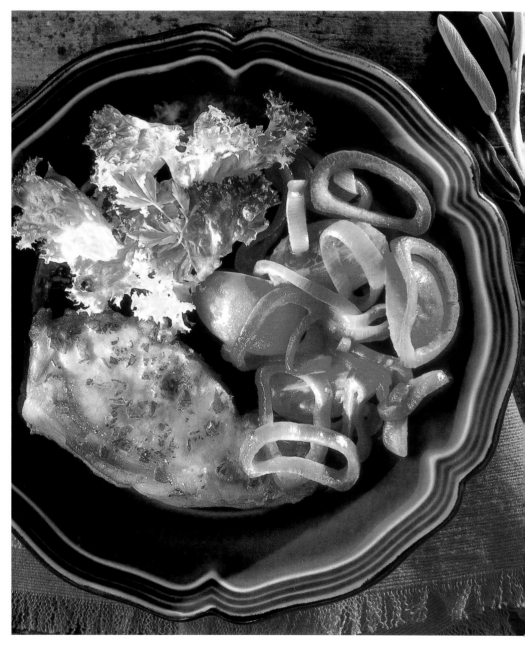

Pasta & Pork in Cream Sauce

This unusual and attractive dish is extremely delicious. Make the Italian Red Wine Sauce well in advance to reduce the preparation time.

NUTRITIONAL INFORMATION

Calories 735   Sugars 4g
Protein ....31g   Fat 52g
Carbohydrate ...37g   Saturates 19g

8¾ HOURS   35 MINS

SERVES 4

INGREDIENTS

1 lb pork tenderloin, thinly sliced

4 tbsp olive oil

8 oz button mushrooms, sliced

⅞ cup Italian Red Wine Sauce
   (see page 15)

1 tbsp lemon juice

pinch of saffron

3 cups dried orecchioni

4 tbsp heavy cream

12 quail eggs (see Cook's Tip)

salt

1 Pound the slices of pork between 2 sheets of plastic wrap until wafer thin, then cut into strips.

2 Heat the olive oil in a large skillet. Add the pork and stir-fry for 5 minutes. Add the mushrooms to the pan and stir-fry for a further 2 minutes.

3 Pour the Italian Red Wine Sauce over, lower the heat, and simmer gently for 20 minutes.

4 Meanwhile, bring a large saucepan of lightly salted water to a boil. Add the lemon juice, saffron, and orecchioni and cook for 8–10 minutes until tender, but still firm to the bite. Drain the pasta and keep warm.

5 Stir the cream into the pan with the pork and heat gently for a few minutes.

6 Boil the quail eggs for 3 minutes, cool them in cold water, and remove the shells.

7 Transfer the pasta to a large, warm serving plate, top with the pork and the sauce, and garnish with the eggs. Serve immediately.

COOK'S TIP

In this recipe, the quail eggs are soft-cooked. As they are extremely difficult to shell when warm, it is important that they are thoroughly cooled first. Otherwise, they will break up.

Pork with Fennel & Juniper

The addition of juniper and fennel to the pork chops gives an unusual and delicate flavor to this dish.

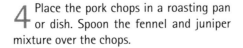

NUTRITIONAL INFORMATION

Calories	277	Sugars	.......0.4g
Protein	........32g	Fat	..........16g
Carbohydrate	...0.4g	Saturates	.......5g

2¼ HOURS   15 MINS

SERVES 4

I N G R E D I E N T S

½ fennel bulb

1 tbsp juniper berries

about 2 tbsp olive oil

finely grated peel and juice of 1 orange

4 pork chops, each about 5½ oz

fresh bread and a crisp salad, to serve

1 Finely chop the fennel bulb, discarding the green parts.

2 Grind the juniper berries in a mortar and pestle. Mix the minced juniper berries with the fennel flesh, olive oil and orange peel.

3 Using a sharp knife, score a few cuts all over each chop.

COOK'S TIP

Juniper berries are most commonly associated with gin, but they are often added to meat dishes in Italy for a delicate citrus flavor. They can be bought dried from most health-food stores and supermarkets.

4 Place the pork chops in a roasting pan or dish. Spoon the fennel and juniper mixture over the chops.

5 Pour the orange juice over the top of each chop, cover, and marinate in the refrigerator for about 2 hours.

6 Broil the pork chops, under a preheated broiler, for 10–15 minutes, depending on the thickness of the meat, or until the meat is tender and cooked through, turning occasionally.

7 Transfer the pork chops to serving plates and serve with a crisp, fresh salad and plenty of fresh bread to mop up the cooking juices.

Pork Cooked in Milk

This traditional dish of boned pork cooked with garlic and milk can be served hot or chilled.

NUTRITIONAL INFORMATION

Calories	498	Sugars	........15g
Protein	........50g	Fat	..........27g
Carbohydrate	...15g	Saturates	.......9g

🍲 20 MINS 🕐 1¾ HOURS

SERVES 4

I N G R E D I E N T S

1 lb 12 oz leg of pork, boned

1 tbsp oil

2 tbsp butter

1 onion, chopped

2 garlic cloves, chopped

¾ cup pancetta, diced

5 cups milk

1 tbsp green peppercorns, minced

2 fresh bay leaves

2 tbsp marjoram

2 tbsp thyme

1 Using a sharp knife, remove the fat from the pork. Shape the meat into a neat form, tying it in place with a piece of string.

2 Heat the oil and butter in a large pan. Add the onion, garlic, and pancetta to the pan and cook for 2–3 minutes.

3 Add the pork to the pan and cook, turning occasionally, until it is browned all over.

4 Pour the milk over, add the peppercorns, bay leaves, marjoram, and thyme and cook over a low heat for 1¼–1½ hours, or until tender. Watch the

liquid carefully for the last 15 minutes of cooking time because it tends to reduce very quickly and will then burn. If the liquid reduces and the pork is still not tender, add another 7 tbsp milk and continue cooking. Reserve the cooking liquid (because the milk reduces naturally in this dish, it forms a thick and creamy sauce, which curdles slightly but tastes very delicious).

5 Remove the pork from the saucepan. Using a sharp knife, cut the meat into slices. Transfer the pork slices to serving plates and serve immediately with the reserved cooking liquid.

Pork with Lemon & Garlic

This is a simplified version of a traditional dish from the Marche region of Italy. Pork tenderloin pockets are stuffed with prosciutto and herbs.

NUTRITIONAL INFORMATION

Calories 428   Sugars 2g
Protein ....31g   Fat 32g
Carbohydrate ....4g   Saturates 4g

25 MINS   1 HOUR

SERVES 4

INGREDIENTS

1 lb pork fillet

1¾ oz chopped almonds

2 tbsp olive oil

3½ oz raw prosciutto, finely chopped

2 garlic cloves, chopped

1 tbsp fresh oregano, chopped

finely grated peel of 2 lemons

4 shallots, finely chopped

¾ cup ham or chicken stock

1 tsp sugar

1 Using a sharp knife, cut the pork tenderloin into 4 equal pieces. Place the pork between sheets of waxed paper and pound each piece with a meat mallet or the end of a rolling pin to flatten.

2 Cut a horizontal slit in each piece of pork to make a pocket.

3 Place the almonds on a cookie sheet. Lightly toast the almonds under a medium-hot broiler for 2–3 minutes, or until golden.

4 Mix the almonds with 1 tbsp oil, prosciutto, garlic, oregano, and the finely grated peel from 1 lemon. Spoon the mixture into the pockets of pork.

5 Heat the remaining oil in a large skillet. Add the shallots and cook for 2 minutes.

6 Add the pork to the skillet and cook for 2 minutes on each side or until browned all over.

7 Add the ham or chicken stock to the pan, bring to a boil, cover and leave to simmer for 45 minutes, or until the pork is tender. Remove the meat from the pan, set aside, and keep warm.

8 Add the lemon peel and sugar to the pan. Boil for 3–4 minutes or until reduced and syrupy. Pour the lemon sauce over the pork tenderloin and serve immediately.

Pork Stuffed with Prosciutto

This sophisticated roast with Mediterranean flavors is ideal served with a pungent olive paste.

NUTRITIONAL INFORMATION

Calories 427	Sugars 0g	
Protein 31g	Fat 34g	
Carbohydrate . . .0.2g	Saturates 7g	

25 MINS   55 MINS

SERVES 4

I N G R E D I E N T S

1 lb 2 oz piece of lean pork tenderloin

small bunch fresh of basil leaves, washed

2 tbsp freshly grated Parmesan

2 tbsp sun-dried tomato paste

6 thin slices prosciutto

1 tbsp olive oil

salt and pepper

O L I V E   P A S T E

⅔ cup pitted black olives

4 tbsp olive oil

2 garlic cloves, peeled

1 Trim away excess fat and membrane from the pork tenderloin. Slice the pork lengthways down the middle, taking care not to cut all the way through.

2 Open out the pork and season the inside. Lay the basil leaves along the center. Mix the cheese and sun-dried tomato paste and spread over the basil.

3 Press the pork back together. Wrap the ham around the pork, overlapping, to cover. Place on a rack in a roasting pan, seamside down, and brush with oil. Bake in a preheated oven, 375°F, for 30–40 minutes, depending on thickness, until cooked through. Allow to stand for 10 minutes.

4 For the olive paste, place all the ingredients in a blender or food processor, and blend until smooth. Alternatively, for a coarser paste, finely chop the olives and garlic, and mix with the oil.

5 Drain the cooked pork and slice thinly. Serve with the olive paste and a salad.

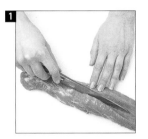

Stuffed Cannelloni

Cannelloni, the thick, round pasta tubes, make perfect containers for close-textured sauces of all kinds.

NUTRITIONAL INFORMATION

Calories	520	Sugars	.........5g
Protein	........21g	Fat	..........39g
Carbohydrate	...23g	Saturates	......18g

  30 MINS · 1¼ HOURS

SERVES 4

INGREDIENTS

8 dried cannelloni tubes

1 tbsp olive oil

¼ cup freshly grated Parmesan cheese

fresh herb sprigs, to garnish

FILLING

2 tbsp butter

10½ oz frozen spinach, thawed
    and chopped

½ cup ricotta cheese

¼ cup freshly grated Parmesan cheese

¼ cup chopped ham

pinch of freshly grated nutmeg

2 tbsp heavy cream

2 eggs, lightly beaten

salt and pepper

SAUCE

2 tbsp butter

¼ cup plain all-purpose flour

1¼ cups milk

2 bay leaves

pinch of freshly grated nutmeg

1 To make the filling, melt the butter in a pan and stir-fry the spinach for 2–3 minutes. Remove from the heat and stir in the ricotta and Parmesan cheeses and the ham. Season to taste with nutmeg, and salt and pepper. Beat in the cream and eggs to make a thick paste.

2 Bring a pan of lightly salted water to a boil. Add the pasta and the oil and cook for 10–12 minutes, or until almost tender; drain and set aside to cool.

3 To make the sauce, melt the butter in a pan. Stir in the flour and cook, stirring, for 1 minute. Gradually stir in the milk. Add the bay leaves and simmer, stirring, for 5 minutes. Add the nutmeg and salt and pepper to taste. Remove from the heat and discard the bay leaves.

4 Spoon the filling into a pastry bag and fill the cannelloni.

5 Spoon a little sauce into the bottom of a baking dish. Arrange the cannelloni in the dish in a single layer and pour over the remaining sauce. Sprinkle the Parmesan cheese over and bake in a preheated oven at 375°F for 40–45 minutes. Garnish with fresh herb sprigs and serve.

Neapolitan Pork Steaks

An Italian version of broiled pork steaks, this dish is easy to make and delicious to eat.

NUTRITIONAL INFORMATION

Calories	353	Sugars	........3g
Protein	........39g	Fat	.........20g
Carbohydrate	....4g	Saturates	.......5g

10 MINS   25 MINS

SERVES 4

INGREDIENTS

2 tbsp olive oil

1 garlic clove, chopped

1 large onion, sliced

14-oz can tomatoes

2 tsp yeast extract

4 pork loin steaks, each about 4½ oz

2¾ oz black olives, pitted

2 tbsp fresh basil, shredded

freshly grated Parmesan cheese, to serve

1 Heat the oil in a large skillet. Add the onions and garlic and cook, stirring, for 3–4 minutes, or until they just begin to soften.

2 Add the tomatoes and yeast extract to the skillet and leave to simmer for about 5 minutes or until the sauce starts to thicken.

COOK'S TIP

Parmesan is a mature and hard cheese produced in Italy. You only need to add a little because it has a very strong flavor.

3 Cook the pork steaks, under a preheated broiler, for 5 minutes on both sides, until the the meat is cooked through; set the pork aside and keep warm.

4 Add the olives and fresh shredded basil to the sauce in the skillet and stir quickly to combine.

5 Transfer the steaks to warm serving plates. Top the steaks with the sauce, sprinkle with freshly grated Parmesan cheese, and serve immediately.

Pasta & Lamb Loaf

Any dried pasta shape can be used for this delicious recipe. It has been adapted for microwave cooking for convenience.

NUTRITIONAL INFORMATION

Calories ....245 Sugars 2g
Protein ....15g Fat 18g
Carbohydrate ....6g Saturates 7g

35 MINS   35 MINS

SERVES 4

INGREDIENTS

1 tbsp butter

½ small eggplant, diced

2 oz multi-colored fusilli

2 tsp olive oil

1 cup ground lamb

½ small onion, chopped

½ red bell pepper, chopped

1 garlic clove, minced

1 tsp dried mixed herbs

2 eggs, beaten

2 tbsp light cream

salt and pepper

TO SERVE

salad

pasta sauce of your choice

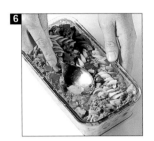

1 Place the butter in a 1 lb 2 oz loaf dish. Cook on HIGH power for 30 seconds until melted. Brush over the bottom and sides of the dish.

2 Sprinkle the eggplant with salt, put in a colander, and leave for 20 minutes. Rinse the eggplant well and pat dry with paper towels.

3 Place the pasta in a bowl, add a little salt and enough boiling water to cover by 1 inch. Cover and cook on HIGH power for 8 minutes, stirring halfway through. Leave to stand, covered, for a few minutes.

4 Place the oil, lamb and onion in a bowl. Cover and cook on HIGH power for 2 minutes.

5 Break up any lumps of meat using a fork. Add the bell pepper, garlic, herbs, and eggplant. Cover and cook on HIGH power for 5 minutes, stirring halfway through.

6 Drain the pasta and add to the lamb with the eggs and cream. Season well. Turn into the loaf dish and pat down using the back of a spoon.

7 Cook on MEDIUM power for 10 minutes until firm to the touch; leave to stand for 5 minutes before turning out. Serve in slices with a salad and a pasta sauce.

Roman Pan-Fried Lamb

Chunks of tender lamb, pan-fried with garlic, and stewed in red wine are a real Roman dish.

NUTRITIONAL INFORMATION

Calories	299	Sugars	.........1g
Protein	........31g	Fat	..........16g
Carbohydrate	....1g	Saturates	.......7g

 15 MINS   50 MINS

SERVES 4

INGREDIENTS

1 tbsp oil

1 tbsp butter

1 lb 5 oz lamb (shoulder or leg),
    cut into 1 inch chunks

4 garlic cloves, peeled

3 sprigs thyme, stalks removed

6 canned anchovy fillets

⅔ cup red wine

⅔ cup lamb or vegetable stock

1 tsp sugar

1¾ oz black olives, pitted and halved

2 tbsp chopped parsley, to garnish

mashed potato, to serve

1 Heat the oil and butter in a large skillet. Add the lamb and cook for 4–5 minutes, stirring, until the meat is browned all over.

2 Using a mortar and pestle, grind together the garlic, thyme, and anchovies to make a smooth paste.

3 Add the wine and lamb or vegetable stock to the skillet. Stir in the garlic and anchovy paste together with the sugar.

4 Bring the mixture to a boil, reduce the heat, cover, and simmer for 30–40 minutes or until the lamb is tender. For the last 10 minutes, of the cooking time, remove the lid to allow the sauce to reduce.

5 Stir the olives into the sauce and mix to combine.

6 Transfer the lamb and the sauce to a serving bowl and garnish. Serve with creamy mashed potatoes.

COOK'S TIP

Rome is the capital of Lazio and Italy and has become a focal point for specialties from all over Italy. Food from this region is fairly simple and quick to prepare, all with plenty of herbs and seasonings producing really robust flavors.

Pot Roasted Leg of Lamb

This dish from the Abruzzi uses a slow cooking method which ensures that the meat absorbs the flavorings and becomes very tender.

NUTRITIONAL INFORMATION

Calories ....734 Sugars 6g
Protein ....71g Fat 42g
Carbohydrate ....7g Saturates 15g

35 MINS   3 HOURS

SERVES 4

I N G R E D I E N T S

3½ lb leg of lamb

3–4 sprigs fresh rosemary

4½ oz streaky bacon rashers

4 tbsp olive oil

2–3 garlic cloves, minced

2 onions, sliced

2 carrots, sliced

2 celery stalks, sliced

1¼ cups dry white wine

1 tbsp tomato paste

1¼ cups stock

12 oz tomatoes, peeled, quartered
    and deseeded

1 tbsp chopped fresh parsley

1 tbsp chopped fresh oregano or marjoram

salt and pepper

fresh rosemary sprigs, to garnish

1 Wipe the joint of lamb all over, trimming off any excess fat, then season well with salt and pepper, rubbing well in. Lay the sprigs of rosemary over the lamb, cover evenly with the bacon sliced, and tie in place with string.

2 Heat the oil in a skillet and fry the lamb for about 10 minutes or until browned all over, turning several times. Remove from the pan.

3 Transfer the oil from the skillet to a large casserole and fry the garlic and onion together for 3–4 minutes until beginning to soften. Add the carrots and celery and continue to cook for a few minutes longer.

4 Lay the lamb on top of the vegetables and press down to partly submerge. Pour the wine over the lamb, add the tomato paste, and simmer for 3–4 minutes. Add the stock, tomatoes, herbs, and seasoning and bring back to a boil for a further 3–4 minutes.

5 Cover the casserole tightly and cook in a preheated oven, 350°F, for 2–2½ hours until very tender.

6 Remove the lamb from the casserole and, if preferred, take off the bacon and herbs along with the string; keep warm. Strain the juices, skimming off any excess fat, and serve in a gravy boat. The vegetables may be put around the joint or in a serving dish. Garnish with fresh sprigs of rosemary.

Lamb Chops with Rosemary

A classic combination of flavors, this dish makes a perfect Sunday lunch. Serve with tomato and onion salad and baked potatoes.

NUTRITIONAL INFORMATION

Calories 560   Sugars 1g
Protein . . . . .48g   Fat 40g
Carbohydrate . . . .1g   Saturates 13g

1¼ HOURS   15 MINS

SERVES 4

I N G R E D I E N T S

8 meaty lamb chop

5 tbsp olive oil

2 tbsp lemon juice

1 clove garlic, minced

½ tsp lemon pepper

salt

8 sprigs rosemary

baked potatoes, to serve

S A L A D

4 tomatoes, sliced

4 scallion, sliced diagonally

D R E S S I N G

2 tbsp olive oil

1 tbsp lemon juice

1 clove garlic, chopped

¼ tsp fresh rosemary, chopped finely

1 Trim the lamb chops by cutting away the flesh with a sharp knife to expose the tips of the bones.

2 Place the oil, lemon juice, garlic, lemon pepper, and salt in a shallow, nonmetallic dish and whisk with a fork to combine.

3 Lay the sprigs of rosemary in the dish and place the lamb on top. Leave to marinate for at least 1 hour, turning the lamb chops once.

4 Remove the chops from the marinade and wrap a little foil around the bones to stop them from burning.

5 Place the rosemary sprigs on the rack and place the lamb on top. Grill for 10–15 minutes, turning once.

6 Meanwhile make the salad and dressing. Arrange the tomatoes on a serving dish and scatter the scallions on top. Place all the ingredients for the dressing in a screw-top jar, shake well, and pour over the salad. Serve with the lamb chops and baked potatoes.

COOK'S TIP

Choose medium to small baking potatoes if you want to cook baked potatoes on the grill. Scrub them well, prick with a fork and wrap in buttered kitchen foil. Bury them in the hot coals and grill for 50–60 minutes.

Lamb with Olives

This is a very simple dish, and the chili adds a bit of spiciness. It is quick to prepare and makes an ideal family dinner dish.

NUTRITIONAL INFORMATION

Calories 577	Sugars 1g	
Protein 62g	Fat 33g	
Carbohydrate 1g	Saturates 10g	

15 MINS   1½ HOURS

SERVES 4

INGREDIENTS

2 lb 12 oz boned leg of lamb

⅓ cup olive oil

2 garlic cloves, minced

1 onion, sliced

1 small red chili, cored, seeded and
    chopped finely

¾ cup dry white wine

1 cup pitted black olives

salt

chopped fresh parsley, to garnish

1 Using a sharp knife, cut the lamb into 1 inch cubes.

2 Heat the oil in a skillet and fry the garlic, onion, and chili for 5 minutes.

3 Add the meat and wine and cook for a further 5 minutes.

4 Stir in the olives, then transfer the mixture to a casserole. Place in a preheated oven, 350°F, and cook for 1 hour 20 minutes, or until the meat is tender. Season with salt to taste, and serve with chopped fresh parsley.

Lamb with Bay & Lemon

These lamb chops quickly become more elegant when the bone is removed to make these delicate noisettes.

NUTRITIONAL INFORMATION

Calories 268   Sugars 0.2g
Protein ....24g   Fat 16g
Carbohydrate ...0.2g   Saturates 7g

10 MINS   35 MINS

SERVES 4

I N G R E D I E N T S

4 lamb chops

1 tbsp oil

1 tbsp butter

⅔ cup white wine

⅔ cup lamb or vegetable stock

2 bay leaves

pared peel of 1 lemon

salt and pepper

1 Using a sharp knife, carefully remove the bone from each lamb chop, keeping the meat intact. Alternatively, ask the butcher to prepare the lamb noisettes for you.

2 Shape the meat into rounds and secure with a piece of string.

3 In a large skillet, heat the oil and butter together until the mixture starts to froth.

4 Add the lamb noisettes to the skillet and cook for 2–3 minutes on each side, or until browned all over.

5 Remove the skillet fom the heat, drain off all of the excess fat, and discard.

6 Return the skillet to the heat. Add the wine, stock, bay leaves, and lemon peel to the skillet and cook for 20–25 minutes, or until the lamb is tender. Season the lamb noisettes and sauce to taste with a little salt and pepper.

7 Transfer to serving plates. Remove the string from each noisette and serve with the sauce.

COOK'S TIP

A butcher will offer you good advice on how to prepare the lamb noisettes, if you are wary of preparing them yourself.

Barbecued Butterflied Lamb

The appearance of the lamb as it is opened out to cook on the barbecue gives this dish its name. Marinate the lamb in advance, if possible.

NUTRITIONAL INFORMATION

Calories	733	Sugars	.........6g
Protein	........69g	Fat	..........48g
Carbohydrate	....6g	Saturates	......13g

 6¼ HOURS   1 HOUR

SERVES 4

INGREDIENTS

boned leg of lamb, about 4 lb

8 tbsp balsamic vinegar

grated peel and juice of 1 lemon

⅔ cup sunflower oil

4 tbsp chopped, fresh mint

2 cloves garlic, minced

2 tbsp light muscovado sugar

salt and pepper

TO SERVE

broiled vegetables

green salad leaves

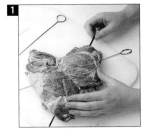

1 Open out the boned leg of lamb so that its shape resembles a butterfly. Thread 2 or 3 skewers through the meat in order to make it easier to turn on the grill.

2 Combine the balsamic vinegar, lemon peel and juice, oil, mint, garlic, sugar, and salt and pepper to taste in a nonmetallic dish that is large enough to hold the lamb.

3 Place the lamb in the dish and turn it over a few times so the meat is coated on both sides with the marinade. Leave to marinate for at least 6 hours or preferably overnight, turning occasionally.

4 Remove the lamb from the marinade and reserve the liquid for basting.

5 Place the rack about 6 inches above the coals and grill the lamb for about 30 minutes on each side, turning once and basting frequently with the marinade.

6 Transfer the lamb to a chopping board and remove the skewers. Cut the lamb into slices across the grain and serve.

COOK'S TIP

If you prefer, cook the lamb for half the cooking time in a preheated oven at 350°F, then finish off on the grill.

Saltimbocca

The Italian name for this dish, *saltimbocca*, means "jump into the mouth". The stuffed rolls are quick and easy to make and taste delicious.

NUTRITIONAL INFORMATION

Calories	303	Sugars	.......0.3g
Protein	........29g	Fat	..........17g
Carbohydrate	....1g	Saturates	.......1g

  15 MINS 🕐 20 MINS

SERVES 4

INGREDIENTS

4 turkey tenderloins or 4 veal escalopes,

about 1 lb in total

3½ oz prosciutto, thinly sliced

8 sage leaves

1 tbsp olive oil

1 onion, finely chopped

¾ cup white wine

¾ cup chicken stock

1 Place the turkey or veal between sheets of waxed paper. Pound the meat with a meat mallet or the end of a rolling pin to flatten it slightly. Cut each piece in half.

2 Trim the prosciutto to fit each piece of turkey or veal and place over the meat. Lay a sage leaf on top. Roll up the meat and secure with a wooden toothpick.

3 Heat the oil in a skillet and cook the onion for 3–4 minutes. Add the turkey or veal rolls cook for 5 minutes until brown.

4 Pour the white wine and chicken stock into the pan and leave to simmer for 15 minutes if using turkey, and 20 minutes if using veal, or until tender. Serve immediately.

VARIATION

Try a similar recipe called *bocconcini*, meaning "little mouthfuls". Follow the same method as given here, but replace the sage leaf with a piece of Gruyère cheese.

Veal in a Rose Petal Sauce

This spectacular dish is equally delicious whether you use veal or pork tenderloin. Make sure the roses are free from blemishes and pesticides.

NUTRITIONAL INFORMATION

Calories	.810	Sugars	.2g
Protein	.31g	Fat	.56g
Carbohydrate	.49g	Saturates	.28g

10 MINS   35 MINS

SERVES 4

INGREDIENTS

1 lb dried fettuccine

7 tbsp olive oil

1 tsp chopped fresh oregano

1 tsp chopped fresh marjoram

¾ cup butter

1 lb veal tenderloin, thinly sliced

⅔ cup rose petal vinegar
(see Cook's Tip)

⅔ cup fish stock

¼ cup grapefruit juice

¼ cup heavy cream

salt

TO GARNISH

12 pink grapefruit segments

12 pink peppercorns

rose petals

fresh herb leaves

1 Bring a large saucepan of lightly salted water to a boil. Add the fettuccine and 1 tablespoon of the oil and cook for 8–10 minutes or until tender, but still firm to the bite. Drain and transfer to a warm serving dish, sprinkle 2 tablespoons of the olive oil, the oregano, and marjoram over.

2 Heat 4 tbsp of the butter with the remaining oil in a large skillet. Add the veal and cook over a low heat for 6 minutes. Remove the veal from the pan and place the meat on top of the pasta.

3 Add the vinegar and fish stock to the pan and bring to a boil. Boil vigorously until reduced by two-thirds. Add the grapefruit juice and cream and simmer over a low heat for 4 minutes. Dice the remaining butter and add to the pan, one piece at a time, whisking constantly until it has been completely incorporated.

4 Pour the sauce around the veal, garnish with grapefruit segments, pink peppercorns, the rose petals (washed), and your favorite herb leaves.

COOK'S TIP

To make rose petal vinegar, infuse the petals of 8 pesticide-free roses in ⅔ cup white wine vinegar for 48 hours.

Vitello Tonnato

Veal dishes are the specialty of Lombardy, with this dish being one of the most sophisticated. Serve cold with seasonal salads.

NUTRITIONAL INFORMATION

Calories	654	Sugars	.........1g
Protein	........49g	Fat	..........47g
Carbohydrate	....1g	Saturates	.......8g

30 MINS   1¼ HOURS

SERVES 4

I N G R E D I E N T S

1 lb 10 oz boned leg of veal, rolled

2 bay leaves

10 black peppercorns

2–3 cloves

½ tsp salt

2 carrots, sliced

1 onion, sliced

2 celery stalks, sliced

3 cups stock or water

⅔ cup dry white wine (optional)

3 oz canned tuna fish, well drained

1½ oz can anchovy fillets, drained

⅔ cup olive oil

2 tsp bottled capers, drained

2 egg yolks

1 tbsp lemon juice

salt and pepper

TO GARNISH

capers

lemon wedges

fresh herbs

1 Put the veal in a saucepan with the bay leaves, peppercorns, cloves, salt and vegetables; add sufficient stock or water and the wine (if using) to barely cover the veal. Bring to a boil, remove any scum from the surface, then cover the pan, and simmer gently for about 1 hour or until tender. Leave in the water until cold, then drain thoroughly. If time allows, chill the veal to make it easier to carve.

2 For the tuna sauce, thoroughly mash the tuna with 4 anchovy fillets, 1 tablespoon of oil, and the capers. Add the egg yolks and press through a strainer in a food processor or blender until the mixture is smooth.

3 Stir in the lemon juice, then gradually whisk in the rest of the oil a few drops at a time until the sauce is smooth and has the consistency of thick cream. Season with salt and pepper to taste.

4 Slice the veal thinly and arrange on a platter in overlapping slices. Spoon the sauce over the veal to cover. Then cover the dish and chill overnight.

5 Before serving, uncover the veal carefully. Arrange the remaining anchovy fillets and the capers in a decorative pattern on top, and then garnish with lemon wedges and sprigs of fresh herbs.

Neapolitan Veal Chops

The delicious combination of apple, onion and mushroom perfectly complements the delicate flavor of veal.

NUTRITIONAL INFORMATION

Calories	1071	Sugars	........13g
Protein	........74g	Fat	..........59g
Carbohydrate	...66g	Saturates	......16g

  20 MINS   45 MINS

SERVES 4

INGREDIENTS

⅞ cup butter

9 oz veal cutlets, trimmed

1 large onion, sliced

2 apples, peeled, cored and sliced

6 oz button mushrooms

1 tbsp chopped fresh tarragon

8 black peppercorns

1 tbsp sesame seeds

14 oz dried marille

scant ½ cup extra virgin olive oil

¾ cup mascarpone cheese,
   broken into small pieces

2 large beef tomatoes, cut in half

leaves of 1 fresh basil sprig

salt and pepper

fresh basil leaves, to garnish

1 Melt 4 tbsp of the butter in a skillet. Fry the veal over a low heat for 5 minutes on each side. Transfer to a dish and keep warm.

2 Fry the onion and apples in the pan until lightly browned. Transfer to a dish, place the veal on top, and keep warm.

3 Melt the remaining butter in the skillet. Gently fry the mushrooms, tarragon, and peppercorns over a low heat for 3 minutes. Sprinkle the sesame seeds over.

4 Bring a pan of salted water to a boil. Add the pasta and 1 tbsp of oil. Cook for 8–10 minutes, or until tender, but still firm to the bite. Drain; transfer to a plate.

5 Broil or fry the tomatoes and basil for 2–3 minutes.

6 Top the pasta with the mascarpone cheese and sprinkle the remaining olive oil over. Place the onions, apples, and veal cutlets on top of the pasta. Spoon the mushrooms, peppercorns, and pan juices on to the cutlets, place the tomatoes and basil leaves around the edge, and place in a preheated oven at 300°F for 5 minutes.

7 Season to taste with salt and pepper, garnish with fresh basil leaves, and serve immediately.

Veal Italienne

This dish is really superb if made with tender veal. However, if veal is unavailable, use pork or turkey scallops instead.

NUTRITIONAL INFORMATION

Calories 592   Sugars 5g
Protein . . . . .44g   Fat 23g
Carbohydrate . . .48g   Saturates 9g

 25 MINS   1 HR 20 MINS

SERVES 4

I N G R E D I E N T S

¼ cup butter

1 tbsp olive oil

1½ lb potatoes, cubed

4 veal escalopes, weighing 6 oz each

1 onion, cut into 8 wedges

2 garlic cloves, minced

2 tbsp all-purpose flour

2 tbsp tomato paste

⅔ cup red wine

1¼ cups chicken stock

8 ripe tomatoes, peeled, seeded and diced

1 oz pitted black olives, halved

2 tbsp chopped fresh basil

salt and pepper

fresh basil leaves, to garnish

1 Heat the butter and oil in a large skillet. Add the potato cubes and cook for 5-7 minutes, stirring frequently, until they begin to brown.

2 Remove the potatoes from the skillet with a perforated spoon and set aside.

3 Place the veal in the skillet and cook for 2-3 minutes on each side until sealed. Remove from the pan and set aside.

4 Stir the onion and garlic into the skillet and cook for 2-3 minutes.

5 Add the flour and tomato paste and cook for 1 minute, stirring. Gradually blend in the red wine and chicken stock, stirring to make a smooth sauce.

6 Return the potatoes and veal to the skillet. Stir in the tomatoes, olives, and chopped basil and season with salt and pepper.

7 Transfer to a casserole dish and cook in a preheated oven, 350°F, for 1 hour or until the potatoes and veal are cooked through. Garnish with basil leaves and serve.

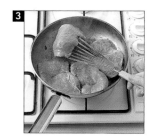

COOK'S TIP

For a quicker cooking time and really tender meat, pound the meat with a meat mallet to flatten it slightly before cooking.

Scallops & Italian Sausage

Anchovies are often used to enhance flavor, particularly in meat dishes. Either veal or turkey scallops can be used for this pan-fried dish.

NUTRITIONAL INFORMATION

Calories 233	Sugars 1g
Protein 28g	Fat 13g
Carbohydrate 1g	Saturates 1g

10 MINS 20 MINS

SERVES 4

INGREDIENTS

1 tbsp olive oil

6 canned anchovy fillets, drained

1 tbsp capers, drained

1 tbsp fresh rosemary, stalks removed

finely grated peel and juice of 1 orange

2¾ oz Italian sausage, diced

3 tomatoes, skinned and chopped

4 turkey or veal escalopes, each about
   4½ oz

salt and pepper

crusty bread or cooked polenta, to serve

1 Heat the oil in a large skillet. Add the anchovies, capers, fresh rosemary, orange peel, and juice, Italian sausage and tomatoes to the pan and cook for 5–6 minutes, stirring occasionally.

2 Meanwhile, place the turkey or veal scallops between sheets of waxed paper. Pound the meat with a meat mallet or the end of a rolling pin to flatten.

3 Add the meat to the mixture in the skillet. Season to taste with salt and pepper, cover, and cook for 3–5 minutes on each side, slightly longer if the meat is thicker.

4 Transfer to serving plates and serve with fresh crusty bread or cooked polenta, if you prefer.

VARIATION

Try 4-minute steaks, slightly flattened, instead of the turkey or veal. Cook them for 4–5 minutes on top of the sauce in the pan.

Sausage & Bean Casserole

In this traditional Tuscan dish, Italian sausages are cooked with cannellini beans and tomatoes.

NUTRITIONAL INFORMATION

Calories 609   Sugars 7g
Protein . . . . .27g   Fat 47g
Carbohydrate . . .20g   Saturates 16g

 15 MINS   35 MINS

SERVES 4

INGREDIENTS

8 Italian sausages

1 tbsp olive oil

1 large onion, chopped

2 garlic cloves, chopped

1 green bell pepper

8 oz fresh tomatoes, skinned and chopped or 14 oz can tomatoes, chopped

2 tbsp sun-dried tomato paste

14 oz can cannellini beans

mashed potato or rice, to serve

1 Using a sharp knife, seed the bell pepper, and cut it into thin strips.

2 Prick the Italian sausages all over with a fork. Cook the sausages, under a preheated broiler, for 10–12 minutes, turning occasionally, until brown all over. Set aside and keep warm.

3 Heat the oil in a large skillet. Add the onion, garlic, and bell pepper to the skillet and cook for 5 minutes, stirring occasionally, or until softened.

4 Add the tomatoes to the skillet and leave the mixture to simmer for about 5 minutes, stirring occasionally, or until slightly reduced and thickened.

5 Stir the sun-dried tomato paste, cannellini beans, and Italian sausages into the mixture in the skillet. Cook for 4–5 minutes or until the mixture is piping hot; add 4–5 tablespoons of water, if the mixture becomes too dry during cooking.

6 Transfer the Italian sausage and bean casserole to serving plates and serve with mashed potato or cooked rice.

COOK'S TIP

Italian sausages are coarse in texture and have a very strong flavor. They can be bought in specialist sausage shops, Italian delicatessens, and supermarkets. They are replaceable in this recipe only by game sausages.

Liver with Wine Sauce

Liver is popular in Italy and is served in many ways. Tender calf liver is the best type to use for this recipe, but you could use lamb liver.

NUTRITIONAL INFORMATION

Calories	435	Sugars	.........2g
Protein	........30g	Fat	..........31g
Carbohydrate	....4g	Saturates	......12g

25 MINS　　20 MINS

SERVES 4

INGREDIENTS

4 slices calf liver or 8 slices lamb liver, about 1 lb 2 oz

flour, for coating

1 tbsp olive oil

2 tbsp butter

4½ oz lean bacon rashers, rinded and cut into narrow strips

1 garlic clove, minced

1 onion, chopped

1 celery stalk, sliced thinly

⅔ cup red wine

⅔ cup beef stock

good pinch of ground allspice

1 tsp Worcestershire sauce

1 tsp chopped fresh sage or ½ tsp dried sage

3–4 tomatoes, peeled, quartered and deseeded

salt and pepper

fresh sage leaves, to garnish

new potatoes or sauté potatoes, to serve

1 Wipe the liver with paper towels, season with salt and pepper to taste, and then coat lightly in flour, shaking off any excess.

2 Heat the oil and butter in a pan and fry the liver until well sealed on both sides and just cooked through – take care not to overcook. Remove the liver from the pan, cover, and keep warm, but do not allow to dry out.

3 Add the bacon to the fat left in the pan, with the garlic, onion, and celery. Fry gently until soft.

4 Add the red wine, beef stock, allspice, Worcestershire sauce, sage, and salt and pepper to taste. Bring to a boil and simmer for 3–4 minutes.

5 Cut each tomato segment in half. Add to the sauce and continue to cook for 2–3 minutes.

6 Serve the liver on a little of the sauce, with the remainder spooned over. Garnish with fresh sage leaves and serve with tiny new potatoes or sauté potatoes.

Chicken & Poultry

Poultry dishes provide some of Italy's finest food. Every part of the chicken is used, including the feet and innards for making soup. Spit-roasted chicken, flavored strongly with aromatic rosemary, has become almost a national dish. Turkey, capon, duck, goose, and guinea fowl are also popular. This chapter contains a superb collection of mouthwatering recipes. You will be astonished at how quickly and easily you can prepare some of these gourmet dishes.

Italian-Style Sunday Roast

A mixture of cheese, rosemary, and sun-dried tomatoes is stuffed under the chicken skin, then roasted with garlic, potatoes, and vegetables.

NUTRITIONAL INFORMATION

Calories 488   Sugars 6g
Protein . . . . .37g   Fat 23g
Carbohydrate . . .34g   Saturates 11g

35 MINS   1½ HOURS

SERVES 6

INGREDIENTS

5 lb 8 oz chicken

sprigs of fresh rosemary

¾ cup feta cheese, coarsely grated

2 tbsp sun-dried tomato paste

4 tbsp butter, softened

1 bulb garlic

2 lb 4 oz new potatoes, halved if large

1 each red, green and yellow bell pepper,
   cut into chunks

3 zucchini, sliced thinly

2 tbsp olive oil

2 tbspall-purpose flour

2½ cups chicken stock

salt and pepper

1 Rinse the chicken inside and out with cold water and drain well. Carefully cut between the skin and the top of the breast meat using a small pointed knife. Slide a finger into the slit and carefully enlarge it to form a pocket. Continue until the skin is completely lifted away from both breasts and the top of the legs.

2 Chop the leaves from 3 rosemary stalks. Mix with the feta cheese, sun-dried tomato paste, butter, and pepper to taste, then spoon under the skin. Put the chicken in a large roasting pan, cover with foil and cook in a preheated oven, 375°F, for 20 minutes per 1 lb 2 oz, plus 20 minutes.

3 Break the garlic bulb into cloves, but do not peel. Add the vegetables to the chicken after 40 minutes.

4 Drizzle with oil, tuck in a few stems of rosemary, and season with salt and pepper. Cook for the remaining calculated time, removing the foil for the last 40 minutes to brown the chicken.

5 Transfer the chicken to a serving platter. Place some of the vegetables around the chicken and transfer the remainder to a warmed serving dish. Pour the fat out of the roasting pan and stir the flour into the remaining pan juices. Cook for 2 minutes then gradually stir in the stock. Bring to a boil, stirring until thickened. Strain into a sauce boat and serve with the chicken.

Garlic & Herb Chicken

There is a delicious surprise of creamy herb and garlic soft cheese hidden inside these chicken bundles!

NUTRITIONAL INFORMATION

Calories 272	Sugars 4g
Protein 29g	Fat 13g
Carbohydrate 4g	Saturates 6g

🔒 🔒 🔒

🥘 20 MINS   🕐 25 MINS

SERVES 4

INGREDIENTS

4 chicken breasts, skin removed

3½ oz full fat soft cheese, flavored
  with herbs and garlic

8 slices prosciutto

⅔ cup red wine

⅔ cup chicken stock

1 tbsp brown sugar

1 Using a sharp knife, make a horizontal slit along the length of the chicken breast to form a pocket.

2 Beat the cheese with a wooden spoon to soften it. Spoon the cheese into the pocket of the chicken breasts.

3 Wrap 2 slices of prosciutto around each chicken breast and secure firmly in place with a piece of string.

4 Pour the wine and chicken stock into a large skillet and bring to a boil. When the mixture is just starting to boil, add the sugar and stir to dissolve.

5 Add the chicken breasts to the mixture in the frying pan (skillet). Leave to simmer for 12–15 minutes, or until the chicken is tender and the juices run clear when a skewer is inserted into the thickest part of the meat.

6 Remove the chicken from the pan, set aside, and keep warm.

7 Reheat the sauce and boil until reduced and thickened. Remove the string from the chicken and cut into slices. Pour the sauce over the chicken to serve.

VARIATION

Add 2 finely chopped sun-dried tomatoes to the soft cheese in step 2.

Chicken & Seafood Rolls

These mouthwatering mini-parcels of tender chicken and shrimp on a bed of pasta will delight your guests.

NUTRITIONAL INFORMATION

Calories 799   Sugars 5g
Protein .... 50g   Fat 45g
Carbohydrate ... 51g   Saturates 13g

 45 MINS   🕐 25 MINS

SERVES 4

INGREDIENTS

4 tbsp butter, plus extra for greasing

7 oz chicken suprêmes, trimmed

4 oz large spinach leaves, trimmed
    and blanched in hot salted water

4 slices of prosciutto

12–16 raw tiger shrimp, shelled
    and deveined

1 lb dried tagliatelle

1 tbsp olive oil

3 leeks, shredded

1 large carrot, grated

⅔ cup thick mayonnaise

2 large cooked beet

salt

1 Grease 4 large pieces of foil and set aside. Place each piece of chicken between 2 pieces of waxed paper and pound with a rolling pin to flatten.

2 Divide half of the spinach between the chicken pieces, add a slice of ham to each, and top with more spinach. Place 3–4 shrimp on top of the spinach. Fold the pointed end of the chicken over the shrimp, then fold over again to form a roll. Wrap in foil, place on a cookie sheet, and bake in a preheated oven at 400°F for 20 minutes.

3 Meanwhile, bring a saucepan of salted water to a boil. Add the pasta and oil and cook for 8–10 minutes, or until tender. Drain and transfer to a serving dish.

4 Melt the butter in a skillet. Fry the leeks and carrots for 3 minutes. Transfer the vegetables to the center of the pasta.

5 Work the mayonnaise and 1 beet in a food processor or blender until smooth. Rub through a strainer and pour around the pasta and vegetables.

6 Cut the remaining beet into diamond shapes and place them neatly around the mayonnaise. Remove the foil from the rolls and, using a sharp knife, cut the pieces into thin slices. Arrange the chicken and shrimp slices on top of the vegetables and pasta. Serve immediately.

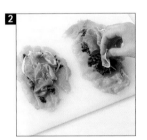

Chicken with Vegetables

This dish combines succulent chicken with tasty vegetables, flavored with wine and olives.

NUTRITIONAL INFORMATION

Calories	.470	Sugars	.7g
Protein	.29g	Fat	.34g
Carbohydrate	.7g	Saturates	.16g

🕐 20 MINS 🕐 1½ HOURS

SERVES 4

INGREDIENTS

4 chicken breasts, halved and part boned

2 tbsp butter

2 tbsp olive oil

1 large onion, chopped finely

2 garlic cloves, crushed

2 bell peppers, red, yellow or green, cored, seeded, and cut into large pieces

8 oz large closed cup mushrooms, sliced or quartered

6 oz tomatoes, peeled and halved

⅔ cup dry white wine

4–6 oz green olives, pitted

4–6 tbsp heavy cream

salt and pepper

chopped flat-leaf parsley, to garnish

1 Season the chicken with salt and pepper to taste. Heat the oil and butter in a skillet, add the chicken, and fry until browned all over. Remove the chicken from the pan.

2 Add the onion and garlic to the skillet and fry gently until just beginning to soften. Add the bell peppers to the pan with the mushrooms and continue to cook for a few minutes longer, stirring occasionally.

3 Add the tomatoes and plenty of seasoning to the pan and then transfer the vegetable mixture to a casserole. Place the chicken on the bed of vegetables.

4 Add the wine to the skillet and bring to a boil. Pour the wine over the chicken and cover the casserole tightly. Cook in a preheated oven, 350°F, for 50 minutes.

5 Add the olives to the chicken, mix lightly, then pour on the cream. Recover the casserole and return to the oven for 10–20 minutes, or until the chicken is very tender.

6 Adjust the seasoning and serve the pieces of chicken, surrounded by the vegetables and sauce, with pasta or tiny new potatoes. Sprinkle with chopped parsley to garnish.

Rich Chicken Casserole

This casserole is packed with the sunshine flavours of Italy. Sun-dried tomatoes add a wonderful richness.

NUTRITIONAL INFORMATION

Calories 320   Sugars 8g
Protein . . . . .34g   Fat 17g
Carbohydrate . . . .8g   Saturates 4g

 15 MINS   🕐 1¼ HOURS

SERVES 4

I N G R E D I E N T S

8 chicken thighs

2 tbsp olive oil

1 medium red onion, sliced

2 garlic cloves, crushed

1 large red bell pepper, sliced thickly

thinly pared peel and juice of 1 small
   orange

½ cup chicken stock

14 oz can chopped tomatoes

½ cup sun-dried tomatoes,
   thinly sliced

1 tbsp chopped fresh thyme

½ cup pitted black olives

salt and pepper

orange rind and thyme sprigs, to garnish

crusty fresh bread, to serve

1 In a heavy or non-stick large skillet, fry the chicken without fat over a fairly high heat, turning occasionally until golden brown. Using a draining spoon, drain off any excess fat from the chicken, and transfer to a casserole.

2 Add the oil to the pan and fry the onion, garlic, and bell pepper over a moderate heat for 3–4 minutes. Transfer the vegetables to the casserole.

3 Add the orange peel and juice, chicken stock, canned tomatoes, and sun-dried tomatoes to the casserole and stir to combine.

4 Bring to a boil, then cover the casserole with a lid and simmer very gently over a low heat for about 1 hour, stirring occasionally. Add the chopped fresh thyme and pitted black olives, then adjust the seasoning with salt and pepper to taste.

5 Scatter orange peel and thyme over the casserole to garnish. Serve with crusty bread.

COOK'S TIP

Sun-dried tomatoes have a dense texture and concentrated taste, and add intense flavor to slow-cooking casseroles.

Chicken Tortellini

Tortellini were said to have been created in the image of the goddess Venus's navel. Whatever the story, they are a delicious blend of Italian flavors.

NUTRITIONAL INFORMATION

Calories	635	Sugars	.........4g
Protein	........31g	Fat	..........36g
Carbohydrate	...50g	Saturates	......16g

 1 HOUR 35 MINS

SERVES 4

I N G R E D I E N T S

4 oz boned chicken breast, skinned

2 oz prosciutto

1½ oz cooked spinach, well drained

1 tbsp finely chopped onion

2 tbsp freshly grated Parmesan cheese

pinch of ground allspice

1 egg, beaten

1 lb pasta dough

salt and pepper

2 tbsp chopped fresh parsley, to garnish

S A U C E

1¼ cups light cream

2 garlic cloves, crushed

4 oz button mushrooms, thinly sliced

4 tbsp freshly grated Parmesan cheese

1 Bring a saucepan of seasoned water to a boil. Add the chicken and poach for about 10 minutes. Leave to cool slightly, then put in a food processor with the prosciutto, spinach, and onion and process until finely chopped. Stir in the Parmesan cheese, allspice, and egg and season with salt and pepper to taste.

2 Thinly roll out the pasta dough and cut into 1½–2 inch rounds.

3 Place ½ tsp of the filling in the center of each round. Fold the pieces in half and press the edges to seal. Then wrap each piece around your index finger, cross over the ends, and curl the rest of the dough backward to make a navel shape. Re-roll the trimmings and repeat until all of the dough is used up.

4 Bring a saucepan of salted water to a boil. Add the tortellini, in batches, bring back to a boil and cook for 5 minutes. Drain well and transfer to a serving dish.

5 To make the sauce, bring the cream and garlic to a boil in a small pan, then simmer for 3 minutes. Add the mushrooms and half of the cheese, season with salt and pepper to taste, and simmer for 2–3 minutes. Pour the sauce over the chicken tortellini. Sprinkle over the remaining Parmesan cheese, garnish with the parsley, and serve.

Pasta & Chicken Medley

Strips of cooked chicken are tossed with coloured pasta, grapes, and carrot sticks in a pesto-flavored dressing.

NUTRITIONAL INFORMATION

Calories 609   Sugars 11g
Protein ....26g   Fat 38g
Carbohydrate ...45g   Saturates 6g

30 MINS   10 MINS

SERVES 2

INGREDIENTS

4½–5½ oz dried pasta shapes,
    such as twists or bows
1 tbsp oil
2 tbsp mayonnaise
2 tsp bottled pesto sauce
1 tbsp sour cream or plain
    fromage blanc
6 oz cooked skinless, boneless
    chicken meat
1–2 celery stalks
1 cup black grapes (preferably seedless)
1 large carrot, trimmed
salt and pepper
celery leaves, to garnish

DRESSING

1 tbsp wine vinegar
3 tbsp extra-virgin olive oil
salt and pepper

1 To make the dressing, whisk all the ingredients together until smooth.

2 Cook the pasta with the oil for 8–10 minutes in plenty of boiling salted water until just tender. Drain thoroughly, rinse, and drain again. Transfer to a bowl and mix in 1 tablespoon of the dressing while hot; set aside until cold.

3 Combine the mayonnaise, pesto sauce and sour cream or fromage blanc in a bowl, and season to taste.

4 Cut the chicken into narrow strips. Cut the celery diagonally into narrow slices. Reserve a few grapes for garnish, halve the rest, and remove any seeds. Cut the carrot into narrow julienne strips.

5 Add the chicken, the celery, the halved grapes, the carrot, and the mayonnaise mixture to the pasta, and toss thoroughly. Check the seasoning, adding more salt and pepper if necessary.

6 Arrange the pasta mixture on two plates and garnish with the reserved black grapes and the celery leaves.

Italian Chicken Packages

This cooking method makes the chicken aromatic and succulent, and reduces the oil needed because the chicken and vegetables cook in their own juices.

NUTRITIONAL INFORMATION

Calories . . . . . . .234 Sugars 5g
Protein . . . . .28g Fat 12g
Carbohydrate . . . .5g Saturates 5g

25 MINS   30 MINS

SERVES 6

I N G R E D I E N T S

1 tbsp olive oil

6 skinless, boneless chicken breast halves

2 cups Mozzarella cheese

3½ cups zucchini, sliced

6 large tomatoes, sliced

1 small bunch fresh basil or oregano

pepper

rice or pasta, to serve

1 Cut 6 pieces of foil, each measuring about 10 inches square. Brush the foil squares lightly with oil and set aside until required.

2 With a sharp knife, slash each chicken breast at regular intervals. Slice the mozzarella cheese and place between the cuts in the chicken.

COOK'S TIP

To aid cooking, place the vegetables and chicken on the shiny side of the foil so once the package is wrapped up the dull surface of the foil is facing outward. This ensures the heat is absorbed into the package and not reflected away from it.

3 Divide the zucchini and tomatoes between the pieces of foil and sprinkle with pepper to taste. Tear or roughly chop the basil or oregano and scatter on the vegetables in each package.

4 Place the chicken on top of each pile of vegetables, then wrap in the foil to enclose the chicken and vegetables, tucking in the ends.

5 Place on a cookie sheet and bake in a preheated oven, at 400°F, for about 30 minutes.

6 To serve, unwrap each foil package and serve with rice or pasta.

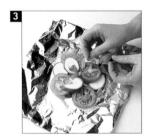

Pasta with Chicken Sauce

Spinach ribbon noodles, topped with a rich tomato sauce and creamy chicken, make a very appetizing dish.

NUTRITIONAL INFORMATION

Calories 995	Sugars 8g
Protein 36g	Fat 74g
Carbohydrate . . .50g	Saturates 34g

15 MINS 45 MINS

SERVES 4

I N G R E D I E N T S

9 oz fresh green tagliatelle

1 tbsp olive oil

salt

fresh basil leaves, to garnish

T O M A T O S A U C E

2 tbsp olive oil

1 small onion, chopped

1 garlic clove, chopped

14-oz can chopped tomatoes

2 tbsp chopped fresh parsley

1 tsp dried oregano

2 bay leaves

2 tbsp tomato paste

1 tsp sugar

salt and pepper

C H I C K E N S A U C E

4 tbsp unsalted butter

14 oz boned and skinned chicken breasts,
  cut into thin strips

¾ cup blanched almonds

1¼ cups heavy cream

salt and pepper

1 To make the tomato sauce, heat the oil in a pan over a medium heat. Add the onion and fry until translucent. Add the garlic and fry for 1 minute. Stir in the tomatoes, parsley, oregano, bay leaves, tomato paste, sugar, and salt and pepper to taste. Bring to a boil and simmer, uncovered, for 15–20 minutes, until reduced by half. Remove the pan from the heat and discard the bay leaves.

2 To make the chicken sauce, melt the butter in a skillet over a medium heat. Add the chicken and almonds and stir-fry for 5–6 minutes, or until the chicken is cooked through.

3 Meanwhile, bring the cream to a boil in a small pan over a low heat and boil for about 10 minutes, until reduced by almost half. Pour the cream over the chicken and almonds, stir and season to taste with salt and pepper. Set aside and keep warm.

4 Bring a large pan of lightly salted water to a boil. Add the tagliatelle and olive oil and cook for 8–10 minutes until tender, but still firm to the bite. Drain and transfer to a warm serving dish. Spoon the tomato sauce over and arrange the chicken sauce down the center. Garnish with the basil leaves and serve immediately.

Chicken & Lobster on Penne

While this is certainly a treat to get the taste buds tingling, it is not as extravagant as it sounds.

NUTRITIONAL INFORMATION

Calories 696	Sugars 4g	
Protein 59g	Fat 32g	
Carbohydrate ...45g	Saturates 9g	

🍲 20 MINS   🕐 30 MINS

SERVES 6

INGREDIENTS

butter, for greasing

6 chicken suprêmes

1 lb dried penne rigate

6 tbsp extra virgin olive oil

1 cup freshly grated
   Parmesan cheese

salt

FILLING

4 oz lobster meat, chopped

2 shallots, very finely chopped

2 figs, chopped

1 tbsp Marsala

2 tbsp breadcrumbs

1 large egg, beaten

salt and pepper

  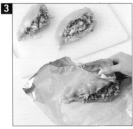

1 Grease 6 pieces of foil large enough to enclose each chicken suprême and lightly grease a cookie sheet.

2 Place all of the filling ingredients into a mixing bowl and blend together thoroughly with a spoon.

3 Cut a pocket in each chicken suprême with a sharp knife and fill with the lobster mixture. Wrap each chicken suprême in foil, place the parcels on the greased cookie sheet and bake in a preheated oven at 400°F for 30 minutes.

4 Meanwhile, bring a large pan of lightly salted water to a boil. Add the pasta and 1 tablespoon of the olive oil and cook for about 10 minutes, or until tender but still firm to the bite. Drain the pasta thoroughly and transfer to a large serving plate. Sprinkle over the remaining olive oil and the grated Parmesan cheese, set aside and keep warm.

5 Carefully remove the foil from around the chicken suprêmes. Slice the suprêmes very thinly, arrange over the pasta and serve immediately.

COOK'S TIP

The cut of chicken known as suprême consists of the breast and wing. It is always skinned.

Roman Chicken

This classic Roman dish makes an ideal light meal. It is equally good cold and can be taken on a picnic – serve with bread to mop up the juices.

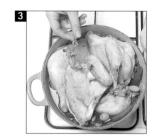

NUTRITIONAL INFORMATION

Calories 317	Sugars 8g
Protein 22g	Fat 22g
Carbohydrate 9g	Saturates 4g

 35 MINS   1 HOUR

SERVES 4

I N G R E D I E N T S

4 tbsp olive oil

6 chicken pieces

2 garlic cloves, crushed with 1 tsp salt

1 large red onion, sliced

4 large mixed red, green, and yellow
  bell peppers, cored, seeded, and
  cut into strips

⅔ cup pitted green olives

½ quantity Tomato Sauce (see page 14)

1¼ cups hot chicken stock

2 sprigs fresh marjoram

salt and pepper

1 Heat half of the oil in a casserole and brown the chicken pieces on all sides. Remove the chicken and set aside.

2 Add the remaining oil to the casserole and fry the garlic and onion until softened. Stir in the bell peppers, olives, and tomato sauce.

3 Return the chicken to the casserole with the stock and marjoram. Cover the casserole and simmer for about 45 minutes, or until the chicken is tender. Season with salt and pepper to taste and serve with crusty bread.

Chicken Pepperonata

All the sunshine, colors, and flavors of Italy are combined in this dish, which is easy to make.

NUTRITIONAL INFORMATION

Calories	328	Sugars	.........7g
Protein	........35g	Fat	..........15g
Carbohydrate	...13g	Saturates	.......4g

15 MINS   40 MINS

SERVES 4

I N G R E D I E N T S

8 skinless chicken thighs

2 tbsp whole wheat flour

2 tbsp olive oil

1 small onion, sliced thinly

1 garlic clove, crushed

1 each large red, yellow, and green bell
    peppers, sliced thinly

14 oz can chopped tomatoes

1 tbsp chopped oregano

salt and pepper

fresh oregano, to garnish

crusty whole wheat bread, to serve

1 Remove the skin from the chicken thighs and toss in the flour.

2 Heat the oil in a wide skillet and fry the chicken quickly until sealed and lightly browned, then remove them from the pan.

3 Add the onion to the pan and gently fry until soft. Add the garlic, bell peppers, tomatoes, and oregano, then bring to a boil, stirring.

4 Arrange the chicken over the vegetables, season well with salt and pepper, cover the pan tightly, and simmer for 20–25 minutes, or until the chicken is completely cooked and tender.

5 Season with salt and pepper to taste, garnish with oregano, and serve with crusty whole wheat bread.

COOK'S TIP

For extra flavor, halve the bell peppers and broil under a preheated broiler until the skins are charred. Leave to cool, then remove the skins and seeds. Slice the bell peppers thinly and use in the recipe.

Chicken with Orange Sauce

The refreshing combination of chicken and orange sauce makes this a ideal dish to serve on a warm summer evening.

NUTRITIONAL INFORMATION

Calories 797   Sugars 28g
Protein . . . . .59g   Fat 25g
Carbohydrate . . .77g   Saturates 6g

15 MINS   25 MINS

SERVES 4

INGREDIENTS

2 tbsp vegetable oil

3 tbsp olive oil

8 oz chicken suprêmes

⅔ cup orange brandy

2 tbsp all-purpose flour

⅔ cup freshly squeezed orange juice

1 oz zucchini, cut into matchstick strips

1 oz red bell pepper, cut into
    matchstick strips

1 oz leek, finely shredded

14 oz dried whole-wheat spaghetti

3 large oranges, peeled and cut into
    segments

peel of 1 orange, cut into very fine strips

2 tbsp chopped fresh tarragon

⅔ cup fromage blanc or ricotta cheese

salt and pepper

fresh tarragon leaves, to garnish

1 Heat the vegetable oil and 1 tablespoon of the olive oil in a skillet. Add the chicken and cook quickly until golden brown. Add the orange brandy and cook for 3 minutes. Sprinkle the flour over and cook for 2 minutes.

2 Lower the heat and add the orange juice, zucchini, bell pepper, and leek and season. Simmer for 5 minutes until the sauce has thickened.

3 Meanwhile, bring a pan of salted water to a boil. Add the spaghetti and

1 tablespoon of the olive oil, and cook for 10 minutes. Drain the spaghetti, transfer to a serving dish, and drizzle the remaining oil over.

4 Add half of the orange segments, half of the orange rind, the tarragon, and fromage blanc or ricotta cheese to the sauce in the pan and cook for 3 minutes.

5 Place the chicken on top of the pasta, pour a little sauce over, garnish with orange segments, peel, and tarragon. Serve immediately.

Skewered Chicken Spirals

These unusual chicken kabobs have a wonderful Italian flavor, and the bacon helps keep them moist during cooking.

NUTRITIONAL INFORMATION

Calories 231   Sugars 1g
Protein . . . . .29g   Fat 13g
Carbohydrate . . . .1g   Saturates 5g

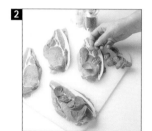  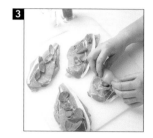

 15 MINS   10 MINS

SERVES 4

I N G R E D I E N T S

4 skinless, boneless chicken breast halves

1 garlic clove, crushed

2 tbsp tomato paste

4 slices smoked back bacon

large handful of fresh basil leaves

oil for brushing

salt and pepper

1 Spread out a piece of chicken between two sheets of plastic wrap and beat firmly with a rolling pin to flatten the chicken to an even thickness. Repeat with the remaining chicken breasts.

2 Mix the garlic and tomato paste and spread over the chicken. Lay a bacon slice over each, then scatter with the basil. Season with salt and pepper.

3 Roll up each piece of chicken firmly, then cut into thick slices.

4 Thread the slices onto 4 skewers, making sure the skewer holds the chicken in a spiral shape.

5 Brush lightly with oil and cook on a preheated hot grill or broiler for about 10 minutes, turning once. Serve hot with a green salad.

Prosciutto-Wrapped Chicken

Stuffed with ricotta, nutmeg, and spinach, then wrapped with wafer-thin slices of prosciutto and gently cooked in white wine.

NUTRITIONAL INFORMATION

Calories	426	Sugars	.........4g
Protein	........44g	Fat	..........21g
Carbohydrate	....9g	Saturates	.......8g

30 MINS   45 MINS

SERVES 4

INGREDIENTS

½ cup frozen spinach, defrosted

½ cup ricotta cheese

pinch of grated nutmeg

4 skinless, boneless chicken breasts, each weighing 6 oz

4 prosciutto slices

2 tbsp butter

1 tbsp olive oil

12 small onions or shallots

1½ cups button mushrooms, sliced

1 tbsp all-purpose flour

⅔ cup dry white or red wine

1¼ cups chicken stock

salt and pepper

1 Put the spinach into a strainer and press out the water with a spoon. Mix with the ricotta and nutmeg and season with salt and pepper to taste.

2 Using a sharp knife, slit each chicken piece through the side and enlarge each cut to form a pocket. Fill with the spinach mixture, reshape the chicken breasts, wrap each breast tightly in a slice of ham and secure with wooden toothpicks. Cover and chill.

3 Heat the butter and oil in a skillet and brown the chicken pieces for 2 minutes on each side. Transfer the chicken to a large, shallow baking dish and keep warm until required.

4 Fry the onions and mushrooms for 2–3 minutes until lightly browned. Stir in the all-purpose flour, then gradually add the wine and stock. Bring to a boil, stirring constantly. Season with salt and pepper and spoon the mixture around the chicken.

5 Cook the chicken uncovered in a preheated oven, 400°F, for 20 minutes. Turn the chicken pieces over and cook for a further 10 minutes. Remove the toothpicks and serve with the sauce, together with carrot purée and green beans, if wished.

Chicken Scallops

Served in scallop shells, this makes a stylish presentation for a dinner-party starter or a light lunch.

NUTRITIONAL INFORMATION

Calories 532	Sugars 3g	
Protein 25g	Fat 34g	
Carbohydrate ...33g	Saturates 14g	

20 MINS   25 MINS

SERVES 4

I N G R E D I E N T S

6 oz short-cut macaroni, or other
short pasta shape

3 tbsp vegetable oil, plus extra for brushing

1 onion, chopped finely

3 slices unsmoked slab bacon, rind
   removed, chopped

4½ oz button mushrooms, sliced
   thinly or chopped

¾ cup cooked chicken, diced

¾ cup crème fraîche or sour cream

4 tbsp dry bread crumbs

½ cup sharp Cheddar, grated

salt and pepper

flat-leaf parsley sprigs, to garnish

1 Cook the pasta in a large pan of boiling salted water, to which you have added 1 tablespoon of the oil, for 8–10 minutes, or until tender. Drain the pasta, return to the pan, and cover.

2 Heat the broiler to medium. Heat the remaining oil in a pan over medium heat and fry the onion until it is translucent. Add the chopped bacon and mushrooms and cook for 3–4 minutes, stirring once or twice.

3 Stir in the pasta, chicken and crème fraîche and season to taste with salt and pepper.

4 Brush four large scallop shells with oil. Spoon in the chicken mixture and smooth to make neat mounds.

5 Mix together the breadcrumbs and cheese, and sprinkle over the top of the shells. Press the topping lightly into the chicken mixture, and broil for 4–5 minutes, until golden brown and bubbling. Garnish with sprigs of flat-leaf parsley, and serve hot.

  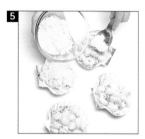

Chicken & Balsamic Vinegar

A rich caramelized sauce, flavored with balsamic vinegar and wine, adds a piquant taste. The chicken needs to be marinated overnight.

NUTRITIONAL INFORMATION

Calories	148	Sugars	.......0.2g
Protein	........11g	Fat	...........8g
Carbohydrate	...0.2g	Saturates	.......3g

10 MINS   35 MINS

SERVES 4

INGREDIENTS

4 chicken thighs, boned

2 garlic cloves, crushed

¾ cup red wine

3 tbsp white-wine vinegar

1 tbsp oil

1 tbsp butter

6 shallots

3 tbsp balsamic vinegar

2 tbsp fresh thyme

salt and pepper

cooked polenta or rice, to serve

1 Using a sharp knife, make a few slashes in the skin of the chicken. Brush the chicken with the crushed garlic and place in a nonmetallic dish.

2 Pour the wine and white-wine vinegar over the chicken and season with salt and pepper to taste. Cover and leave to marinate in the refrigerator overnight.

3 Remove the chicken pieces with a draining spoon, draining well, and reserve the marinade.

4 Heat the oil and butter in a skillet. Add the shallots and cook for 2–3 minutes, or until they begin to soften.

5 Add the chicken pieces to the pan and cook for 3-4 minutes, turning, until browned all over. Reduce the heat and add half of the reserved marinade. Cover and cook for 15–20 minutes, adding more marinade when necessary.

6 Once the chicken is tender, add the balsamic vinegar and thyme, and cook for a further 4 minutes.

7 Transfer the chicken and marinade to serving plates and serve with polenta or rice.

COOK'S TIP

To make the chicken pieces look neater, use wooden skewers to hold them together or secure them with a piece of string.

Chicken with Green Olives

Olives are a popular flavoring for poultry and game in the Apulia region of Italy, where this recipe originates.

NUTRITIONAL INFORMATION

Calories 614   Sugars 6g
Protein . . . . .34g   Fat 30g
Carbohydrate . . .49g   Saturates 11g

 15 MINS   1½ HOURS

SERVES 4

I N G R E D I E N T S

3 tbsp olive oil

2 tbsp butter

4 chicken breast halves, part boned

1 large onion, finely chopped

2 garlic cloves, crushed

2 red, yellow, or green bell peppers, cored,
 seeded, and cut into large pieces

9 oz button mushrooms, sliced
 or quartered

6 oz tomatoes, skinned and halved

⅔ cup dry white wine

1½ cups pitted green olives

4–6 tbsp heavy cream

14 oz dried pasta

salt and pepper

chopped flat leaf parsley, to garnish

1 Heat 2 tbsp of the oil and the butter in a skillet. Add the chicken breast halves and fry until golden brown all over. Remove the chicken from the pan.

2 Add the onion and garlic to the pan and fry over a medium heat until beginning to soften. Add the bell peppers and mushrooms and cook for 2–3 minutes.

3 Add the tomatoes and season to taste with salt and pepper. Transfer the vegetables to a casserole and arrange the chicken on top.

4 Add the wine to the pan and bring to a boil. Pour the wine over the chicken. Cover and cook in a preheated oven at 350°F for 50 minutes.

5 Add the olives to the casserole and mix in. Pour in the cream, cover, and return to the oven for 10–20 minutes.

6 Meanwhile, bring a large pan of lightly salted water to a boil. Add the pasta and the remaining oil and cook for 8–10 minutes, or until tender, but still firm to the bite. Drain the pasta well and transfer to a serving dish.

7 Arrange the chicken on top of the pasta, spoon over the sauce, garnish with the parsley, and serve immediately. Alternatively, place the pasta in a large serving bowl and serve separately.

Chicken Lasagne

You can use your favorite mushrooms, such as chanterelles or oyster mushrooms, for this delicately flavored dish.

NUTRITIONAL INFORMATION

Calories 708   Sugars 17g
Protein . . . . .35g   Fat 35g
Carbohydrate . . .57g   Saturates 14g

    40 MINS   1¾ HOURS

SERVES 4

I N G R E D I E N T S

butter, for greasing

14 sheets pre-cooked lasagne

3¾ cups Béchamel Sauce (see page 14)

1 cup grated Parmesan cheese

W I L D   M U S H R O O M   S A U C E

2 tbsp olive oil

2 garlic cloves, crushed

1 large onion, finely chopped

8 oz wild mushrooms, sliced

2½ cups ground chicken

3 oz chicken livers, finely chopped

4 oz prosciutto, diced

⅔ cup Marsala wine

10 oz can chopped tomatoes

1 tbsp chopped fresh basil leaves

2 tbsp tomato paste

salt and pepper

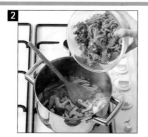

1 To make the chicken and wild mushroom sauce, heat the olive oil in a large saucepan. Add the garlic, onion, and mushrooms and cook, stirring frequently, for 6 minutes.

2 Add the ground chicken, chicken livers, and prosciutto and cook over a low heat for 12 minutes, or until the meat has browned.

3 Stir the Marsala wine, tomatoes, basil, and tomato paste into the mixture in the pan and cook for 4 minutes. Season with salt and pepper to taste, cover, and leave to simmer for 30 minutes. Uncover the pan, stir, and leave to simmer for a further 15 minutes.

4 Lightly grease a baking dish with butter. Arrange sheets of lasagne over the base of the dish, spoon over a layer of wild mushroom sauce, then spoon a layer of Béchamel Sauce over. Place another layer of lasagne on top and repeat the process twice, finishing with a layer of Béchamel Sauce. Sprinkle over the grated cheese and bake in a preheated oven at 375°F for 35 minutes until golden brown and bubbling. Serve immediately.

Broiled Chicken

This Italian-style dish is richly flavored with pesto, a mixture of basil, olive oil, pine nuts, and Parmesan cheese.

NUTRITIONAL INFORMATION

Calories	787	Sugars	.........6g
Protein	........45g	Fat	..........38g
Carbohydrate	...70g	Saturates	.......9g

10 MINS   25 MINS

SERVES 4

I N G R E D I E N T S

8 part-boned chicken thighs

olive oil, for brushing

1⅔ cups sieved tomatoes

½ cup green or red pesto sauce

12 slices French bread

1 cup freshly grated Parmesan cheese

½ cup pine nuts or slivered almonds

salad leaves, to serve

1 Arrange the chicken in a single layer in a wide flameproof dish and brush lightly with oil. Place under a preheated broiler for about 15 minutes, turning occasionally, until golden brown.

COOK'S TIP

Although leaving the skin on the chicken means that it will have a higher fat content, many people like the rich taste and crispy skin especially when it is blackened by the grill. The skin also keeps in the cooking juices.

2 Pierce the chicken with a skewer to test if it is cooked through – the juices will run clear, not pink, when it is ready.

3 Pour off any excess fat. Warm the sieved tomatoes and half the pesto sauce in a small pan and pour over the chicken. Broil for a few more minutes, turning until coated.

4 Meanwhile, spread the remaining pesto onto the slices of bread. Arrange the bread over the chicken and sprinkle with the Parmesan cheese. Scatter the pine nuts over the cheese. Broil for 2–3 minutes, or until browned and bubbling. Serve with salad leaves.

Barbecued Chicken

You need a bit of brute force to prepare the chicken, but once marinated it's an easy and tasty candidate for the barbecue.

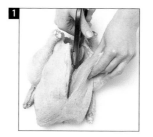

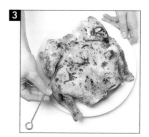

NUTRITIONAL INFORMATION

Calories 129	Sugars 0g
Protein 22g	Fat 5g
Carbohydrate 0g	Saturates 1g

   2½ HOURS   30 MINS

SERVES 4

INGREDIENTS

3 lb 5 oz chicken

grated peel of 1 lemon

4 tbsp lemon juice

2 sprigs rosemary

1 small red chili, chopped finely

⅔ cup olive oil

1 Split the chicken down the breast bone and open it out. Trim off excess fat, and remove the pope's nose, wing, and leg tips. Break the leg and wing joints to enable you to pound the bird flat. This ensures that it cooks evenly. Cover the split chicken with plastic wrap and pound it as flat as possible with a rolling pin.

2 Mix the lemon peel and juice, rosemary sprigs, chili, and olive oil together in a small bowl. Place the chicken in a large dish and pour the marinade over, turning the chicken to coat it evenly. Cover the dish and leave the chicken to marinate for at least 2 hours.

3 Cook the chicken over a hot barbecue (the coals should be white, and red when fanned) for about 30 minutes, turning it regularly until the skin is golden and crisp. To test if it is cooked, pierce one of the chicken thighs: the juices will run clear, not pink, when it is ready. Serve.

Chicken Cacciatora

This is a popular Italian classic in which browned chicken quarters are cooked in a tomato and bell pepper sauce.

NUTRITIONAL INFORMATION

Calories 397	Sugars 4g	
Protein 37g	Fat 17g	
Carbohydrate ...22g	Saturates 4g	

 20 MINS   1 HOUR

SERVES 4

INGREDIENTS

1 roasting chicken, about 3 lb 5 oz,
   cut into 6 or 8 serving pieces

1 cup all-purpose flour

3 tbsp olive oil

⅔ cup dry white wine

1 green bell pepper, seeded and sliced

1 red bell pepper, seeded and sliced

1 carrot, chopped finely

1 celery stalk, chopped finely

1 garlic clove, crushed

7 oz can of chopped tomatoes

salt and pepper

1 Rinse and pat dry the chicken pieces with paper towels. Lightly dust them with seasoned flour.

2 Heat the oil in a large skillet. Add the chicken and fry over a medium heat until browned all over. Remove from the pan and set aside.

3 Drain off all but 2 tablespoons of the fat in the pan. Add the wine and stir for a few minutes. Then add the bell peppers, carrots, celery, and garlic, season with salt and pepper to taste and simmer together for about 15 minutes.

4 Add the chopped tomatoes to the pan. Cover and simmer for 30 minutes, stirring often, until the chicken is completely cooked through.

5 Check the seasoning before serving piping hot.

Boned Chicken & Parmesan

It's really very easy to bone a whole chicken, but if you prefer, you can ask your butcher to do this for you.

NUTRITIONAL INFORMATION

Calories ....578 Sugars 0.4g
Protein ....42g Fat 42g
Carbohydrate ....9g Saturates 15g

35 MINS   1½ HOURS

SERVES 6

INGREDIENTS

1 chicken, weighing about 5 lb

8 slices mortadella or salami

2 cups fresh white or brown breadcrumbs

1 cup freshly grated Parmesan cheese

2 garlic cloves, crushed

6 tbsp chopped fresh basil or parsley

1 egg, beaten

pepper

fresh spring vegetables, to serve

1 Bone the chicken, keeping the skin intact. Dislocate each leg by breaking it at the thigh joint. Cut down each side of the backbone, taking care not to pierce the breast skin.

2 Pull the backbone clear of the flesh and discard. Remove the ribs, severing any attached flesh with a sharp knife.

3 Scrape the flesh from each leg and cut away the bone at the joint with a knife or shears. Use the bones for stock.

4 Lay out the boned chicken on a board, skin side down. Arrange the mortadella slices over the chicken, overlapping slightly.

5 Put the bread crumbs, Parmesan, garlic, and basil or parsley in a bowl.

Season with pepper to taste and mix together well. Stir in the beaten egg to bind the mixture together. Spoon the mixture along the middle of the boned chicken, roll the meat around it, and then tie securely with string.

6 Place in a roasting dish and brush lightly with olive oil. Roast in a preheated oven, 400°F, for 1½ hours, or until the juices run clear when pierced.

7 Serve hot or cold, in slices, with fresh spring vegetables.

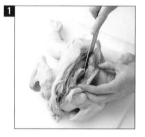 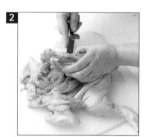 

VARIATION

Replace the mortadella with rashers of sliced bacon, if preferred.

Pan-Cooked Chicken

Artichokes are a familiar ingredient in Italian cooking. In this dish, they are used to delicately flavor chicken.

NUTRITIONAL INFORMATION

Calories	296	Sugars	.........2g
Protein	........27g	Fat	..........15g
Carbohydrate	....7g	Saturates	.......6g

  15 MINS · 55 MINS

SERVES 4

INGREDIENTS

4 chicken breast halves, part boned

2 tbsp butter

2 tbsp olive oil

2 red onions, cut into wedges

2 tbsp lemon juice

⅔ cup dry white wine

⅔ cup chicken stock

2 tsp all-purpose flour

14-oz can artichoke halves,

   drained and halved

salt and pepper

chopped fresh parsley, to garnish

1 Season the chicken with salt and pepper to taste. Heat the oil and 1 tablespoon of the butter in a large skillet. Add the chicken and fry for 4–5 minutes on each side until lightly golden. Remove from the pan using a draining spoon.

2 Toss the onion in the lemon juice, and add to the skillet. Gently fry, stirring, for 3–4 minutes until just beginning to soften.

3 Return the chicken to the pan. Pour in the wine and stock, bring to a boil, cover, and simmer gently for 30 minutes.

4 Remove the chicken from the pan, reserving the cooking juices, and keep warm. Bring the juices to a boil, and boil rapidly for 5 minutes.

5 Blend the remaining butter with the flour to form a paste. Reduce the juices to a simmer and spoon the paste into the skillet, stirring until thickened.

6 Adjust the seasoning according to taste, stir in the artichoke hearts and cook for a further 2 minutes. Pour the mixture over the chicken and garnish with chopped parsley.

Mustard-Baked Chicken

Chicken pieces are cooked in a succulent, mild mustard sauce, then coated in poppy seeds and served on a bed of fresh pasta shells.

NUTRITIONAL INFORMATION

Calories	652	Sugars	.........5g
Protein	........51g	Fat	..........31g
Carbohydrate	...46g	Saturates	......12g

10 MINS   35 MINS

SERVES 4

I N G R E D I E N T S

8 chicken pieces (about 4 oz each)

4 tbsp butter, melted

4 tbsp mild mustard (see Cook's Tip)

2 tbsp lemon juice

1 tbsp brown sugar

1 tsp paprika

3 tbsp poppy seeds

14 oz pasta shells

1 tbsp olive oil

salt and pepper

1 Arrange the chicken pieces in a single layer in a large baking dish.

2 Mix together the butter, mustard, lemon juice, sugar, and paprika in a bowl and season with salt and pepper to taste. Brush the mixture over the upper

COOK'S TIP

Dijon is the type of mustard most often used in cooking, as it has a clean and mildly spicy flavor. German mustard has a sweet-sour taste, with Bavarian mustard is slightly sweeter. American mustard is mild and sweet.

surfaces of the chicken pieces and bake in a preheated oven at 400°F for 15 minutes.

3 Remove the dish from the oven and carefully turn over the chicken pieces. Coat the upper surfaces of the chicken with the remaining mustard mixture, sprinkle the chicken pieces with poppy seeds, and return to the oven for a further 15 minutes.

4 Meanwhile, bring a large saucepan of lightly salted water to a boil. Add the pasta shells and olive oil, and cook for 8–10 minutes, or until tender, but still firm to the bite.

5 Drain the pasta thoroughly and arrange on a warmed serving dish. Top the pasta with the chicken, pour the sauce over, and serve immediately.

Chicken Marengo

Napoleon's chef was ordered to cook a sumptuous meal on the eve of the battle of Marengo – this feast of flavours was the result.

NUTRITIONAL INFORMATION

Calories 521	Sugars 6g
Protein 47g	Fat 19g
Carbohydrate . . .34g	Saturates 8g

🍳 20 MINS   🕑 50 MINS

SERVES 4

I N G R E D I E N T S

8 chicken pieces

2 tbsp olive oil

10½ oz strained puréed tomatoes

¾ cup white wine

2 tsp dried Italian seasoning

3 tbsp butter, melted

2 garlic cloves, crushed

8 slices white bread

3½ oz mixed mushrooms
   (such as button, oyster, and ceps)

1½ oz pitted black olives, chopped

1 tsp sugar

fresh basil, to garnish

1 Using a sharp knife, remove the bone from each of the chicken pieces.

2 Heat 1 tbsp of oil in a large skillet. Add the chicken pieces and cook for about 4–5 minutes, turning occassionally, or until browned all over.

3 Add the strained tomatoes, wine, and Italian seasoning to the skillet. Bring to a boil and then leave to simmer for 30 minutes or until the chicken is tender and the juices run clear when a skewer is inserted into the thickest part of the meat.

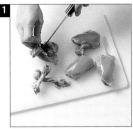  

4 Mix the melted butter and crushed garlic together. Lightly toast the slices of bread and brush with the garlic butter.

5 Add the remaining oil to a separate skillet, and cook the mushrooms for 2–3 minutes or until just browned.

6 Add the olives and sugar to the chicken mixture and warm through.

7 Transfer the chicken and sauce to serving plates. Serve with the fried bread and fried mushrooms.

Italian Chicken Spirals

These little foil rolls retain all the natural juices of the chicken when it cooks conveniently over the pasta while it boils.

NUTRITIONAL INFORMATION

Calories	...... .367	Sugars	.... .1g
Protein	.... .33g	Fat	.... .12g
Carbohydrate	...35g	Saturates	...... .2g

🍲 20 MINS   🕐 20 MINS

SERVES 4

INGREDIENTS

4 skinless, boneless chicken breast halves

1 cup fresh basil leaves

2 tbsp hazelnuts

1 garlic clove, crushed

2 cups whole-wheat pasta spirals

2 sun-dried tomatoes or fresh tomatoes

1 tbsp lemon juice

1 tbsp olive oil

1 tbsp capers

½ cup black olives

1 Beat the chicken breasts with a rolling pin to flatten evenly.

2 Place the basil and hazelnuts in a food processor and process until finely chopped. Mix with the garlic and salt and pepper to taste.

3 Spread the basil mixture over the chicken pieces and roll up from a short end to enclose the filling. Wrap the chicken roll tightly in foil so they hold their shape, then seal the ends well.

4 Bring a pan of lightly salted water to a boil and cook the pasta for 8–10 minutes, or until tender, but firm to the bite. Meanwhile, place the chicken rolls in a steamer or colander set over the pan, cover tightly, and steam for 10 minutes.

5 Using a sharp knife, dice the tomatoes.

6 Drain the pasta and return to the pan with the lemon juice, olive oil, tomatoes, capers, and olives. Heat through.

7 Pierce the chicken with a skewer to make sure that the juices run clear and not pink (this shows that the chicken is cooked through). Slice the chicken, arrange over the pasta, and serve.

COOK'S TIP

Sun-dried tomatoes have a wonderful, rich flavor but if they're unavailable, use fresh tomatoes instead.

Slices of Duckling with Pasta

A raspberry and honey sauce superbly counterbalances the richness of the duckling.

NUTRITIONAL INFORMATION

Calories	686	Sugars	........15g
Protein	........62g	Fat	..........20g
Carbohydrate	...70g	Saturates	.......7g

15 MINS   25 MINS

SERVES 4

I N G R E D I E N T S

4 x 9 oz boned breasts of duckling

2 tbsp butter

½ cup finely chopped carrots

4 tbsp finely chopped shallots

1 tbsp lemon juice

⅔ cup meat stock

4 tbsp clear honey

¾ cup fresh or thawed frozen raspberries

¼ cup all-purpose flour

1 tbsp Worcestershire sauce

14 oz fresh linguine

1 tbsp olive oil

salt and pepper

TO GARNISH

fresh raspberries

fresh sprig of flat-leaf parsley

1 Trim and score the duck breasts with a sharp knife and season well all over. Melt the butter in a skillet, add the duck breasts and fry all over until lightly colored.

2 Add the carrots, shallots, lemon juice, and half the meat stock and simmer over a low heat for 1 minute. Stir in half of the honey and half of the raspberries.

Sprinkle half of the flour over and cook, stirring constantly for 3 minutes. Season with pepper to taste and add the Worcestershire sauce.

3 Stir in the remaining stock and cook for 1 minute. Stir in the remaining honey and remaining raspberries and sprinkle the remaining flour over. Cook for a further 3 minutes.

4 Remove the duck breasts from the pan, but leave the sauce to continue simmering over a very low heat.

5 Meanwhile, bring a large saucepan of lightly salted water to a boil. Add the linguine and olive oil and cook for 8–10 minutes, or until tender, but still firm to the bite. Drain and divide between 4 individual plates.

6 Slice the duck breast lengthways into ¼ inch thick pieces. Pour a little sauce over the pasta and arrange the sliced duck in a fan shape on top of it. Garnish with raspberries and flat-leaf parsley and serve immediately.

Pheasant Lasagne

This scrumptious and unusual baked lasagne is virtually a meal in itself. It is served with pearl onions and green peas.

NUTRITIONAL INFORMATION

Calories	1038	Sugars	........13g
Protein	........65g	Fat	..........64g
Carbohydrate	...54g	Saturates	......27g

40 MINS   1¼ HOURS

SERVES 4

INGREDIENTS

butter for greasing

14 sheets precooked lasagne

3¾ cups Béchamel Sauce (see page 14)

¾ cup grated mozzarella cheese

FILLING

8 oz pork fat, diced

2 tbsp butter

16 pearl onions

8 large pheasant breasts, thinly sliced

¼ cup plain all-purpose flour

2½ cups chicken stock

bouquet garni

3 cups fresh peas, shelled

salt and pepper

1 To make the filling, put the pork fat into a saucepan of boiling, salted water and simmer for 3 minutes, drain, and pat dry.

2 Melt the butter in a large skillet. Add the pork fat and onions to the pan and cook for about 3 minutes, or until lightly browned.

3 Remove the pork fat and onions from the pan and set aside. Add the slices of pheasant and cook over a low heat for 12 minutes, until browned all over. Transfer to a baking dish.

4 Stir the flour into the pan and cook until just brown, then blend in the stock. Pour the mixture over the pheasant, add the bouquet garni and cook in a preheated oven, at 400°F, for 5 minutes. Remove the bouquet garni. Add the onions, pork fat, and peas and return to the oven for 10 minutes.

5 Put the pheasant and pork fat in a food processor and grind finely.

6 Lower the oven temperature to 375°F. Grease a baking dish with butter. Make layers of lasagne, pheasant sauce, and Béchamel Sauce in the dish, ending with Béchamel Sauce. Sprinkle the cheese over and bake for 30 minutes.

Pesto Baked Partridge

Partridge has a more delicate flavor than many game birds and this subtle sauce complements it perfectly.

NUTRITIONAL INFORMATION

Calories 895	Sugars 5g	
Protein 79g	Fat 45g	
Carbohydrate ...45g	Saturates 18g	

15 MINS   40 MINS

SERVES 4

INGREDIENTS

8 partridge pieces (about 4 oz each)

4 tbsp butter, melted

4 tbsp Dijon mustard

2 tbsp lime juice

1 tbsp brown sugar

6 tbsp bottled pesto sauce

1 lb dried rigatoni

1 tbsp olive oil

1⅓ cups freshly grated Parmesan cheese

salt and pepper

1 Arrange the partridge pieces, smooth side down, in a single layer in a large baking dish.

2 Mix together the butter, Dijon mustard, lime juice, and brown sugar in a bowl. Season to taste. Brush this mixture over the partridge pieces and bake in a preheated oven at 400°F for 15 minutes.

3 Remove the dish from the oven and coat the partridge pieces with 3 tbsp of the pesto sauce. Return to the oven and bake for a further 12 minutes.

4 Remove the dish from the oven and carefully turn over the partridge pieces. Coat the top of the partridges with the remaining mustard mixture and return to the oven for a further 10 minutes.

5 Meanwhile, bring a large pan of lightly salted water to a boil. Add the rigatoni and olive oil and cook for 8–10 minutes until tender, but still firm to the bite. Drain and transfer to a serving dish. Toss the pasta with the remaining pesto sauce and the Parmesan cheese.

6 Serve the partridge with the pasta, pouring over the cooking juices.

VARIATION

You can prepare young pheasant in the same way.

Pasta

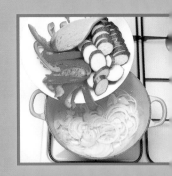

The simplicity and satisfying nature of pasta in all its varieties makes it a universal favorite. Easy to cook and economical, pasta is wonderfully versatile. It can be served with sauces made from meat, fish or vegetables, or baked in the oven. The classic spaghetti sauce needs no introduction, and yet it is said that there are almost as

many versions of this delicious regional dish as there are lovers of Italian food! Fish and seafood are irresistible combined with pasta and need only the briefest of cooking times. Pasta combined with vegetables provides inspiration for countless dishes that will please vegetarians and meat-eaters alike. The delicious pasta dishes in this chapter range from easy, economic midweek suppers to sophisticated and elegant meals for special occasions.

Spaghetti Bolognese

The original recipe takes about 4 hours to cook and should be left overnight to let the flavors mingle. This version is much quicker.

NUTRITIONAL INFORMATION

Calories	.591	Sugars	.7g
Protein	.29g	Fat	.24g
Carbohydrate	.64g	Saturates	.9g

20 MINS   1 HR 5 MINS

SERVES 4

INGREDIENTS

1 tbsp olive oil

1 onion, finely chopped

2 garlic cloves, chopped

1 carrot, scraped and chopped

1 stalk celery, chopped

1¾ oz pancetta or streaky bacon, diced

12 oz lean minced beef

14-oz can chopped tomatoes

2 tsp dried oregano

scant ½ cup red wine

2 tbsp tomato paste

salt and pepper

1½ lb fresh spaghetti or 12 oz
   dried spaghetti

1 Heat the oil in a large skillet. Add the onions and cook for 3 minutes.

2 Add the garlic, carrot, celery, and pancetta or bacon and sauté for 3–4 minutes or until just beginning to brown.

3 Add the beef and cook over a high heat for another 3 minutes, or until all of the meat is brown.

4 Stir in the tomatoes, oregano, and red wine and bring to a boil. Reduce the heat and leave to simmer for about 45 minutes.

5 Stir in the tomato paste and season with salt and pepper.

6 Cook the spaghetti in a pan of boiling water for 8–10 minutes until tender, but still has bite. Drain thoroughly.

7 Transfer the spaghetti to a serving plate and pour the bolognese sauce over. Toss to mix well and serve hot.

VARIATION

Add 1 oz dried porcini, soaked for 10 minutes in 2 tablespoons of warm water, to the sauce in step 4, if you wish.

Pasta Carbonara

Lightly cooked eggs and pancetta are combined with cheese to make this rich, classic sauce.

NUTRITIONAL INFORMATION

Calories 547   Sugars 1g
Protein . . . . .21g   Fat 31g
Carbohydrate . . .49g   Saturates 14g

  15 MINS   20 MINS

SERVES 4

I N G R E D I E N T S

1 tbsp olive oil

3 tbsp butter

3½ oz pancetta or unsmoked bacon, diced

3 eggs, beaten

2 tbsp milk

1 tbsp thyme, stems removed

1½ lb fresh or 12 oz dried conchigoni rigati

1¾ oz Parmesan cheese, grated

salt and pepper

1 Heat the oil and butter in a skillet until the mixture is just beginning to froth.

2 Add the pancetta or bacon to the pan and cook for 5 minutes, or until browned all over.

3 Mix together the eggs and milk in a small bowl. Stir in the thyme and season to taste with salt and pepper.

4 Cook the pasta in a saucepan of boiling water for 8–10 minutes until tender, but still has bite. Drain thoroughly.

5 Add the cooked, drained pasta to the skillet with the eggs and cook over a high heat for about 30 seconds, or until the eggs just begin to cook and set. Do not overcook the eggs or they will become rubbery.

6 Add half of the grated Parmesan cheese, stirring to combine.

7 Transfer the pasta to a serving plate, pour the sauce over and toss to mix well.

8 Sprinkle the rest of the grated Parmesan over the top and serve immediately.

VARIATION

For an extra rich carbonara sauce, stir in 4 tablespoons of heavy cream with the eggs and milk in step 3. Follow exactly the same cooking method.

Three-Cheese Macaroni

Based on a traditional family favorite, this pasta bake has plenty of flavor. Serve with a crisp salad for a quick, tasty supper.

NUTRITIONAL INFORMATION

Calories	672	Sugars	........10g
Protein	........31g	Fat	..........44g
Carbohydrate	...40g	Saturates	......23g

30 MINS   45 MINS

SERVES 4

I N G R E D I E N T S

2½ cups Béchamel Sauce (see page 14)

2 cups macaroni

1 egg, beaten

1 cup grated sharp Cheddar cheese

1 tbsp wholegrain mustard

2 tbsp chopped fresh chives

4 tomatoes, sliced

1 cup grated brick cheese

½ cup crumbled blue cheese

2 tbsp sunflower seeds

salt and pepper

snipped fresh chives, to garnish

1 Make the Béchamel Sauce, put into a bowl and cover with plastic wrap to prevent a skin forming. Set aside.

2 Bring a saucepan of salted water to a boil and cook the macaroni for 8–10 minutes or until just tender. Drain well and place in a baking dish.

3 Stir the beaten egg, Cheddar, mustard, chives, and seasoning into the Béchamel Sauce and spoon over the macaroni, making sure it is well covered. Top with a layer of sliced tomatoes.

4 Sprinkle over the brick and blue cheeses, and add the sunflower seeds. Put on a cookie sheet and bake in a preheated oven, at 375°F, for 25–30 minutes, or until bubbling and golden. Garnish with chives and serve immediately.

Italian Tomato Sauce & Pasta

Fresh tomatoes make a delicious Italian-style sauce that goes particularly well with pasta.

NUTRITIONAL INFORMATION

Calories	304	Sugars	.........8g
Protein	........15g	Fat	..........14g
Carbohydrate	...31g	Saturates	.......5g

 10 MINS 25 MINS

SERVES 2

INGREDIENTS

1 tbsp olive oil

1 small onion, chopped finely

1–2 cloves garlic, crushed

12 oz tomatoes, peeled and chopped

2 tsp tomato paste

2 tbsp water

10½–12 oz dried pasta shapes

¾ cup lean diced bacon

½ cup mushrooms, sliced

1 tbsp chopped fresh parsley or 1 tsp
    chopped fresh cilantro

2 tbsp sour cream or natural fromage

blanc (optional)

salt and pepper

1 To make the tomato sauce, heat the oil in a saucepan and fry the onion and garlic gently until soft.

2 Add the tomatoes, tomato paste, water, and salt and pepper to taste to the mixture in the pan and bring to a boil. Cover and simmer gently for 10 minutes.

3 Meanwhile, cook the pasta in a saucepan of boiling salted water for 8–10 minutes, or until tender. Drain the pasta and transfer to serving dishes.

4 Heat the bacon gently in a skillet until the fat runs, then add the mushrooms and continue cooking for 3–4 minutes. Drain off any excess oil.

5 Add the bacon and mushrooms to the tomato mixture, together with the parsley or cilantro and the sour cream or fromage blanc, if using. Reheat and serve with the pasta.

COOK'S TIP

Sour cream contains 18–20 per cent fat, so if you are following a low-fat diet, leave it out of this recipe or substitute a low-fat alternative.

Pasta with Green Vegetables

The different shapes and textures of the vegetables make a mouthwatering presentation in this light, summery dish.

NUTRITIONAL INFORMATION

Calories	...517	Sugars	...5g
Protein	...17g	Fat	...32g
Carbohydrate	...42g	Saturates	...18g

10 MINS   25 MINS

SERVES 4

INGREDIENTS

8 oz gemelli or other pasta shapes

1 tbsp olive oil

2 tbsp chopped fresh parsley

2 tbsp freshly grated Parmesan

salt and pepper

SAUCE

1 head of green broccoli, cut into flowerets

2 zucchini, sliced

8 oz asparagus spears, trimmed

4½ oz snow peas, trimmed

1 cup frozen peas

2 tbsp butter

3 tbsp vegetable stock

5 tbsp heavy cream

large pinch of freshly grated nutmeg

1 Cook the pasta in a large pan of salted boiling water, adding the olive oil, for 8–10 minutes, or until tender. Drain the pasta in a colander, return to the pan, cover, and keep warm.

2 Steam the broccoli, zucchini, asparagus spears, and snow peas over a pan of boiling, salted water until just beginning to soften. Remove from the heat and plunge into cold water to prevent more cooking. Drain and set aside.

3 Cook the peas in boiling salted water for 3 minutes, then drain. Refresh in cold water and drain again.

4 Put the butter and vegetable stock in a pan over a medium heat. Add all the vegetables, except for the asparagus spears, and toss carefully with a wooden spoon to heat through, taking care not to break them up. Stir in the cream, allow the sauce to heat through and season with salt, pepper, and nutmeg.

5 Transfer the pasta to a warmed serving dish and stir in the chopped parsley. Spoon the sauce over and sprinkle with the freshly grated Parmesan. Arrange the asparagus spears on top. Serve hot.

Pasta & Vegetable Sauce

A Mediterranean mixture of bell peppers, garlic, and zucchini cooked in olive oil and tossed with pasta.

NUTRITIONAL INFORMATION

Calories	.341	Sugars	.8g
Protein	.13g	Fat	.20g
Carbohydrate	.30g	Saturates	.8g

 15 MINS   20 MINS

SERVES 4

INGREDIENTS

3 tbsp olive oil

1 onion, sliced

2 garlic cloves, chopped

3 red bell peppers, seeded and cut into strips

3 zucchini, sliced

14-oz can chopped tomatoes

3 tbsp sun-dried tomato paste

2 tbsp chopped fresh basil

8 oz fresh pasta spirals

1 cup grated Swiss cheese

salt and pepper

fresh basil sprigs, to garnish

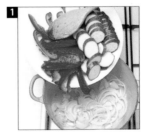

1 Heat the oil in a heavy-based saucepan or casserole. Add the onion and garlic and cook, stirring occasionally, until softened. Add the bell peppers and zucchini and fry for 5 minutes, stirring occasionally.

2 Add the tomatoes, sun-dried tomato paste, basil, and seasoning. Cover and cook for 5 minutes.

3 Meanwhile, bring a large saucepan of salted water to a boil and add the pasta. Stir and bring back to a boil.

Reduce the heat slightly and cook, uncovered, for 3 minutes, or until just tender. Drain thoroughly and add to the vegetables; toss gently to mix well.

4 Put the mixture into a shallow baking dish and sprinkle the cheese over.

5 Cook under a preheated broiler for 5 minutes until the cheese is golden. Garnish with basil sprigs and serve.

COOK'S TIP

Be careful not to overcook fresh pasta – it should be al dente. It takes only a few minutes to cook as it is still full of moisture.

Basil & Pine Nut Pesto

Delicious stirred into pasta, soups, and salad dressings, pesto is available in all supermarkets, but making your own gives a concentrated flavor.

NUTRITIONAL INFORMATION

Calories 321   Sugars 1g
Protein . . . . .11g   Fat 17g
Carbohydrate . . .32g   Saturates 4g

15 MINS   10 MINS

SERVES 4

INGREDIENTS

about 40 fresh basil leaves,
    washed and dried

3 garlic cloves, crushed

¼ cup pine kernels

½ cup Parmesan cheese, finely grated

2–3 tbsp extra-virgin olive oil

salt and pepper

1½ lb fresh pasta or 12 oz dried pasta

1 Rinse the basil leaves and pat them dry with paper towels.

2 Put the basil leaves, garlic, pine kernels, and grated Parmesan into a food processor and blend for about 30 seconds or until smooth. Alternatively, pound all of the ingredients by hand, using a mortar and pestle.

3 If you are using a food processor, keep the motor running and slowly add the olive oil. Alternatively, add the oil drop by drop while stirring briskly. Season with salt and pepper to taste.

4 Cook the pasta in a saucepan of boiling water allowing 3–4 minutes for fresh pasta or 8–10 minutes for dried, or until it is cooked through, but still has bite.

Drain the pasta thoroughly in a colander.

5 Transfer the pasta to a serving plate and serve with the pesto. Toss to mix well and serve hot.

COOK'S TIP

You can store pesto in the refrigerator for about 4 weeks. Cover the surface of the pesto with olive oil before sealing the container or bottle, to prevent the basil from oxidizing and turning black.

Tagliatelle with Pumpkin

This unusual pasta dish comes from the Emilia Romagna region of Italy.

NUTRITIONAL INFORMATION

Calories 454	Sugars 4g	
Protein 9g	Fat 33g	
Carbohydrate ...33g	Saturates 12g	

15 MINS   35 MINS

SERVES 4

I N G R E D I E N T S

1 lb 2 oz pumpkin or butternut squash

2 tbsp olive oil

1 onion, chopped finely

2 garlic cloves, crushed

4–6 tbsp chopped fresh parsley

good pinch of ground or freshly grated
  nutmeg

about 1 cup chicken or vegetable stock

4½ oz prosciutto, cut into thin strips

9 oz tagliatelle, green or white, fresh
  or dried

⅔ cup heavy cream

salt and pepper

freshly grated Parmesan, to serve

1 Peel the pumpkin or squash and scoop out the seeds and membrane. Cut the flesh into ½ inch dice.

2 Heat the olive oil in a pan and gently fry the onion and garlic until softened. Add half of the parsley and fry for 1–2 minutes.

3 Add the pumpkin or squash and continue to cook for 2–3 minutes. Season well with salt, pepper, and nutmeg.

4 Add half of the stock, bring to a boil, cover and simmer for about 10 minutes, or until the pumpkin is tender, adding more stock as necessary. Add the prosciutto and continue to cook for 2 minutes, stirring frequently.

5 Meanwhile, cook the tagliatelle in a large saucepan of boiling salted water, allowing 3–4 minutes for fresh pasta or 8–10 minutes for dried. Drain thoroughly and turn into a warmed dish.

6 Add the cream to the ham mixture and heat gently. Season and spoon over the pasta. Sprinkle with the remaining parsley and grated Parmesan separately.

Pasta with Cheese & Broccoli

Some of the simplest and most satisfying dishes are made with pasta, such as this delicious combination of tagliatelle with two-cheese sauce.

NUTRITIONAL INFORMATION

Calories 624	Sugars 2g	
Protein 22g	Fat 45g	
Carbohydrate ...34g	Saturates 28g	

🧀 5 MINS   🕐 15 MINS

SERVES 4

I N G R E D I E N T S

10½ oz dried tagliatelle tricolore (plain, spinach-, and tomato-flavored noodles)

2½ cups broccoli, broken into small flowerets

1½ cups mascarpone cheese

1 cup blue cheese, crumbled

1 tbsp chopped fresh oregano

2 tbsp butter

salt and pepper

sprigs of fresh oregano, to garnish

freshly grated Parmesan, to serve

1 Cook the tagliatelle in plenty of boiling salted water for 8–10 minutes, or until just tender.

2 Meanwhile, cook the broccoli flowerets in a small amount of lightly salted, boiling water. Avoid overcooking the broccoli, so it retains much of its color and texture.

3 Heat the mascarpone and blue cheeses together gently in a large saucepan until they are melted. Stir in the oregano and season with salt and pepper to taste.

4 Drain the pasta thoroughly. Return it to the saucepan and add the butter, tossing the tagliatelle to coat it. Drain the broccoli well and add to the pasta with the sauce, tossing gently to mix.

5 Divide the pasta between 4 warmed serving plates. Garnish with sprigs of fresh oregano and serve with freshly grated Parmesan.

Spicy Tomato Tagliatelle

A deliciously fresh and slightly spicy tomato sauce that is excellent for lunch or a light supper.

NUTRITIONAL INFORMATION

Calories 306	Sugars 7g
Protein 8g	Fat 12g
Carbohydrate ...45g	Saturates 7g

15 MINS   35 MINS

SERVES 4

I N G R E D I E N T S

3 tbsp butter

1 onion, finely chopped

1 garlic clove, crushed

2 small red chilies, seeded and diced

1 lb fresh tomatoes, skinned, seeded and diced

¾ cup vegetable stock

2 tbsp tomato paste

1 tsp sugar

salt and pepper

1½ lb fresh green and white tagliatelle, or 12 oz dried

VARIATION

Try topping your pasta dish with 1¾ oz pancetta or unsmoked bacon, diced and dry-fried for 5 minutes until crispy.

1 Melt the butter in a large saucepan. Add the onion and garlic and cook for 3–4 minutes, or until softened.

2 Add the chilies to the pan and continue cooking for about 2 minutes.

3 Add the tomatoes and stock, reduce the heat, and leave to simmer for 10 minutes, stirring.

4 Pour the sauce into a food processor and blend for 1 minute until smooth.

Alternatively, push the sauce through a strainer.

5 Return the sauce to the pan and add the tomato paste, sugar, and salt and pepper to taste. Gently reheat over a low heat until piping hot.

6 Cook the tagliatelle in a pan of boiling water for 8–10 minutes, or until it is tender, but still has bite. Drain the tagliatelle, transfer to serving plates, and serve with the tomato sauce.

Pasta & Bean Casserole

A satisfying winter dish, this is a slow-cooked, one-pot meal. The navy beans need to be soaked overnight, so prepare well in advance.

NUTRITIONAL INFORMATION

Calories ....323 Sugars 5g
Protein ....13g Fat 12g
Carbohydrate ...41g Saturates 2g

 25 MINS   3½ HOURS

SERVES 6

INGREDIENTS

1⅓ cups dried navy beans, soaked overnight
  and drained

8 oz penne, or other short pasta shapes

6 tbsp olive oil

3½ cups vegetable stock

2 large onions, sliced

2 cloves garlic, chopped

2 bay leaves

1 tsp dried oregano

1 tsp dried thyme

5 tbsp red wine

2 tbsp tomato paste

2 celery stalks, sliced

1 fennel bulb, sliced

1½ cups mushrooms, sliced

1½ cups tomatoes, sliced

1 tsp dark muscovado sugar

4 tbsp dry white bread crumbs

salt and pepper

TO SERVE

salad leaves

crusty bread

1 Put the beans in a large pan, cover them with water, and bring to a boil. Boil the beans rapidly for 20 minutes, then drain them.

2 Cook the pasta for only 3 minutes in a large pan of boiling salted water, with 1 tablespoon of the oil. Drain in a colander and set aside.

3 Put the beans in a large casserole, pour on the vegetable stock, and stir in the remaining olive oil, the onions, garlic, bay leaves, herbs, wine, and tomato paste.

4 Bring to a boil, cover the casserole, and cook in a preheated oven, 350°F, for 2 hours.

5 Add the reserved pasta, the celery, fennel, mushrooms, and tomatoes, and season with salt and pepper.

6 Stir in the sugar and sprinkle with the bread crumbs. Cover the casserole and continue cooking for 1 hour. Serve hot, with salad leaves and crusty bread.

Pasta & Cheese Puddings

These delicious pasta puddings are served with a flavorful tomato and bay leaf sauce.

NUTRITIONAL INFORMATION

Calories	.517	Sugars	.8g
Protein	.19g	Fat	.27g
Carbohydrate	.47g	Saturates	.13g

45 MINS   50 MINS

SERVES 4

INGREDIENTS

1 tbsp butter or margarine, softened

½ cup dried white bread crumbs

6 oz tricolour spaghetti

1¼ cups Béchamel Sauce (see page 14)

1 egg yolk

1 cup Swiss cheese, grated

salt and pepper

fresh flat-leaf parsley, to garnish

TOMATO SAUCE

2 tsp olive oil

1 onion, chopped finely

1 bay leaf

⅔ cup dry white wine

⅔ cup strained puréed tomatoes

1 tbsp tomato paste

1 Grease four ¾ cup molds or ramekins with the butter or margarine. Evenly coat the insides with half the bread crumbs.

2 Break the spaghetti into 2-inch pieces. Bring a saucepan of lightly salted water to a boil and cook the spaghetti for 5–6 minutes, or until just tender. Drain well and put in a bowl.

3 Mix the Béchamel Sauce, egg yolk, cheese, and seasoning into the cooked pasta and pack into the molds.

4 Sprinkle with the remaining bread crumbs and place the molds on a cookie sheet. Bake in a preheated oven, at 425°F, for 20 minutes until golden. Leave to stand for 10 minutes.

5 Meanwhile, make the sauce. Heat the oil in a pan and fry the onion and bay leaf for 2–3 minutes, or until softened.

6 Stir in the wine, strained puréed tomatoes, tomato paste, and seasoning. Bring to a boil and simmer for 20 minutes, or until thickened. Discard the bay leaf.

7 Run a spatula around the inside of the molds. Turn on to serving plates, garnish, and serve with the tomato sauce.

Tagliatelle with Garlic Butter

Pasta is not difficult to make yourself, just a little time consuming. The resulting pasta only takes a couple of minutes to cook and tastes wonderful.

NUTRITIONAL INFORMATION

Calories ....642 Sugars 2g
Protein ....16g Fat 29g
Carbohydrate ...84g Saturates 13g

45 MINS   5 MINS

SERVES 4

INGREDIENTS

1 lb strong white flour, plus extra for
  dredging

2 tsp salt

4 eggs, beaten

3 tbsp olive oil

5 tbsp butter, melted

3 garlic cloves, finely chopped

2 tbsp chopped, fresh parsley

pepper

  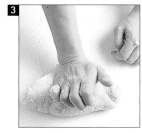

1 Sift the flour into a large bowl and stir in the salt.

2 Make a well in the middle of the dry ingredients and add the eggs and 2 tablespoons of oil. Using a wooden spoon, stir in the eggs, gradually drawing in the flour. After a few minutes the dough will be too stiff to use a spoon and you will need to use your hands.

3 Once all of the flour has been incorporated, turn the dough out onto a floured surface and knead for about 5 minutes, or until smooth and elastic. If you find the dough is too wet, add a little more flour and continue kneading. Cover with plastic wrap and leave to rest for at least 15 minutes.

4 The basic dough is now ready to use; roll out the pasta thinly and create the pasta shapes required. This can be done by hand or using a pasta machine. Results from a machine are usually neater and thinner, but not necessarily better.

5 To make the tagliatelle by hand, fold the thinly rolled pasta sheets into thirds and cut out long, thin stips, about ½ inch wide.

6 To cook, bring a pan of water to a boil, add 1 tbsp of oil and the pasta. It will take 2–3 minutes to cook, and the texture should have a slight bite to it. Drain.

7 Mix together the butter, garlic, and parsley. Stir into the pasta, season with a little pepper to taste, and serve immediately.

COOK'S TIP

Generally allow about 5½ oz fresh pasta or about 3½ oz dried pasta per person.

Spaghetti with Ricotta Sauce

This makes a quick-and-easy starter, and is particularly ideal for the summer.

NUTRITIONAL INFORMATION

Calories 688	Sugars 5g
Protein 17g	Fat 51g
Carbohydrate . . .43g	Saturates 16g

15 MINS   20 MINS

SERVES 4

INGREDIENTS

12 oz dried spaghetti

3 tbsp olive oil

3 tbsp butter, cut into small pieces

2 tbsp chopped parsley

SAUCE

1 cup freshly ground almonds

½ cup ricotta

large pinch of grated nutmeg

large pinch of ground cinnamon

⅔ cup crème fraîche or sour cream

½ cup hot chicken stock

1 tbsp pine kernels

pepper

cilantro leaves, to garnish

COOK'S TIP

To toss spaghetti and coat it with a sauce or dressing, use the 2 largest forks you can find. Holding one fork in each hand, ease the prongs under the spaghetti from each side and lift them toward the center. Repeat evenly until the pasta is well coated.

1 Cook the spaghetti in a large pan of boiling salted water, to which you have added 1 tablespoon of the oil, for 8–10 minutes, or until tender. Drain the pasta in a colander, return to the pan, and toss with the butter and parsley. Cover the pan and keep warm.

2 To make the sauce, mix together the ground almonds, ricotta, nutmeg, cinnamon, and crème fraîche or sour cream, to make a thick paste. Gradually pour on the remaining oil, stirring constantly until it is well blended. Gradually pour on the hot stock, stirring all the time, until the sauce is smooth.

3 Transfer the spaghetti to warmed serving dishes, pour on the sauce, and toss well. Sprinkle each serving with pine kernels and garnish with cilantro leaves. Serve warm.

Artichoke & Olive Spaghetti

The tasty flavors of artichoke hearts and black olives are a winning combination.

NUTRITIONAL INFORMATION

Calories	393	Sugars	........11g
Protein	........14g	Fat	...........11g
Carbohydrate	...63g	Saturates	.......2g

20 MINS   35 MINS

SERVES 4

INGREDIENTS

2 tbsp olive oil

1 large red onion, chopped

2 garlic cloves, crushed

1 tbsp lemon juice

4 baby eggplant, quartered

2½ cups strained puréed tomatoes

2 tsp superfine sugar

2 tbsp tomato paste

14-oz can artichoke hearts, drained
    and halved

¾ cup pitted black olives

12 oz dried wholewheat spaghetti

salt and pepper

sprigs of fresh basil, to garnish

olive bread, to serve

1 Heat 1 tablespoon of the oil in a large skillet and gently fry the onion, garlic, lemon juice, and eggplant for 4–5 minutes, or until lightly browned.

2 Pour in the strained puréed tomatoes, season with salt and pepper to taste, and add the sugar and tomato paste. Bring to a boil, reduce the heat, and simmer for 20 minutes.

3 Gently stir in the artichoke halves and olives and cook for 5 minutes.

4 Meanwhile, bring a large saucepan of lightly salted water to a boil, and cook the spaghetti for 8–10 minutes or until just tender. Drain well, toss in the remaining olive oil, and season with salt and pepper to taste.

5 Transfer the spaghetti to a warmed serving bowl and top with the vegetable sauce. Garnish with basil sprigs and serve with olive bread.

Chili & Bell Pepper Pasta

This roasted bell pepper and chili sauce is sweet and spicy – the perfect combination!

NUTRITIONAL INFORMATION

Calories	423	Sugars	.........5g
Protein	.........9g	Fat	..........27g
Carbohydrate	...38g	Saturates	.......4g

🕑 25 MINS   🕐 30 MINS

SERVES 4

I N G R E D I E N T S

2 red bell peppers, halved and seeded

1 small red chili

4 tomatoes, halved

2 garlic cloves

1¾ oz ground blanched almonds

7 tbsp olive oil

1½ lb fresh pasta or 12 oz dried pasta

fresh oregano leaves, to garnish

1 Place the bell peppers, skin-side up, on a cookie sheet, with the chili and tomatoes. Cook under a preheated broiler for 15 minutes, or until charred. After 10 minutes turn the tomatoes skin-side up. Place the bell peppers and chilies in a plastic bag and leave to sweat for 10 minutes.

VARIATION

Add 2 tablespoons red-wine vinegar to the sauce and use as a dressing for a cold pasta salad, if you wish.

2 Remove the skin from the bellpeppers and chilies, and slice the flesh into strips, using a sharp knife.

3 Peel the garlic, and peel and seed the tomatoes.

4 Place the almonds on a cookie sheetand place under the broiler for 2–3 minutes until golden.

5 Using a food processor, blend the bell pepper, chili, garlic, and tomatoes to make a purée. Keep the motor running and slowly add the olive oil to form a thick sauce. Alternatively, mash the mixture with a fork and beat in the olive oil, drop by drop.

6 Stir the toasted ground almonds into the mixture.

7 Warm the sauce in a saucepan until it is heated through.

8 Cook the pasta in a saucepan of boiling water for 8–10 minutes if using dried, or 3–5 minutes if using fresh. Drain the pasta thoroughly and transfer to a serving dish. Pour over the sauce and toss to mix. Garnish with the fresh oregano leaves.

Tagliatelle & Garlic Sauce

This pasta dish can be prepared in a moment – the intense flavors are sure to make this a popular recipe.

NUTRITIONAL INFORMATION

Calories	.501	Sugars	.3g
Protein	.15g	Fat	.31g
Carbohydrate	.43g	Saturates	.11g

 15 MINS   20 MINS

SERVES 4

INGREDIENTS

2 tbsp walnut oil

1 bunch scallions, sliced

2 garlic cloves, sliced thinly

3 cups mushrooms, sliced

1 lb 2 oz fresh green and white tagliatelle

1½ cups frozen chopped leaf spinach, thawed and drained

½ cup full-fat soft cheese with garlic and herbs

4 tbsp light cream

½ cup chopped, unsalted pistachio nuts

2 tbsp shredded fresh basil

salt and pepper

sprigs of fresh basil, to garnish

Italian bread, to serve

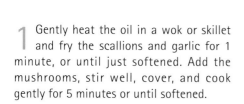

1 Gently heat the oil in a wok or skillet and fry the scallions and garlic for 1 minute, or until just softened. Add the mushrooms, stir well, cover, and cook gently for 5 minutes or until softened.

2 Meanwhile, bring a large saucepan of lightly salted water to a boil and cook the pasta for 3–5 minutes or until just tender. Drain the pasta thoroughly and return to the saucepan.

3 Add the spinach to the mushrooms and heat through for 1–2 minutes. Add the cheese and allow to melt slightly. Stir in the cream and continue to heat without allowing to boil.

4 Pour the mixture over the pasta, season to taste, and mix well. Heat gently, stirring, for 2–3 minutes.

5 Pile into a warmed serving bowl and sprinkle the pistachio nuts and shredded basil over. Garnish with basil sprigs and serve with Italian bread.

Pasta with Nuts & Cheese

Simple and inexpensive, this tasty pasta dish can be prepared fairly quickly.

NUTRITIONAL INFORMATION

Calories 531   Sugars 4g
Protein . . . . .20g   Fat 35g
Carbohydrate . . .35g   Saturates 16g

10 MINS   30 MINS

SERVES 4

INGREDIENTS

1 cup pine kernels

12 oz dried pasta shapes

2 zucchini, sliced

1¼ cups broccoli, broken into flowerets

1 cup full-fat soft cheese

⅔ cup milk

1 tbsp chopped fresh basil

4½ oz button mushrooms, sliced

3 oz blue cheese, crumbled

salt and pepper

sprigs of fresh basil, to garnish

green salad, to serve

1 Scatter the pine kernels onto a cookie sheet and broil, turning occasionally, until lightly browned all over; set aside.

2 Cook the pasta in plenty of boiling salted water for 8–10 minutes, or until just tender.

3 Meanwhile, cook the zucchini and broccoli in a small amount of boiling, lightly salted water for about 5 minutes, or until just tender.

4 Put the soft cheese into a pan and heat gently, stirring constantly. Add the milk and stir to mix. Add the basil and mushrooms and cook for 2–3 minutes. Stir in the blue cheese and season.

5 Drain the pasta and the vegetables and mix together. Pour the cheese and mushroom sauce over and add the pine kernels. Toss to mix. Garnish with basil sprigs and serve with a green salad.

Macaroni & Tuna Fish Layer

A layer of tuna fish with garlic, mushroom, and red bell pepper is sandwiched between two layers of macaroni with a crunchy topping.

NUTRITIONAL INFORMATION

Calories . . . . .691 Sugars 10g
Protein . . . . .41g Fat 33g
Carbohydrate . . .62g Saturates 15g

20 MINS   50 MINS

SERVES 2

INGREDIENTS

4½–5½ oz dried macaroni

2 tbsp oil

1 garlic clove, crushed

¾ cup button mushrooms, sliced

½ red bell pepper, thinly sliced

7 oz can tuna in brine, drained and flaked

½ tsp dried oregano

salt and pepper

SAUCE

2 tbsp butter or margarine

1 tbsp all-purpose flour

1 cup milk

2 tomatoes, sliced

2 tbsp dried bread crumbs

¼ cup sharp cheese, grated

1 Cook the macaroni in boiling salted water, with 1 tablespoon of the oil added, for 10–12 minutes, or until tender. Drain, rinse, and drain thoroughly.

2 Heat the remaining oil in a saucepan or skillet and fry the garlic, mushrooms, and bell pepper until soft. Add the tuna, oregano, and seasoning, and heat through.

3 Grease a 1-quart baking dish, and add half of the cooked macaroni. Cover with the tuna mixture and then add the remaining macaroni.

4 To make the sauce, melt the butter or margarine in a saucepan, stir in the flour, and cook for 1 minute. Add the milk gradually and bring to a boil. Simmer for 1–2 minutes, stirring continuously, until thickened. Season to taste and pour the sauce over the macaroni.

5 Lay the sliced tomatoes over the sauce and sprinkle with the bread crumbs and cheese.

6 Place in a preheated oven, at 400°F, for about 25 minutes, or until piping hot and the top is browned.

VARIATION

Replace the tuna with chopped cooked chicken, beef, pork, or ham, or 3–4 sliced hard-cooked eggs for a vegetarian version.

Fish & Vegetable Lasagne

Layers of cheese sauce, smoked cod, and wholewheat lasagne can be assembled overnight and left ready to cook on the following day.

NUTRITIONAL INFORMATION

Calories	.456	Sugars	.8g
Protein	.33g	Fat	.24g
Carbohydrate	.24g	Saturates	.15g

 25 MINS   50 MINS

SERVES 6

INGREDIENTS

8 sheets wholewheat lasagne

1 lb 2 oz smoked cod

2½ cups milk

1 tbsp lemon juice

8 peppercorns

2 bay leaves

a few parsley stalks

½ cup sharp cheese, grated

¼ cup Parmesan, grated

salt and pepper

a few whole shrimp, to garnish

SAUCE

¼ cup butter, plus extra for greasing

1 large onion, sliced

1 green bell pepper, cored, seeded, and
   chopped

1 small zucchini, sliced

½ cup all-purpose flour

⅔ cup white wine

⅔ cup light cream

4½ oz shelled shrimp

½ cup sharp cheese, grated

1 Cook the lasagne in a pan of boiling, salted water until almost tender. Drain and reserve.

2 Place the smoked cod, milk, lemon juice, peppercorns, bay leaves, and parsley stems in a skillet. Bring to a boil, cover, and simmer for 10 minutes.

3 Lift the fish from the pan with a draining spoon. Remove the skin and any bones and flake the fish. Strain and reserve the cooking liquid.

4 To make the sauce, melt the butter in a pan and fry the onion, bell pepper and zucchini for 2–3 minutes. Stir in the flour and cook for 1 minute. Gradually add the fish cooking liquid, then stir in the wine, cream, and shrimp. Simmer for 2 minutes. Remove from the heat, add the cheese, and season.

5 Grease a shallow baking dish. Pour in one quarter of the sauce and spread evenly over the base. Cover the sauce with three sheets of lasagne, then with another quarter of the sauce.

6 Arrange the fish on top, then cover with half of the remaining sauce. Finish with the remaining lasagne, then the rest of the sauce. Sprinkle the cheese over the sauce.

7 Bake in a preheated oven at 375°F for 25 minutes, or until the top is golden brown and bubbling. Garnish and serve.

Pasta with Chili & Tomatoes

The pappardelle and vegetables are tossed in a delicious chili and tomato sauce for a quick and economical meal.

NUTRITIONAL INFORMATION

Calories	353	Sugars	.........7g
Protein	........10g	Fat	..........24g
Carbohydrate	...26g	Saturates	.......4g

 15 MINS   20 MINS

SERVES 4

INGREDIENTS

10 oz pappardelle

3 tbsp peanut oil

2 cloves garlic, crushed

2 shallots, sliced

8 oz green beans, sliced

3½ oz cherry tomatoes, halved

1 tsp chili flakes

4 tbsp crunchy peanut butter

⅔ cup coconut milk

1 tbsp tomato paste

sliced scallions, to garnish

1 Cook the pappardelle in a large saucepan of boiling lightly salted water for 5-6 minutes.

2 Heat the peanut oil in a large pan or preheated wok.

3 Add the garlic and shallots and stir-fry for 1 minute.

4 Drain the pappardelle thoroughly and set aside.

5 Add the green beans and drained pasta to the wok and stir-fry for 5 minutes.

6 Add the cherry tomatoes to the wok and mix well.

7 Mix together the chili flakes, peanut butter, coconut milk, and tomato paste.

8 Pour the chili mixture over the noodles, toss well to combine, and heat through.

9 Transfer to warm serving dishes and garnish. Serve immediately.

VARIATION

Add slices of chicken or beef to the recipe and stir-fry with the beans and pasta in step 5 for a more substantial main meal.

Vermicelli & Clam Sauce

This recipe is quick to prepare and cook – it's so delicious that it will be devoured even faster!

NUTRITIONAL INFORMATION

Calories 502   Sugars 2g
Protein . . . . .27g   Fat 17g
Carbohydrate . . .58g   Saturates 7g

 15 MINS   🕐 25 MINS

SERVES 4

I N G R E D I E N T S

14 oz vermicelli, spaghetti, or other long
   pasta

1 tbsp olive oil

2 tbsp butter

2 tbsp Parmesan shavings, to garnish

sprig of basil, to garnish

S A U C E

1 tbsp olive oil

2 onions, chopped

2 garlic cloves, chopped

2 x 7-oz jars clams in brine

½ cup white wine

4 tbsp chopped fresh parsley

½ tsp dried oregano

pinch of freshly grated nutmeg

salt and pepper

1 Cook the pasta in a large pan of boiling salted water, with the olive oil, for 8–10 minutes, or until tender. Drain the pasta in a colander and return to the pan. Add the butter, cover, and shake the pan. Keep warm until required.

2 To make the clam sauce, heat the oil in a pan over a medium heat and fry the onion until it is translucent. Stir in the garlic and cook for 1 minute.

3 Strain the liquid from one jar of clams, pour it into the pan, and add the wine. Stir, bring to simmering point, and simmer for 3 minutes. Drain the brine from the second jar of clams and discard.

4 Add the shellfish and herbs to the pan, and season with pepper to taste and the nutmeg. Lower the heat and cook until the sauce is heated through.

5 Transfer the pasta to a warmed serving dish and pour over the sauce.

6 Sprinkle with the Parmesan and garnish with the basil sprig. Serve hot.

Macaroni & Squid Casserole

This pasta dish is easy to make and is a very hearty meal for a large number of guests.

🕒 15 MINS   🕐 35 MINS

SERVES 6

I N G R E D I E N T S

8 oz short-cut macaroni, or other
　short pasta shapes

1 tbsp olive oil

2 tbsp chopped fresh parsley

salt and pepper

S A U C E

12 oz cleaned squid, cut into ½-in strips

6 tbsp olive oil

2 onions, sliced

1 cup fish stock

⅔ cup red wine

12 oz tomatoes, peeled and thinly sliced

2 tbsp tomato paste

1 tsp dried oregano

2 bay leaves

1 Cook the pasta for only 3 minutes in a large pan of boiling salted water, with the oil. Drain in a colander, return to the pan, cover, and keep warm.

2 To make the sauce, heat the oil in a pan over medium heat and fry the onion until translucent. Add the squid and stock and simmer for 5 minutes. Pour over the wine and add the tomatoes, tomato

paste, oregano, and bay leaves. Bring the sauce to a boil, season with salt and pepper to taste, and cook, uncovered, for 5 minutes.

3 Add the pasta, stir well, cover the pan and continue simmering for 10 minutes, or until the macaroni and squid are almost tender. By this time the sauce should be thick and syrupy. If it is too

liquid, uncover the pan and continue cooking for a few minutes. Taste the sauce and adjust the seasoning if necessary.

4 Remove the bay leaves and stir in most of the parsley, reserving a little to garnish. Transfer to a warmed serving dish. Sprinkle on the remaining parsley and serve hot. Serve with warm, crusty bread, such as ciabatta.

Spaghetti & Salmon Sauce

The smoked salmon ideally complements the spaghetti to make a very luxurious dish.

NUTRITIONAL INFORMATION

Calories	782	Sugars	.........3g
Protein	........20g	Fat	..........48g
Carbohydrate	...48g	Saturates	......27g

 10 MINS   15 MINS

SERVES 4

I N G R E D I E N T S

1 lb 2 oz buckwheat spaghetti

2 tbsp olive oil

½ cup feta cheese, crumbled

cilantro or parsley, to garnish

S A U C E

1¼ cups heavy cream

⅔ cup whiskey or brandy

4½ oz smoked salmon

large pinch of cayenne pepper

2 tbsp chopped cilantro or parsley

salt and pepper

1 Cook the spaghetti in a large saucepan of salted boiling water, with 1 tablespoon of the olive oil, for 8–10 minutes or until tender. Drain the pasta in a colander. Return the pasta to the pan, sprinkle the remaining oil over, cover, and shake the pan. Set aside and keep warm until required.

2 In separate small saucepans, heat the cream and the whiskey or brandy to simmering point. Do not let them boil.

3 Combine the cream with the whiskey or brandy.

4 Cut the smoked salmon into thin strips and add to the cream mixture. Season with a little black pepper and cayenne pepper to taste, and then stir in the chopped cilantro or parsley.

5 Transfer the spaghetti to a warmed serving dish, pour over the sauce and toss thoroughly using 2 large forks. Scatter the crumbled cheese over the pasta and garnish with the cilantro or parsley. Serve at once.

Pasta & Mussel Sauce

Serve this aromatic seafood dish with plenty of fresh, crusty bread to soak up the delicious sauce.

NUTRITIONAL INFORMATION

Calories 735   Sugars 3g
Protein . . . . .37g   Fat 46g
Carbohydrate . . .41g   Saturates 26g

25 MINS   25 MINS

SERVES 6

INGREDIENTS

14 oz pasta shells

1 tbsp olive oil

SAUCE

6 pints mussels, scrubbed

1 cup dry white wine

2 large onions, chopped

½ cup unsalted butter

6 large garlic cloves, chopped finely

5 tbsp chopped fresh parsley

1¼ cups heavy cream

salt and pepper

crusty bread, to serve

1 Pull off the beards from the mussels and rinse well in several changes of water; discard any mussels that refuse to close when tapped. Put the mussels in a large pan with the white wine and half of the onions. Cover the pan, shake, and cook over a medium heat for 2–3 minutes until the mussels open.

2 Remove the pan from the heat, lift out the mussels with a draining spoon, reserving the liquid, and set aside until they are cool enough to handle. Discard any mussels that have not opened.

3 Melt the butter in a pan over medium heat and fry the remaining onion for 3–4 minutes, or until translucent. Stir in the garlic and cook for 1 minute. Gradually pour over the reserved cooking liquid, stirring to blend thoroughly. Stir in the parsley and cream. Season to taste and bring to simmering point. Taste and adjust the seasoning if necessary.

4 Cook the pasta in a large pan of salted boiling water, with the oil, for 8–10 minutes, or until tender. Drain the pasta in a colander, return to the pan, cover, and keep warm.

5 Remove the mussels from their shells, reserving a few shells for garnish. Stir the mussels into the cream sauce. Tip the pasta into a warmed serving dish, pour in the sauce, and, using 2 large spoons, toss it together well. Garnish with a few of the reserved mussel shells. Serve hot, with warm, crusty bread.

Pasta & Sicilian Sauce

This Sicilian recipe of anchovies mixed with pine kernels and golden raisins in a tomato sauce is delicious with all types of pasta.

NUTRITIONAL INFORMATION

Calories	286	Sugars	14g
Protein	11g	Fat	8g
Carbohydrate	46g	Saturates	1g

25 MINS   30 MINS

SERVES 4

I N G R E D I E N T S

1 lb tomatoes, halved

1 oz pine kernels

1¾ oz golden raisins

1¾ oz can anchovies, drained and halved

2 tbsp concentrated tomato paste

1½ lb fresh penne or 12 oz dried penne

1 Broil the tomatoes under a preheated broiler for about 10 minutes. Leave to cool slightly, then once cool enough to handle, peel off the skin, and dice the flesh.

2 Place the pine kernels on a cookie sheet and lightly toast under the broiler for 2–3 minutes, or until golden brown.

3 Soak the golden raisins in a bowl of warm water for about 20 minutes; drain them thoroughly.

4 Place the tomatoes, pine kernels, and golden raisins in a small saucepan and gently heat.

5 Add the anchovies and tomato paste, heating the sauce for a further 2–3 minutes, or until hot.

6 Cook the pasta in a saucepan of boiling water for 8–10 minutes or until it is cooked through, but still has bite. Drain thoroughly.

7 Transfer the pasta to a serving plate and serve with the hot Sicilian sauce.

VARIATION

Add 3½ oz bacon, broiled for 5 minutes until crispy, then chopped, instead of the anchovies, if you prefer.

Pasta Pudding

A tasty mixture of creamy fish and pasta cooked in a bowl, unmolded, and drizzled with tomato sauce presents macaroni in a new guise.

NUTRITIONAL INFORMATION

Calories	536	Sugars	........4g
Protein	........35g	Fat	.........35g
Carbohydrate	...21g	Saturates	......17g

🍲 35 MINS   🕐 2 HOURS

SERVES 4

INGREDIENTS

4½ oz short-cut macaroni, or other

   short pasta shapes

1 tbsp olive oil

1 tbsp butter, plus extra for greasing

1 lb 2 oz white fish fillets, such as cod,

   haddock, or coley

a few parsley stems

6 black peppercorns

½ cup heavy cream

2 eggs, separated

2 tbsp chopped dill, or parsley

pinch of grated nutmeg

½ cup Parmesan, grated

Basic Tomato Sauce (see page 14), to serve

pepper

dill or parsley sprigs, to garnish

1 Cook the pasta in a pan of salted boiling water, adding the oil, for 8–10 minutes. Drain, return to the pan, add the butter, and cover. Keep warm.

2 Place the fish in a skillet with the parsley stems and peppercorns and pour on just enough water to cover. Bring to a boil, cover, and simmer for 10 minutes. Lift out the fish with a pancake turner, reserving the liquid. When the fish is cool enough to handle, skin and remove any bones. Cut into bite-sized pieces.

3 Transfer the pasta to a large bowl and stir in the cream, egg yolks, and dill. Stir in the fish, taking care not to break it up, and enough liquid to make a moist but firm mixture. It should fall easily from a spoon, but not be too runny. Whisk the egg whites until stiff but not dry, then fold into the mixture.

4 Grease a heatproof bowl or pudding basin and spoon in the mixture to within ½ inches of the rim. Cover the top with greased waxed paper and a cloth, or with foil, and tie firmly around the rim. Do not use foil if you cook the pudding in a microwave.

5 Stand the pudding on a trivet in a large pan of boiling water to come halfway up the sides. Cover and steam for 1½ hours, topping up a boiling water as needed, or cook in a microwave on maximum power for 7 minutes.

6 Run a knife around the inside of the bowl and invert onto a warm serving dish. Pour some tomato sauce over the top; serve the rest separately. Garnish and serve.

Spaghetti & Shellfish

Frozen shelled shrimp from the freezer becomes the star ingredient in this colorful and flavorsome dish.

NUTRITIONAL INFORMATION

Calories	510	Sugars	. . . . . . .38g
Protein	. . . . .33g	Fat	. . . . .24g
Carbohydrate	. . .44g	Saturates	. . . . . .11g

35 MINS 30 MINS

SERVES 4

INGREDIENTS

8 oz short-cut spaghetti, or long spaghetti
   broken into 6-inch pieces

2 tbsp olive oil

1¼ cups chicken stock

1 tsp lemon juice

1 small cauliflower, cut into flowerets

2 carrots, sliced thinly

4½ oz snow peas, trimmed

¼ cup butter

1 onion, sliced

1½ cups zucchini, sliced thinly

1 garlic clove, chopped

12 oz frozen shelled shrimp, defrosted

2 tbsp chopped fresh parsley

¼ cup Parmesan, grated

salt and pepper

½ tsp paprika, to sprinkle

4 unshelled shrimp, to garnish (optional)

1 Cook the spaghetti in a large pan of boiling salted water, adding 1 tbsp of the oil, for 8–10 minutes, or until tender. Drain, then return to the pan and stir in the remaining oil; cover and keep warm.

2 Bring the chicken stock and lemon juice to a boil. Add the cauliflower and carrots and cook for 3–4 minutes until they are barely tender. Remove with a draining spoon and set aside. Add the snow peas and cook for 1–2 minutes, until they begin to soften. Remove with a draining spoon and add to the other vegetables. Reserve the stock.

3 Melt half of the butter in a skillet over a medium heat and fry the onion and zucchini for about 3 minutes. Add the garlic and shrimp and cook for a further 2–3 minutes, until heated through.

4 Stir in the reserved vegetables and heat through. Season with salt and pepper, then stir in the remaining butter.

5 Transfer the spaghetti to a warmed serving dish. Pour the sauce and parsley over and toss well using 2 forks, until thoroughly coated. Sprinkle on the grated cheese and paprika, and garnish with unshelled shrimp, if using. Serve.

Pasta Vongole

Fresh clams are available from most good fishmongers. If you prefer, used canned clams, which are less messy to eat but not as attractive.

NUTRITIONAL INFORMATION

Calories	.410	Sugars	.1g
Protein	.39g	Fat	.9g
Carbohydrate	.39g	Saturates	.1g

20 MINS   20 MINS

SERVES 4

INGREDIENTS

1½ lb fresh clams or 1 x 10 oz can clams, drained

14 oz mixed seafood, such as shrimp, squid, and mussels, defrosted if frozen

2 tbsp olive oil

2 garlic cloves, finely chopped

⅔ cup white wine

⅔ cup fish stock

2 tbsp chopped tarragon

salt and pepper

1½ lb fresh pasta or 12 oz dried pasta

1 If you are using fresh clams, scrub them clean and discard any that are already open.

2 Heat the oil in a large skillet. Add the garlic and the clams to the pan and cook for 2 minutes, shaking the pan to make sure all the clams are coated in oil.

3 Add the remaining seafood mixture to the pan and cook for a further 2 minutes.

4 Pour the wine and stock over the mixed seafood and garlic and bring to a boil. Cover the pan, reduce the heat and leave to simmer for 8–10 minutes, or until the shells open; discard any clams or mussels that do not open.

5 Meanwhile, cook the pasta in a saucepan of boiling water for 8–10 minutes or until it is cooked through, but still has bite. Drain the pasta thoroughly.

6 Stir the tarragon into the sauce and season with salt and pepper to taste.

7 Transfer the pasta to a serving plate and pour the sauce over. Serve immediately.

VARIATION

Red clam sauce can be made by adding 8 tablespoons of strained puréed tomatoes to the sauce along with the stock in step 4. Follow the same cooking method.

Spaghetti, Tuna, & Parsley

This is a recipe to look forward to when parsley is at its most prolific, during its growing season.

NUTRITIONAL INFORMATION

Calories	970	Sugars	.....2g
Protein	.....23g	Fat	.....80g
Carbohydrate	...42g	Saturates	.....18g

 10 MINS   15 MINS

SERVES 4

I N G R E D I E N T S

1 lb 2 oz spaghetti

1 tbsp olive oil

2 tbsp butter

black olives, to serve (optional)

S A U C E

7-oz can tuna, drained

2-oz can anchovies, drained

1 cup olive oil

1 cup roughly chopped fresh, flat-leaf
  parsley

⅔ cup crème fraîche or sour cream

salt and pepper

1 Cook the spaghetti in a large saucepan of salted boiling water, with the olive oil, for 8–10 minutes, or until tender. Drain the spaghetti in a colander and return to the pan. Add the butter, toss thoroughly to coat, and keep warm until required.

2 Remove any bones from the tuna and flake into smaller pieces, using 2 forks. Put the tuna in a blender or food processor with the anchovies, olive oil, and parsley and process until the sauce is smooth. Pour in the crème fraîche and process for a few seconds to blend. Taste the sauce and season with salt and pepper.

3 Warm 4 plates. Shake the saucepan of spaghetti over a medium heat for a few minutes, or until it is thoroughly warmed through.

4 Pour the sauce over the spaghetti and toss quickly, using 2 forks. Serve immediately with a small dish of black olives, if liked.

Penne & Butternut Squash

The creamy, nutty flavor of squash complements the al dente texture of the pasta perfectly. This recipe has been adapted for the microwave.

NUTRITIONAL INFORMATION

Calories	499	Sugars	.........4g
Protein	........20g	Fat	..........26g
Carbohydrate	...49g	Saturates	......13g

15 MINS   30 MINS

SERVES 4

INGREDIENTS

2 tbsp olive oil

1 garlic clove, crushed

1 cup fresh white bread crumbs

1 lb 2 oz peeled and seeded
   butternut squash

½ cup water

1 lb 2 oz fresh penne, or other pasta shape

1 tbsp butter

1 onion, sliced

½ cup cooked ham, cut into strips

scant cup light cream

½ cup Cheddar cheese, grated

2 tbsp chopped fresh parsley

salt and pepper

1 Mix together the oil, garlic, and bread crumbs and spread out on a large plate. Cook on HIGH power for 4–5 minutes, stirring every minute, until crisp and beginning to brown; set aside.

2 Dice the squash. Place in a large bowl with half of the water. Cover and cook on HIGH power for 8–9 minutes, stirring occasionally; leave to stand for 2 minutes.

3 Place the pasta in a large bowl, add a little salt and pour boiling water over to cover by 1 inch. Cover and cook on HIGH power for 5 minutes, stirring once, until the pasta is just tender, but still firm to the bite. Leave to stand, covered, for 1 minute before draining.

4 Place the butter and onion in a large bowl. Cover and cook on HIGH power for 3 minutes.

5 Coarsely mash the squash, using a fork. Add to the onion with the pasta, ham, cream, cheese, parsley, and remaining water. Season generously and mix well. Cover and cook on HIGH power for 4 minutes until heated through.

6 Serve the pasta sprinkled with the crisp garlic crumbs.

COOK'S TIP

If the squash weighs more than is needed for this recipe, blanch the excess for 3–4 minutes on HIGH power in a covered bowl with a little water. Drain, cool, and place in a freezer bag. Store in the freezer for up to 3 months.

Sicilian Spaghetti Cake

Any variety of long pasta could be used for this very tasty dish from Sicily.

NUTRITIONAL INFORMATION

Calories	876	Sugars	........10g
Protein	........37g	Fat	..........65g
Carbohydrate	...39g	Saturates	......18g

30 MINS   50 MINS

SERVES 4

INGREDIENTS

2eggplants, about 1 lb 7 oz

⅔ cup olive oil

12 oz finely groundlean beef

1 onion, chopped

2 garlic cloves, crushed

2 tbsp tomato paste

14-oz can chopped tomatoes

1 tsp Worcestershire sauce

1 tsp chopped fresh oregano or marjoram
    or ½ tsp dried oregano or marjoram

⅓ cup stoned black olives, sliced

1 green, red, or yellow bell pepper, cored,
    seeded, and chopped

6 oz spaghetti

1 cup Parmesan, grated

1 Brush a 8-inch loose-based round cake pan with olive oil, place a disc of baking parchment in the base, and brush with oil. Trim the eggplants and cut into slanting slices, ¼ inch thick. Heat some of the oil in a skillet. Fry a few slices of eggplant at a time until lightly browned, turning once, and adding more oil as necessary. Drain on paper towels.

2 Put the ground beef, onion, and garlic into a saucepan and cook, stirring frequently, until browned all over. Add the tomato paste, tomatoes, Worcestershire sauce, herbs, and seasoning. Simmer for 10 minutes, stirring occasionally, then add the olives and bell pepper and cook for 10 minutes.

3 Bring a large saucepan of salted water to a boil. Cook the spaghetti for 8–10 minutes or until just tender; drain the spaghetti thoroughly. Turn the spaghetti into a bowl and stir in the meat mixture and Parmesan, tossing together with 2 forks.

4 Lay overlapping slices of eggplant over the bottom of the cake pan and up the sides. Add the meat mixture, pressing it down, and cover with the remaining eggplant slices.

5 Stand the cake pan in a baking pan and cook in a preheated oven at 400°F for 40 minutes. Leave to stand for 5 minutes, then loosen around the edges and invert onto a warmed serving dish, releasing the pan clip. Remove the baking parchment. Serve immediately.

Vegetable-Pasta Nests

These large pasta nests look impressive when presented filled with broiled mixed vegetables, and taste delicious.

NUTRITIONAL INFORMATION

Calories 392   Sugars 1g
Protein . . . . .6g   Fat 28g
Carbohydrate . . .32g   Saturates 9g

25 MINS   40 MINS

SERVES 4

I N G R E D I E N T S

6 oz spaghetti

1 eggplant, halved and sliced

1 zucchini, diced

1 red bell pepper, seeded and chopped
  diagonally

6 tbsp olive oil

2 garlic cloves, crushed

4 tbsp butter or margarine, melted

1 tbsp dry white bread crumbs

salt and pepper

fresh parsley sprigs, to garnish

1 Bring a large saucepan of water to a boil and cook the spaghetti for 8–10 minutes, or until al dente. Drain the spaghetti in a colander and set aside until required.

2 Place the eggplant, zucchini, and bellpepper on a cookie sheet.

3 Mix the oil and garlic together and pour the vegetables over, tossing to coat all over.

4 Cook under a preheated hot broiler for about 10 minutes, turning, until tender and lightly charred. Set aside.

5 Divide the spaghetti between 4 lightly greased Yorkshire pudding pans or giant mufin molds. Using 2 forks, curl the spaghetti to form nests.

6 Brush the pasta nests with melted butter or margarine and sprinkle with the bread crumbs. Bake in a preheated oven at 400°F for 15 minutes or until they are lightly golden. Remove the pasta nests from the pans or muffin molds and transfer to serving plates. Divide the broiled vegetables between the pasta nests, season, and garnish.

COOK'S TIP

"Al dente" means "to the bite" and describes cooked pasta that is not too soft, but still has a bite to it.

Lasagne Verde

The sauce in this delicious baked pasta dish can be used as an alternative sauce for Spaghetti Bolognese (see page 184).

NUTRITIONAL INFORMATION

Calories 619   Sugars 7g
Protein . . . . .29g   Fat 45g
Carbohydrate . . .21g   Saturates 19g

1¾ HOURS   55 MINS

SERVES 6

I N G R E D I E N T S

Ragù Sauce (see page 9)

1 tbsp olive oil

8 oz lasagne verde

Béchamel Sauce (see page 14)

½ cup Parmesan, grated

salt and pepper

green salad, tomato salad, or black olives,
    to serve

1 Begin by making the Ragù Sauce as described on page 9, but cook for 10–12 minutes longer than the time given, in an uncovered pan, to allow the excess liquid to evaporate. To layer the sauce with lasagne, it needs to be reduced to the consistency of a thick paste.

2 Have ready a large saucepan of boiling salted water and add the olive oil. Drop the pasta sheets into a boiling water a few at a time, and return the water to a boil before adding more pasta sheets. If you are using fresh lasagne, cook the sheets for a total of 8 minutes. If you are using dried or partly precooked pasta, cook it according to the directions given on the package.

3 Remove the pasta sheets from the saucepan with a draining spoon.

Spread them in a single layer on damp dish cloths.

4 Grease a rectangular ovenproof dish, about 10–11 inches long. To assemble the dish, spoon a little of the meat sauce into the prepared dish, cover with a layer of lasagne, then spoon a little Béchamel Sauce over, and sprinkle with some of the cheese. Continue making layers in this way, covering the final layer of lasagne with the remaining Béchamel Sauce.

5 Sprinkle on the remaining cheese and bake in a preheated oven at 375°F for 40 minutes, or until the sauce is golden brown and bubbling. Serve with a green salad, a tomato salad, or a bowl of black olives.

Pasticcio

A recipe that has both Italian and Greek origins, this dish can be served hot or cold, cut into thick, satisfying squares.

NUTRITIONAL INFORMATION

Calories	590	Sugars	.........8g
Protein	........34g	Fat	..........39g
Carbohydrate	...23g	Saturates	......16g

 35 MINS   1¼ HOURS

SERVES 6

INGREDIENTS

8 oz fusilli, or other short pasta shapes

1 tbsp olive oil

4 tbsp heavy cream

salt

rosemary sprigs, to garnish

SAUCE

2 tbsp olive oil, plus extra for brushing

1 onion, sliced thinly

1 red bell pepper, cored, seeded and chopped

2 garlic cloves, chopped

1 lb 6 oz ground lean beef

14-oz can chopped tomatoes

½ cup dry white wine

2 tbsp chopped fresh parsley

1¾ oz can anchovies, drained and chopped

salt and pepper

TOPPING

1¼ cups plain yogurt

3 eggs

pinch of freshly grated nutmeg

⅓ cup Parmesan cheese, grated

1 To make the sauce, heat the oil in a large skillet and fry the onion and red bell pepper for 3 minutes. Stir in the garlic and cook for 1 minute more. Stir in the beef and cook, stirring frequently, until no longer pink.

2 Add the tomatoes and wine, stir well, and bring to a boil. Simmer, uncovered, for 20 minutes, or until the sauce is fairly thick. Stir in the parsley and anchovies, and season to taste.

3 Cook the pasta in a large pan of boiling salted water, with the oil, for 8–10 minutes, or until tender. Drain the pasta in a colander, then transfer to a bowl. Stir in the cream and set aside.

4 To make the topping, beat together the yogurt and eggs and season with nutmeg and salt and pepper to taste.

5 Brush a shallow baking dish with oil. Spoon in half of the pasta and cover with half of the meat sauce. Repeat these layers, then spread the topping evenly over the final layer. Sprinkle the cheese on top.

6 Bake in a preheated oven at 375°F for 25 minutes, or until the topping is golden brown and bubbling. Garnish with sprigs of rosemary and serve with a selection of raw vegetable crudités.

Chicken & Tomato Lasagne

This variation of the traditional beef dish has layers of pasta and chicken or turkey baked in red wine, tomatoes, and a delicious cheese sauce.

NUTRITIONAL INFORMATION

Calories ....550 Sugars 11g
Protein ....35g Fat 29g
Carbohydrate ...34g Saturates 12g

 20 MINS 1¹/₄ HOURS

SERVES 4

I N G R E D I E N T S

12 oz fresh lasagne (about 9 sheets) or 5½ oz dried lasagne (about 9 sheets)

1 tbsp olive oil

1 red onion, finely chopped

1 garlic clove, crushed

3½ oz mushrooms, wiped and sliced

12 oz skinless chicken or turkey breast, cut into chunks

⅔ cup red wine, diluted with ⅓ cup water

9 oz strained puréd tomatoes

1 tsp sugar

B E C H A M E L   S A U C E

5 tbsp butter

4 tbsp all-purpose flour

2½ cups milk

1 egg, beaten

¾ cup Parmesan cheese, grated

salt and pepper

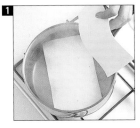  

1 Cook the lasagne in a pan of boiling water according to the directions. Lightly grease a deep baking dish.

2 Heat the oil in a pan. Add the onion and garlic and cook for 3–4 minutes. Add the mushrooms and chicken and stir-fry for 4 minutes, or until the meat browns.

3 Add the wine and bring to a boil, then simmer for 5 minutes. Stir in the strained purée tomatoes and sugar and cook for 3–5 minutes until the meat is tender and cooked through. The sauce should have thickened, but still be quite runny.

4 To make the Béchamel Sauce, melt the butter in a pan, stir in the flour and cook for 2 minutes. Remove the pan from the heat and gradually add the milk, mixing to form a smooth sauce. Return the pan to the heat and bring to a boil, stirring until thickened. Leave to cool slightly, then beat in the egg and half of the cheese; season to taste.

5 Place 3 sheets of lasagne in the bottom of the dish and spread with half of the chicken; repeat the layers. Top with the last 3 sheets of lasagne, pour over the Béchamel Sauce, and sprinkle with the Parmesan. Bake in a preheated oven, at 375°F for 30 minutes until golden and the pasta is cooked.

Tagliatelle with Meatballs

There is an appetizing contrast of textures and flavors in this satisfying family dish.

NUTRITIONAL INFORMATION

Calories 910   Sugars 13g
Protein . . . . .40g   Fat 54g
Carbohydrate . . .65g   Saturates 19g

 45 MINS   1 HR 5 MINS

SERVES 4

I N G R E D I E N T S

1 lb 2 oz ground lean beef

1 cup soft white bread crumbs

1 garlic clove, crushed

2 tbsp chopped fresh parsley

1 tsp dried oregano

large pinch of freshly grated nutmeg

¼ tsp ground coriander

½ cup Parmesan cheese, grated

2–3 tbsp milk

flour, for dusting

4 tbsp olive oil

4 oz tagliatelle

2 tbsp butter, diced

salt and pepper

S A U C E

3 tbsp olive oil

2 large onions, sliced

2 celery stalks, sliced thinly

2 garlic cloves, chopped

14-oz can chopped tomatoes

4½-oz bottled sun-dried tomatoes, drained and chopped

2 tbsp tomato paste

1 tbsp dark muscovado sugar

⅔ cup white wine, or water

1 To make the sauce, heat the oil in a skillet, and fry the onions and celery until translucent. Add the garlic and cook for 1 minute. Stir in the tomatoes, tomato paste, sugar, and wine, and season. Bring to a boil and simmer for 10 minutes.

2 Meanwhile, break up the meat in a bowl with a wooden spoon until it becomes a sticky paste. Stir in the bread crumbs, garlic, herbs, and spices. Stir in the cheese and enough milk to make a firm paste. Flour your hands, take large spoonfuls of the mixture and shape it into 12 balls. Heat 3 tbsp of the oil in a skillet and fry the meatballs for 5–6 minutes until browned.

3 Pour the tomato sauce over the meatballs. Lower the heat, cover the pan, and simmer for 30 minutes, turning once or twice. Add a little extra water if the sauce begins to dry.

4 Cook the pasta in a large saucepan of boiling salted water, with the remaining oil, for 8–10 minutes, or until tender. Drain the pasta, then turn into a warmed serving dish, dot with the butter, and toss with 2 forks. Spoon the meatballs and sauce over the pasta and serve.

Tortelloni

These delicious squares of pasta stuffed with mushrooms and cheese are surprisingly filling. This recipe makes 36 tortelloni.

NUTRITIONAL INFORMATION

Calories	360	Sugars	.........1g
Protein	.........9g	Fat	..........21g
Carbohydrate	...36g	Saturates	......12g

1¼ HOURS   25 MINS

SERVES 4

I N G R E D I E N T S

10½ oz fresh pasta, rolled out to thin sheets

5 tbsp butter

⅓ cup shallots, finely chopped

3 garlic cloves, crushed

⅔ oz mushrooms, wiped and finely
  chopped

½ stick celery, finely chopped

1 oz Pecorino cheese, finely grated,
  plus extra to garnish

1 tbsp oil

salt and pepper

1 Using a serrated pasta cutter, cut 2 inch squares from the sheets of fresh pasta. To make 36 tortelloni you will need 72 squares. Once the pasta is cut, cover the squares with plastic wrap to stop them drying out.

2 Heat 2 tbsp of the butter in a skillet. Add the shallots, 1 crushed garlic clove, the mushrooms, and celery and cook for 4–5 minutes.

3 Remove the pan from the heat, stir in the cheese and season with salt and pepper to taste.

4 Spoon ½ teaspoon of the mixture on to the middle of 36 pasta squares. Brush the edges of the squares with water and top with the remaining 36 squares. Press the edges together to seal; leave to rest for 5 minutes.

5 Bring a large pan of water to a boil, add the oil and cook the tortelloni, in batches, for 2–3 minutes. The tortelloni will rise to the surface when cooked and the pasta should be tender with a slight bite. Remove from the pan with a perforated spoon and drain thoroughly.

6 Meanwhile, melt the remaining butter in a pan. Add the remaining garlic and plenty of pepper and cook for 1–2 minutes. Transfer the tortelloni to serving plates and pour the garlic butter over. Garnish with grated pecorino cheese and serve immediately.

Meat & Pasta Loaf

The cheesy pasta layer comes as a pleasant surprise inside this lightly spiced meat loaf.

NUTRITIONAL INFORMATION

Calories 497   Sugars 4g
Protein ....26g   Fat 37g
Carbohydrate ...16g   Saturates 16g

45 MINS   1¼ HOURS

SERVES 6

INGREDIENTS

2 tbsp butter, plus extra for greasing

1 onion, chopped finely

1 small red bell pepper, cored, seeded, and chopped

1 garlic clove, chopped

1 lb 2 oz ground lean beef

½ cup soft white bread crumbs

½ tsp cayenne pepper

1 tbsp lemon juice

½ tsp grated lemon rind

2 tbsp chopped fresh parsley

3 oz short pasta, such as fusilli

4 bay leaves

1 tbsp olive oil

Cheese Sauce (see page 15)

6 oz bacon rashers

salt and pepper

salad leaves, to garnish

1 Melt the butter in a pan over a medium heat and fry the onion and pepper for about 3 minutes until the onion is translucent. Stir in the garlic and cook for 1 minute.

2 Put the meat into a large bowl and mash it with a wooden spoon until it becomes a sticky paste. Tip in the fried vegetables and stir in the bread crumbs, cayenne, lemon juice, lemon peel, and parsley. Season with salt and pepper and set aside.

3 Cook the pasta in a large pan of salted boiling water and olive oil, for 8–10 minutes or until tender. Drain the pasta, then stir it into the cheese sauce.

4 Grease a bread pan and arrange the bay leaves in the bottom. Stretch the bacon with a knife blade and arrange them to line the bottom and sides of the pan.

5 Spoon in half of the meat mixture, level the surface, and cover it with the pasta. Spoon in the remaining meat mixture, level the top and cover the pan with foil.

6 Cook the meat loaf in a preheated oven at 350°F, for 1 hour, or until the juices run clear and the loaf has shrunk away from the sides of the pan. Pour off any excess fat from the pan and turn the loaf out onto a warmed serving dish. Garnish with salad leaves and serve hot.

Tagliatelle & Chicken Sauce

Spinach ribbon noodles covered with a rich tomato sauce and topped with creamy chicken makes a very appetizing dish.

NUTRITIONAL INFORMATION

Calories	853	Sugars	.........6g
Protein	........32g	Fat	...........71g
Carbohydrate	...23g	Saturates	......34g

 30 MINS   25 MINS

SERVES 4

I N G R E D I E N T S

Basic Tomato Sauce (see page 14)

8 oz fresh green ribbon noodles

1 tbsp olive oil

salt

basil leaves, to garnish

CHICKEN SAUCE

¼ cup unsalted butter

14 oz boned, skinned chicken breast, thinly sliced

¾ cup blanched almonds

1¼ cups heavy cream

salt and pepper

basil leaves, to garnish

1 Make the tomato sauce, and keep warm.

2 To make the chicken sauce, melt the butter in a pan over a medium heat, and fry the chicken strips and almonds for 5–6 minutes, stirring frequently, until the chicken is cooked through.

3 Meanwhile, pour the cream into a small pan over a low heat. Bring it to a boil and boil for about 10 minutes, until reduced by almost half. Pour the cream over the chicken and almonds, stir well, and season with salt and pepper to taste. Set aside and keep warm.

4 Cook the pasta in a pan of boiling salted water with the oil, for 8–10 minutes or until tender. Drain, then return to the pan, cover, and keep warm.

5 Turn the pasta into a warmed serving dish and spoon the tomato sauce over. Spoon the chicken and cream over the center, scatter over the basil leaves, and serve at once.

Pizzas & Breads

There is little to beat the irresistible aroma and taste of a freshly made pizza cooked in a wood-fired oven. The recipes for the homemade dough crust and freshly made

tomato sauce in this chapter will give you the closest thing possible to an authentic Italian pizza. You can add any type of topping, from salamis and cooked meats, to vegetables and fragrant herbs – the choice is yours! The Italians make delicious bread, combining all of the flavors of the Mediterranean. You can use the breads in this chapter to mop up the juices from a range of Italian dishes, or you can eat them on their own as a tasty snack.

Bread Dough Crust

Traditionally, pizza crusts are made from bread dough; this recipe will give you a crust similar to an authentic Italian pizza.

NUTRITIONAL INFORMATION

Calories 182   Sugars 2g
Protein . . . . .5g   Fat 3g
Carbohydrate . . .36g   Saturates 0.5g

1½ HOURS   0 MINS

SERVES 4

I N G R E D I E N T S

½ oz fresh yeast, or 1 tsp active-dry, or
    instant yeast

6 tbsp lukewarm water

½ tsp sugar

1 tbsp olive oil

6 oz all-purpose flour

1 tsp salt

1 Combine the fresh yeast with the water and sugar in a bowl. If using active-dry yeast, sprinkle over the surface of the water and whisk until dissolved.

2 Leave the mixture to rest in a warm place for 10–15 minutes until frothy on the surface. Stir in the olive oil.

3 Sift the flour and salt into a large bowl. If using instant yeast, stir it in here. Make a well in the center and pour in the yeast liquid, or water and oil (without the sugar for instant yeast).

4 Using either floured hands or a wooden spoon, mix together to form a dough. Turn out onto a floured work surface and knead for about 5 minutes, or until smooth and elastic.

5 Place the dough in a large greased plastic bag and leave in a warm place for about 1 hour, or until doubled in size.

6 Turn out onto a lightly floured work surface and "knock back" by punching the dough: this releases any air bubbles which can make the pizza uneven. Knead 4 or 5 times. The dough is ready to use.

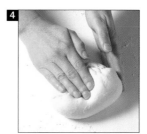

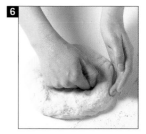

Biscuit Crust

This is a quicker alternative to the bread dough crust. If you do not have time to wait for bread dough to rise, a biscuit crust is ideal.

NUTRITIONAL INFORMATION

Calories 215	Sugars 3g	
Protein 5g	Fat 7g	
Carbohydrate ...35g	Saturates 4g	

  20 MINS   0 MINS

SERVES 4

INGREDIENTS

⅓ cup self-raising flour

½ tsp salt

2 tbs butter

½ cup milk

1 Sift the flour and salt into a large mixing bowl.

2 Rub in the butter with your fingertips until it resembles fine bread crumbs.

3 Make a well in the center of the flour and butter mixture and pour in nearly all of the milk at once. Mix in quickly with a knife. Add the remaining milk only if necessary to mix to a soft dough.

4 Turn the dough out onto a floured work surface and knead by turning and pressing with the heel of your hand 3 or 4 times.

5 Either roll out or press the dough into a 10-inch circle on a lightly greased cookie sheet or pizza pan. Push up the edge slightly all around to form a ridge and use immediately.

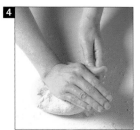

Potato Crust

This is an unusual pizza crust made from mashed potatoes and flour. It is a great way to use up any leftover boiled potatoes.

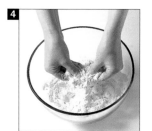

NUTRITIONAL INFORMATION

Calories 170	Sugars 1g	
Protein 4g	Fat 3g	
Carbohydrate . . .34g	Saturates 1g	

 2¼ HOURS   0 MINS

SERVES 4

INGREDIENTS

8 oz boiled potatoes

4 tbsp butter or margarine

1 cup selfraising flour

½ tsp salt

1 If the potatoes are hot, mash them, then stir in the butter until it has melted and is distributed evenly throughout the potatoes; leave to cool.

2 Sift the flour and salt together and stir into the mashed potato to form a soft dough.

3 If the potatoes are cold, mash them without adding the butter. Sift the flour and salt into a bowl.

4 Rub in the butter with your fingertips until the mixture resembles fine bread crumbs. Stir the flour and butter mixture into the mashed potatoes to form a soft dough.

5 Either roll out or press the dough into a 10-inch circle on a lightly greased cookie sheet or pizza pan, pushing up the edge slightly all around to form a ridge before adding the topping of your choice. This potato crust is tricky to lift before it is cooked, so you will find it much easier to

handle if you roll it out directly onto the cookie sheet.

6 If the crust is not required for cooking immediately, cover it with plastic wrap and chill it for up to 2 hours.

Tomato Sauce

This is a basic topping sauce for pizzas. Using canned chopped tomatoes for this dish saves time.

NUTRITIONAL INFORMATION

Calories . . . . .41 Sugars 3g
Protein . . . . .1g Fat 3g
Carbohydrate . . . .3g Saturates 0.4g

 5 MINS 25 MINS

SERVES 4

I N G R E D I E N T S

1 small onion, chopped

1 garlic clove, crushed

1 tbsp olive oil

7-oz can chopped tomatoes

2 tsp tomato paste

½ tsp sugar

½ tsp dried oregano

1 bay leaf

salt and pepper

1 Fry the onion and garlic gently in the oil for 5 minutes, or until softened but not browned.

2 Add the tomatoes, tomato paste, sugar, oregano, bay leaf, and salt and pepper to taste. Stir well.

3 Bring the sauce to a boil, cover and leave to simmer gently for 20 minutes, stirring occasionally, until you have a thick sauce.

4 Remove the bay leaf and season to taste. Leave to cool completely before using. This sauce keeps well in a screw-top jar in the refrigerator for up to 1 week.

Special Tomato Sauce

This sauce is made with fresh tomatoes. Use the plum variety whenever available and always choose the reddest ones for the best flavor.

NUTRITIONAL INFORMATION

Calories 81   Sugars 6g
Protein . . . . .1g   Fat 6g
Carbohydrate . . . .6g   Saturates 1g

  10 MINS   🕐 35 MINS

SERVES 4

I N G R E D I E N T S

1 small onion, chopped

1 small red bell pepper, chopped

1 garlic clove, crushed

2 tbsp olive oil

8 oz tomatoes

1 tbsp tomato paste

1 tsp soft brown sugar

2 tsp chopped fresh basil

½ tsp dried oregano

1 bay leaf

salt and pepper

1 Fry the onion, bell pepper, and garlic gently in the oil for 5 minutes until softened but not browned.

2 Cut a cross in the bottom of each tomato and place them in a heatproof bowl. Pour in boiling water and leave for about 45 seconds. Drain, then plunge in cold water; the skins will slide off easily.

3 Chop the tomatoes, discarding any hard cores.

4 Add the tomatoes to the onion mixture with the tomato paste, sugar, herbs, and seasoning. Stir well. Bring to a boil, cover, and leave to simmer gently for about 30 minutes, stirring occasionally, or until you have a thick sauce.

5 Remove the bay leaf and adjust the seasoning to taste. Leave to cool completely before using.

6 This sauce will keep well in a screw-top jar in the refrigerator for up to 1 week.

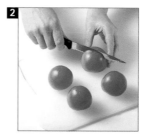

Pizza Margherita

Pizza means "pie" in Italian. The fresh bread dough is not difficult to make but it does take a little time.

NUTRITIONAL INFORMATION

Calories	456	Sugars	.........7g
Protein	........16g	Fat	..........13g
Carbohydrate	...74g	Saturates	.......5g

 1 HOUR   45 MINS

SERVES 4

INGREDIENTS

BASIC PIZZA DOUGH

½ oz active-dry yeast

1 tsp sugar

1 cup hand-hot water

2½ cups 12 oz strong flour

1 tsp salt

1 tbsp olive oil

TOPPING

14-oz can tomatoes, chopped

2 garlic cloves, crushed

2 tsp dried basil

1 tbsp olive oil

2 tbsp tomato paste

½ cups Mozzarella cheese, chopped

2 tbsp freshly grated Parmesan cheese

salt and pepper

1 Place the yeast and sugar in a measuring jug and mix with 2 oz of the water. Leave the yeast mixture in a warm place for 15 minutes, or until frothy.

2 Mix the flour with the salt and make a well in the center. Add the oil, the yeast mixture, and the remaining water. Using a wooden spoon, mix to form a smooth dough.

3 Turn out the dough onto a floured surface and knead for 4–5 minutes, or until smooth.

4 Return the dough to the bowl, cover with an oiled sheet of plastic wrap, and leave to rise for 30 minutes, or until doubled in size.

5 Knead the dough for 2 minutes. Stretch the dough with your hands, then place it on a greased cookie sheet, pushing out the edges until even. The dough should be no more than ¼ inch thick because it will rise during baking.

6 To make the topping, place the tomatoes, garlic, dried basil, olive oil, and salt and pepper to taste in a large skillet and simmer for 20 minutes or until the sauce has thickened. Stir in the tomato paste and leave to cool slightly.

7 Spread the topping evenly over the pizza crust. Top with the mozzarella and Parmesan cheeses and bake in a preheated oven, at 400°F, for 20–25 minutes. Serve hot.

Vegetable & Goat Cheese

Wonderfully colorful vegetables are roasted in olive oil with thyme and garlic. The goat cheese adds a nutty, piquant flavor.

NUTRITIONAL INFORMATION

Calories	387	Sugars	.........9g
Protein	........10g	Fat	..........21g
Carbohydrate	...42g	Saturates	.......5g

2½ HOURS   40 MINS

SERVES 4

INGREDIENTS

2 baby zucchini, halved lengthways

2 baby eggplants, quartered lengthways

½ red bell pepper, cut into 4 strips

½ yellow bell pepper, cut into 4 strips

1 small red onion, cut into wedges

2 garlic cloves, unpeeled

4 tbsp olive oil

1 tbsp red-wine vinegar

1 tbsp chopped fresh thyme

Bread Dough Crust (see page 226)

Tomato Sauce (see page 14)

3 oz goat cheese

salt and pepper

fresh basil leaves, to garnish

1 Place all of the prepared vegetables in a large roasting pan. Mix together the olive oil, vinegar, thyme, and plenty of seasoning and pour over, coating well.

2 Roast the vegetables in a preheated oven, at 400°F, for 15–20 minutes, or until the skins have started to blacken in places, turning half-way through; leave to rest for 5 minutes after roasting.

3 Carefully peel off the skins from the roast bell peppers and the garlic cloves. Slice the garlic.

4 Roll out or press the dough, using a rolling pin or your hands, into a 10-inch circle on a lightly floured work surface. Place on a large greased cookie sheet or pizza pan and raise the edge a little. Cover and leave for 10 minutes to rise slightly in a warm place. Spread with the tomato sauce almost to the edge.

5 Arrange the roasted vegetables on top and dot with the cheese. Drizzle the oil and juices from the roasting pan over the pizza and season.

6 Bake in a preheated oven, at 400°F, for 18–20 minutes, or until the edge is crisp and golden. Serve immediately, garnished with basil leaves.

Tomato Sauce & Bell Pepper

This pizza is made with a pastry crust flavored with cheese and topped with a delicious tomato sauce and roasted bell peppers.

NUTRITIONAL INFORMATION

Calories . . . . .611 Sugars 8g
Protein . . . . .14g Fat 38g
Carbohydrate . . .56g Saturates 21g

1½ HOURS   55 MINS

SERVES 4

I N G R E D I E N T S

1⅔ cups all-purpose flour

1½ cups butter, diced

½ tsp salt

2 tbsp dried Parmesan cheese

1 egg, beaten

2 tbsp cold water

2 tbsp olive oil

1 large onion, finely chopped

1 garlic clove, chopped

14-oz can chopped tomatoes

4 tbsp concentrated tomato paste

1 red bell pepper, halved

5 sprigs of thyme, stalks removed

6 black olives, pitted and halved

2 tbsp Parmesan cheese, grated

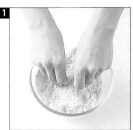

1 Sift the flour and rub in the butter to make bread crumbs. Stir in the salt and dried Parmesan. Add the egg and 1 tablespoon of the water and mix with a round-bladed knife. Add more water if necessary to make a soft dough. Cover with plastic wrap and chill for 30 minutes.

2 Meanwhile, heat the oil in a skillet and cook the onions and garlic for 5 minutes. Add the tomatoes and cook for 8–10 minutes. Stir in the tomato paste.

3 Place the bell peppers, skin-side up, on a cookie sheet and cook under a preheated broiler for 15 minutes until charred. Place in a plastic bag and leave to sweat for 10 minutes. Peel off the skin and slice the flesh into thin strips.

4 Roll out the dough to fit a 9 inch loose base fluted tart pan. Line with foil and bake in a preheated oven, at 400°F, for 10 minutes or until just set. Remove the foil and bake for a further 5 minutes until lightly golden. Leave to cool.

5 Spoon the tomato sauce over the pastry crust and top with the bell peppers, thyme, olives, and fresh Parmesan. Return to the oven for 15 minutes or until the pastry is crisp. Serve warm or cold.

Mushroom Pizza

Juicy mushrooms and stringy Mozzarella top this tomato-based pizza.
Use wild mushrooms or a combination of wild and cultivated mushrooms.

NUTRITIONAL INFORMATION

Calories	302	Sugars	.........7g
Protein	........10g	Fat	..........12g
Carbohydrate	...41g	Saturates	.......4g

1¼ HOURS   45 MINS

SERVES 4

INGREDIENTS

1 portion Basic Pizza Dough (see page 231)

TOPPING

14-oz can chopped tomatoes

2 garlic cloves, crushed

1 tsp dried basil

1 tbsp olive oil

2 tbsp tomato paste

7 oz mushrooms

1½ cups Mozzarella cheese, grated

salt and pepper

basil leaves, to garnish

1 Place the yeast and sugar in a measuring jug and mix with 2 oz of the water. Leave the yeast mixture in a warm place for 15 minutes, or until frothy.

2 Mix the flour with the salt and make a well in the center. Add the oil, the yeast mixture, and the remaining water. Using a wooden spoon, mix to form a smooth dough.

3 Turn out the dough onto a floured surface and knead for 4–5 minutes, or until smooth. Return the dough to the bowl, cover with a greased sheet of plastic wrap and leave to rise for 30 minutes, or until doubled in size.

4 Remove the dough from the bowl. Knead the dough for 2 minutes. Using

a rolling pin, roll out the dough to form an oval or a circular shape, then place it on a greased cookie sheet, pushing out the edges until even. The dough should be no more than ¼ inch thick because it will rise during cooking.

5 Using a sharp knife, cut the mushrooms into slices.

6 To make the topping, place the tomatoes, garlic, dried basil, olive oil,

and salt and pepper in a large pan and simmer for 20 minutes, or until the sauce has thickened. Stir in the tomato paste and leave to cool slightly.

7 Spread the sauce over the bottom of the pizza, top with the mushrooms, and scatter the Mozzarella over. Bake in a preheated oven, at 400°F, for 25 minutes. Garnish with basil leaves.

Bell Peppers & Red Onion

The vibrant colors of the bell peppers and onion make this a delightful pizza. Served cut into fingers, it is ideal for a party or buffet.

NUTRITIONAL INFORMATION

Calories 380	Sugars 19g
Protein 7g	Fat 17g
Carbohydrate ...53g	Saturates 2g

2½ HOURS   25 MINS

SERVES 8

I N G R E D I E N T S

Bread crust base (see page 226)

2 tbsp olive oil

½ each red, green, and yellow bell pepper, sliced thinly

1 small red onion, sliced thinly

1 garlic clove, crushed

Tomato Sauce (see page 14)

3 tbsp raisins

2 tbsp pine kernels

1 tbsp chopped fresh thyme

olive oil, for drizzling

salt and pepper

1 Roll out or press the dough, using a rolling pin or your hands, on a lightly floured work surface to fit a 12 x 7 inch greased jelly roll pan. Place in the pan and push up the edges slightly.

2 Cover and leave the dough to rise slightly in a warm place for about 10 minutes.

3 Heat the oil in a large skillet. Add the bell peppers, onion, and garlic, and fry gently for 5 minutes, until they have softened but not browned; leave to cool.

4 Spread the tomato sauce over the pizza, almost to the edge.

5 Sprinkle the raisins over and top with the cooled bell pepper mixture. Add the pine kernels and thyme. Drizzle with a little olive oil and season well.

6 Bake in a preheated oven, at 400°F, for 18–20 minutes, or until the edges are crisp and golden. Cut into fingers and serve immediately.

Gorgonzola & Pumpkin Pizza

A combination of blue Gorgonzola cheese and pears combine to make a colorful pizza. The whole-wheat base adds a nutty flavor and texture.

NUTRITIONAL INFORMATION

Calories 470   Sugars 5g
Protein . . . . .17g   Fat 15g
Carbohydrate . . .72g   Saturates 6g

  1¼ HOURS   35 MINS

SERVES 4

INGREDIENTS

PIZZA DOUGH

¼ oz active-dry yeast

1 tsp sugar

1 cup hand-hot water

1¼ whole-wheat flour

1¼ cups hard flour

1 tsp salt

1 tbsp olive oil

TOPPING

2½ cups pumpkin or squash, peeled
   and cubed

1 tbsp olive oil

1 pear, cored, peeled, and sliced

3½ oz Gorgonzola cheese

1 sprig fresh rosemary, to garnish

1 Place the yeast and sugar in a measuring jug and mix with 2 oz of the water. Leave the yeast mixture in a warm place for 15 minutes, or until frothy.

2 Mix both of the flours with the salt and make a well in the center. Add the oil, the yeast mixture, and the remaining water. Using a wooden spoon, mix to form a dough.

3 Turn out the dough onto a floured surface and knead for 4–5 minutes, or until smooth.

4 Return the dough to the bowl, cover with a greased sheet of plastic wrap, and leave to rise for 30 minutes, or until doubled in size.

5 Remove the dough from the bowl and knead for 2 minutes. Roll out the dough to form an oval, then place it on an oiled cookie sheet, pushing out the edges until even. The dough should be no more than ¼ inch thick and rises during baking.

6 To make the topping, place the pumpkin in a shallow roasting pan. Drizzle with the olive oil and cook under a preheated broiler for 20 minutes or until soft and lightly golden.

7 Top the dough with the pear and the pumpkin, brushing with the oil from the pan. Sprinkle the Gorgonzola over. Bake in a preheated oven, at 400°F for 15 minutes or until the crust is golden. Garnish with rosemary.

Giardiniera Pizza

As the name implies, this colorful pizza should be topped with fresh vegetables from the garden, especially in the summer months.

NUTRITIONAL INFORMATION

Calories ......362 Sugars 10g

Protein ....13g Fat 15g

Carbohydrate ...48g Saturates 5g

  3½ HOURS 20 MINS

SERVES 4

INGREDIENTS

6 spinach leaves

Potato crust (see page 228)

Basic Tomato Sauce (see page 14)

1 tomato, sliced

1 celery stalk, sliced thinly

½ green bell pepper, sliced thinly

1 baby zucchini, sliced

1 oz asparagus tips

¼ cup sweetcorn, defrosted if frozen

¼ cup peas, defrosted if frozen

4 scallions, trimmed and chopped

1 tbsp chopped fresh mixed herbs

½ cup Mozzarella cheese, grated

2 tbsp freshly grated Parmesan

1 artichoke heart

olive oil, for drizzling

salt and pepper

1 Remove any tough stems from the spinach and wash the leaves in cold water. Pat dry with paper towels.

2 Roll out or press the potato crust, using a rolling pin or your hands, into a large 10-inch circle on a lightly floured work surface. Place the crust on a large greased cookie sheet or pizza pan and push up the edge a little. Spread with the tomato sauce.

3 Arrange the spinach leaves on the sauce, followed by the tomato slices. Top with the remaining vegetables and the herbs.

4 Mix together the cheeses and sprinkle over. Place the artichoke heart in the center. Drizzle the pizza with a little olive oil and season.

5 Bake in a preheated oven, at 400°F, for 18–20 minutes, or until the edges are crisp and golden brown. Serve immediately.

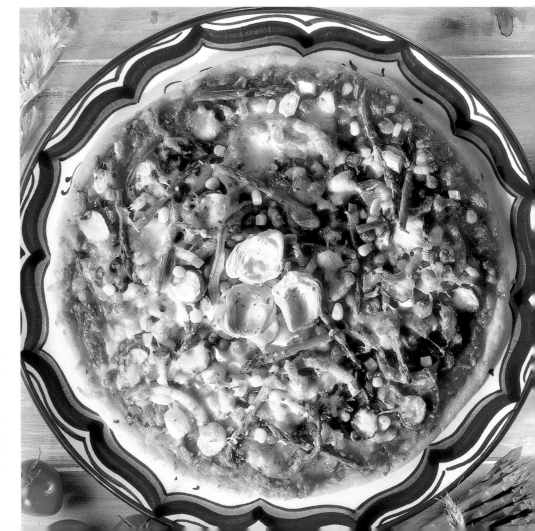

Tomato & Ricotta Pizza

This is a traditional dish from the Calabrian Mountains in southern Italy, where it is made with naturally sun-dried tomatoes and ricotta cheese.

NUTRITIONAL INFORMATION

Calories	274	Sugars	.........4g
Protein	.........8g	Fat	............11g
Carbohydrate	...38g	Saturates	.......4g

1¼ HOURS   30 MINS

SERVES 4

INGREDIENTS

1 portion basic pizza dough (see page 231)

TOPPING

4 tbsp sun-dried tomato paste

⅔ cup ricotta cheese

10 sun-dried tomatoes

1 tbsp fresh thyme

salt and pepper

1 Place the yeast and sugar in a measuring jug and mix with 2 oz of the water. Leave the yeast mixture in a warm place for 15 minutes or until frothy.

2 Mix the flour with the salt and make a well in the center. Add the oil, the yeast mixture and the remaining water. Using a wooden spoon, mix to form a dough.

3 Turn out the dough onto a floured surface and knead for 4–5 minutes, or until smooth.

4 Return the dough to the bowl, cover with a greased sheet of plastic wrap, and leave to rise for 30 minutes or until doubled in size.

5 Remove the dough from the bowl and knead for 2 minutes.

6 Using a rolling pin, roll out the dough to form a circle, then place it on a greased cookie sheet, pushing out the edges until even. The dough should be no more than ¼ inch thick because it will rise during baking.

7 Spread the sun-dried tomato paste over the dough, then add spoonfuls of ricotta cheese.

8 Cut the sun-dried tomatoes into strips and arrange these on top of the pizza.

9 Sprinkle the thyme and salt and pepper to taste over the top of the pizza. Bake in a preheated oven at 400°F for 30 minutes, or until the crust is golden. Serve hot.

Florentine Pizza

A pizza adaptation of Eggs Florentine – sliced hard-cooked eggs on freshly cooked spinach, with a crunchy almond topping.

NUTRITIONAL INFORMATION

Calories 462   Sugars 6g
Protein . . . . .18g   Fat 26g
Carbohydrate . . .41g   Saturates 8g

 3 HOURS   20 MINS

SERVES 4

I N G R E D I E N T S

2 tbsp freshly grated Parmesan

Potato crust (see page 228)

Basic Tomato Sauce (see page 14)

6 oz spinach

1 small red onion, sliced thinly

2 tbsp olive oil

¼ tsp freshly grated nutmeg

2 hard-cooked eggs

¼ cup fresh white bread crumbs

¼ cup grated Jarlsberg (or Cheddar or
   Gruyère, if not available)

2 tbsp slivered almonds

olive oil, for drizzling

salt and pepper

1 Mix the Parmesan with the potato crust ingredients. Roll out or press the dough, using a rolling pin or your hands, into a 10-inch circle on a lightly floured work surface. Place on a large greased cookie sheet or pizza pan and push up the edge slightly. Spread the tomato sauce almost to the edge.

2 Remove the stems from the spinach and wash the leaves thoroughly in plenty of cold water. Drain well and pat off the excess water with paper towels.

3 Fry the onion gently in the oil for 5 minutes, or until softened. Add the spinach and continue to fry until just wilted; drain off any excess liquid. Arrange on the pizza and sprinkle the nutmeg over.

4 Remove the shells from the eggs and slice. Arrange the slices of egg on top of the spinach.

5 Mix together the bread crumbs, cheese, and almonds and sprinkle over. Drizzle with a little olive oil and season with salt and pepper to taste.

6 Bake in a preheated oven at 400°F for 18–20 minutes, or until the edge is crisp and golden. Serve immediately.

Cheese & Artichoke Pizza

Sliced artichokes combined with sharp Cheddar, Parmesan, and blue cheeses give a really delicious topping to this unconventional pizza.

NUTRITIONAL INFORMATION

Calories ....424 Sugars 9g
Protein ....16g Fat 20g
Carbohydrate ...47g Saturates 8g

1³⁄₄ HOURS   20 MINS

SERVES 4

I N G R E D I E N T S

Bread dough crust (see page 226)

Basic Tomato Sauce (see page 14)

2 oz blue cheese, sliced

1 cup artichoke hearts in oil, sliced

½ small red onion, chopped

⅓ cup sharp Cheddar cheese, grated

2 tbsp Parmesan, freshly grated

1 tbsp chopped fresh thyme

oil from artichokes for drizzling

salt and pepper

TO SERVE

salad leaves

cherry tomatoes, halved

1 Roll out or press the dough, using a rolling pin or your hands to form a 10-inch circle on a lightly floured work surface.

2 Place the pizza crust on a large greased cookie sheet or pizza pan and push up the edge slightly. Cover and leave to rise for 10 minutes in a warm place.

3 Spread the tomato sauce almost to the edge of the crust. Arrange the blue cheese on top of the tomato sauce, followed by the artichoke hearts and red onion.

4 Mix the Cheddar and Parmesan cheeses together with the thyme and sprinkle the mixture over the pizza. Drizzle a little of the oil from the jar of artichokes over the pizza and season to taste.

5 Bake in a preheated oven at 400°F for 18–20 minutes, or until the edge is

crisp and golden and the cheese is bubbling.

6 Mix the fresh salad leaves and cherry tomato halves together and serve with the pizza, cut into slices.

Cheese & Garlic Mushroom

This pizza dough is flavored with garlic and herbs and topped with mixed mushrooms and melted cheese for a really delicious pizza.

NUTRITIONAL INFORMATION

Calories 541   Sugars 5g
Protein . . . . .16g   Fat 15g
Carbohydrate . . .91g   Saturates 6g

  45 MINS   30 MINS

SERVES 4

I N G R E D I E N T S

D O U G H

3½ cups strong white flour

2 tsp instant yeast

2 garlic cloves, crushed

2 tbsp chopped thyme

2 tbsp olive oil

1¼ cups tepid water

T O P P I N G

2 tbsp butter or margarine

5 cups mixed mushrooms, sliced

2 garlic cloves, crushed

2 tbsp chopped parsley

2 tbsp tomato paste

6 tbsp strained puréed tomatoes

½ cup Mozzarella cheese, grated

salt and pepper

chopped parsley, to garnish

1 Put the flour, yeast, garlic, and thyme in a bowl. Make a well in the center and gradually stir in the oil and water. Bring together to form a soft dough.

2 Turn out the dough onto a floured surface and knead for 5 minutes or until smooth. Roll into a 14-inch round and place on a greased cookie sheet. Leave in a warm place for 20 minutes, or until the dough puffs up.

3 Meanwhile, make the topping. Melt the margarine or butter in a skillet and sauté the mushrooms, garlic, and parsley for 5 minutes.

4 Mix the tomato paste and strained puréed tomatoes and spoon onto the pizza base, leaving a ½-inch edge of dough. Spoon the mushroom mixture on top. Season well, and sprinkle the cheese on top.

5 Bake the pizza in a preheated oven 375°F for 20–25 minutes, or until the base is crisp and the cheese has melted. Garnish with chopped parsley and serve.

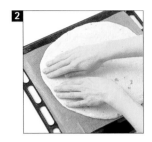

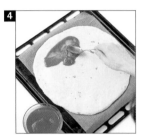

Wild Mushroom & Walnut

Wild mushrooms make a delicious pizza topping, especially when mixed with walnuts and Roquefort cheese.

NUTRITIONAL INFORMATION

Calories . . . . . . .499 Sugars 9g
Protein . . . . .13g Fat 32g
Carbohydrate . . .42g Saturates 11g

  1¼ HOURS   25 MINS

SERVES 4

INGREDIENTS

Biscuit base (see page 227)

Basic Tomato Sauce (see page 14)

4 oz soft cheese

1 tbsp chopped fresh mixed herbs, such as
    parsley, oregano, and basil

8 oz wild mushrooms, such as oyster,
    shiitake, or ceps, or 4 oz each
    wild and button mushrooms

2 tbsp olive oil

¼ tsp fennel seeds

2 tbsp walnuts, chopped roughly

1½ oz blue cheese

olive oil, for drizzling

salt and pepper

sprig of flat-leaf parsley, to garnish

1 Roll out or press the biscuit base, using a rolling pin or your hands, into a 10-inch circle on a lightly floured work surface. Place on a large greased cookie sheet or pizza pan and push up the edge a little with your fingers to form a rim.

2 Carefully spread the tomato sauce almost to the edge of the pizza crust. Dot with the soft cheese and chopped fresh herbs.

3 Wipe and slice the mushrooms. Heat the oil in a large skillet or wok and stir-fry the mushrooms and fennel seeds for 2–3 minutes. Spread over the pizza with the walnuts.

4 Crumble the cheese over the pizza, drizzle with a little olive oil, and season with salt and pepper to taste.

5 Bake in a preheated oven, at 400°F for 18–20 minutes, or until the edge is crisp and golden. Serve immediately, garnished with a sprig of flat-leaf parsley.

Tomato & Olive Pizzas

Halved ciabatta bread or baguettes make instant pizza crusts. The colors of the tomatoes and cheese contrast beautifully on top.

NUTRITIONAL INFORMATION

Calories 181	Sugars 4g
Protein 7g	Fat 10g
Carbohydrate . . .18g	Saturates 4g

45 MINS   25 MINS

SERVES 4

INGREDIENTS

2 loaves of ciabatta, or 2 baguettes

Basic Tomato Sauce (see page 14)

4 plum tomatoes, sliced thinly lengthways

1¼ cups Mozzarella, sliced thinly

10 black olives, sliced

8 fresh basil leaves, shredded

olive oil, for drizzling

salt and pepper

1 Cut the bread in half lengthways and toast the cut side of the bread lightly. Carefully spread the toasted bread with the tomato sauce.

2 Arrange the tomato and Mozzarella slices alternately along the length.

3 Top with the olive slices and half of the basil. Drizzle over a little olive oil and season with salt and pepper.

4 Either place under a preheated medium broiler and cook until the cheese is melted and bubbling, or bake in a preheated oven at 400°F for 15–20 minutes.

5 Sprinkle the remaining basil over and serve immediately.

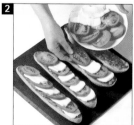

Four Seasons Pizza

This is a traditional pizza on which the toppings are divided into four sections, each of which is supposed to depict a season of the year.

NUTRITIONAL INFORMATION

Calories . . . . .313 Sugars 8g
Protein . . . . .8g Fat 13g
Carbohydrate . . .44g Saturates 3g

2¾ HOURS   20 MINS

SERVES 4

INGREDIENTS

Bread dough crust (see page 226)

Basic Tomato Sauce (see page 14)

1 oz chorizo sausage, sliced thinly

1 oz button mushrooms, wiped and
   sliced thinly

1½ oz artichoke hearts, sliced thinly

¼ cup Mozzarella, sliced thinly

3 anchovies, halved lengthways

2 tsp capers

4 pitted black olives, sliced

4 fresh basil leaves, shredded

olive oil, for drizzling

salt and pepper

1 Roll out or press the dough, using a rolling pin or your hands, into a 10-inch circle on a lightly floured surface. Place on a large greased cookie sheet or pizza pan and push up the edge a little.

2 Cover and leave to rise for 10 minutes in a warm place. Spread the tomato sauce over the crust, almost to the edge.

3 Put the sliced chorizo on to one quarter of the pizza, the sliced mushrooms on another, the artichoke hearts on a third, and the Mozzarella and anchovies on the fourth.

4 Dot with the capers, olives, and basil leaves. Drizzle with a little olive oil and season to taste. Do not put any salt on the anchovy section because the fish are salty.

5 Bake in a preheated oven at 400°F for 18–20 minutes, or until the crust is golden and crisp. Serve immediately.

Onion & Anchovy Pizza

This tasty onion pizza is topped with a lattice pattern of anchovies and black olives. Cut the pizza into squares to serve.

NUTRITIONAL INFORMATION

Calories . . . . . . .373 Sugars 5g
Protein . . . . .12g Fat 20g
Carbohydrate . . .39g Saturates 4g

 1¾ HOURS   🕐 30 MINS

MAKES 6

INGREDIENTS

4 tbsp olive oil

3 onions, sliced thinly

1 garlic clove, crushed

1 tsp light brown sugar

½ tsp crushed fresh rosemary

7-oz can chopped tomatoes

Bread dough crust (see page 226)

2 tbsp freshly grated Parmesan

1¾ oz can anchovies

12–14 black olives

salt and pepper

1 Heat 3 tablespoons of the oil in a large saucepan and add the onions, garlic, sugar, and rosemary. Cover and fry gently, stirring occasionally, for 10 minutes, or until the onions are soft but not brown.

2 Add the tomatoes to the pan, stir, and season with salt and pepper to taste; leave to cool slightly.

3 Roll out or press the dough, using a rolling pin or your hands, on a lightly floured work surface to fit a 12 x 7 inch greased jelly-roll pan. Place in the pan and push up the edges slightly to form a rim.

4 Brush the remaining oil over the dough and sprinkle with the cheese. Cover and leave to rise slightly in a warm place for about 10 minutes.

5 Spread the onion and tomato topping over the crust. Drain the anchovies, reserving the oil. Split each anchovy in half lengthways and arrange on the pizza in a lattice pattern. Place olives in between the anchovies and drizzle a little of the reserved oil over. Season to taste.

6 Bake in a preheated oven, at 400°F for 18–20 minutes, or until the edges are crisp and golden. Cut the pizza into 6 squares and serve immediately.

Eggplant & Lamb

An unusual fragrant, spiced pizza topped with ground lamb and eggplant on a thin crust.

NUTRITIONAL INFORMATION

Calories 430   Sugars 10g
Protein . . . . .18g   Fat 22g
Carbohydrate . . .44g   Saturates 7g

 3 HOURS   30 MINS

SERVES 4

INGREDIENTS

1 small eggplant, diced

Bread dough crust (see page 226)

1 small onion, sliced thinly

1 garlic clove, crushed

1 tsp cumin seeds

1 tbsp olive oil

6 oz ground lamb

2 tbsp canned pimiento, thinly sliced

2 tbsp chopped fresh cilantro

Basic Tomato Sauce (see page 14)

3 oz Mozzarella, sliced thinly

olive oil, for drizzling

salt and pepper

1 Place the diced eggplant in a colander, sprinkle with the salt, and let the bitter juices drain for about 20 minutes. Rinse thoroughly, then pat dry with paper towels.

2 Roll out or press the dough, using a rolling pin or your hands, into a 10-inch circle on a lightly floured work surface. Place on a large greased cookie sheet or pizza pan and push up the edge to form a rim.

3 Cover and leave to rise slightly for 10 minutes in a warm place.

4 Fry the onion, garlic, and cumin seeds gently in the oil for 3 minutes. Increase the heat slightly and add the lamb, eggplant, and pimiento. Fry for 5 minutes, stirring occasionally. Add the cilantro and season with salt and pepper to taste.

5 Spread the tomato sauce over the dough crust, almost to the edge, and then top with the lamb mixture.

6 Arrange the Mozzarella slices on top. Drizzle a little olive oil over, and season with salt and pepper.

7 Bake in a preheated oven, at 400°F for 18–20 minutes, or until the crust is crisp and golden. Serve immediately.

Onion, Ham, & Cheese Pizza

This pizza is a favorite of the Romans. It is slightly unusual because the topping is made without a tomato sauce base.

NUTRITIONAL INFORMATION

Calories .... 333 Sugars 8g
Protein .... 12g Fat 14g
Carbohydrate ...43g Saturates 4g

🖐 1 HOUR   🕐 40 MINS

SERVES 4

INGREDIENTS

Basic pizza crust (see page 231)

TOPPING

2 tbsp olive oil

1¾ cups onions, sliced into rings

2 garlic cloves, crushed

1 red bell pepper, diced

3 oz prosciutto, cut into strips

¾ cup Mozzarella cheese, sliced

2 tbsp rosemary, stems removed and
  roughly chopped

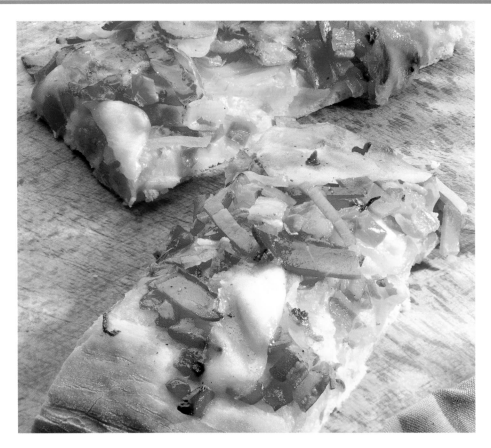

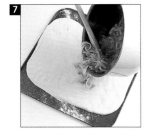

1 Place the yeast and sugar in a measuring jug and mix with 2 oz of the water. Leave the mixture in a warm place for 15 minutes, or until frothy.

2 Mix the flour with the salt and make a well in the center. Add the oil, the yeast mixture, and the remaining water. Using a wooden spoon, mix to form a smooth dough.

3 Turn out the dough onto a floured surface and knead for 4–5 minutes or until smooth. Return the dough to the bowl, cover with a greased sheet of plastic wrap, and leave to rise for 30 minutes, or until doubled in size.

4 Remove the dough from the bowl. Knead the dough for 2 minutes. Using a rolling pin, roll out the dough to form a square shape, then place it on a greased cookie sheet, pushing out the edges until even. The dough should be no more than ¼ inch thick because it will rise during baking.

5 To make the topping, heat the oil in a pan. Add the onions and garlic and cook for 3 minutes. Add the bell pepper and fry for 2 minutes.

6 Cover the pan and cook the vegetables over a low heat for 10 minutes, stirring occasionally, until the onions are slightly caramelized; leave to cool slightly.

7 Spread the topping evenly over the pizza crust. Arrange the prosciutto, Mozzarella, and rosemary over the top.

8 Bake in a preheated oven at 400°F for 20–25 minutes. Serve hot.

Smoky Bacon & Pepperoni

This more traditional pizza is topped with peperoni, smoked bacon, and bell peppers covered in a smoked cheese.

NUTRITIONAL INFORMATION

Calories	450	Sugars	.........6g
Protein	........19g	Fat	..........24g
Carbohydrate	...41g	Saturates	.......6g

  1½ HOURS   20 MINS

SERVES 4

INGREDIENTS

Bread dough crust (see page 226)

1 tbsp olive oil

1 tbsp freshly grated Parmesan

Basic Tomato Sauce (see page 14)

1 cup lightly smoked slab bacon

½ green bell pepper, sliced thinly

½ yellow bell pepper, sliced thinly

2 oz pepperoni-style sliced spicy sausage

½ cup smoked Bavarian cheese, grated

½ tsp dried oregano

olive oil, for drizzling

salt and pepper

1 Roll out or press the dough, using a rolling pin or your hands, into a 10-inch circle on a lightly floured work surface.

2 Place the dough crust on a large greased cookie sheet or pizza pan and push up the edge a little with your fingers, to form a rim.

3 Brush the crust with the olive oil and sprinkle with the Parmesan. Cover and leave to rise slightly in a warm place for about 10 minutes.

4 Spread the tomato sauce over the crust almost to the edge. Top with the bacon and bell peppers. Arrange the pepperoni on top and sprinkle with the smoked cheese.

5 Sprinkle the oregano over and drizzle with a little olive oil; season well.

6 Bake in a preheated oven at 400°F for 18–20 minutes, or until the crust is golden and crisp around the edge. Cut the pizza into wedges and serve immediately.

Marinara Pizza

This pizza is topped with a cocktail of mixed seafood, such as shrimp, mussels, cockles, and squid rings.

NUTRITIONAL INFORMATION

Calories 359	Sugars 9g	
Protein 19g	Fat 14g	
Carbohydrate . . .42g	Saturates 4g	

  3¼ HOURS   20 MINS

SERVES 4

INGREDIENTS

Potato crust (see page 228)

Basic Tomato Sauce (see page 14)

7 oz frozen mixed seafood, defrosted

1 tbsp capers

1 small yellow bell pepper, chopped

1 tbsp chopped fresh marjoram

½ tsp dried oregano

½ cup Mozzarella, grated

1 tbsp Parmesan, grated

12 black olives

olive oil, for drizzling

salt and pepper

sprig of fresh marjoram or oregano, to
    garnish

1 Roll out or press out the potato dough, using a rolling pin or your hands, into a 10-inch circle on a lightly floured work surface.

2 Place the dough on a large greased cookie sheet or pizza pan and push up the edge a little with your fingers to form a rim.

3 Spread the tomato sauce evenly over the crust almost to the edge.

4 Arrange the mixed seafood, capers, and yellow bell pepper on top of the tomato sauce.

5 Sprinkle the herbs and cheeses over. Arrange the olives on top. Drizzle a little olive oil over and season with salt and pepper to taste.

6 Bake in a preheated oven at 400°F for 18–20 minutes or until the edge of the pizza is crisp and golden brown.

7 Transfer to a warmed serving plate, garnish with a sprig of marjoram or oregano and serve immediately.

Salmon Pizza

You can use either red or pink salmon for this unusual pizza. Red salmon gives a better color and flavor but it is expensive.

NUTRITIONAL INFORMATION

Calories 321   Sugars 6g
Protein . . . . .12g   Fat 14g
Carbohydrate . . .39g   Saturates 6g

  1¼ HOURS   20 MINS

SERVES 4

INGREDIENTS

1 quantity biscuit crust (see page 227)

1 quantity Tomato Sauce (see page 14)

1 zucchini, grated

1 tomato, sliced thinly

3½-oz can red or pink salmon

2 oz button mushrooms, wiped and sliced

1 tbsp chopped fresh dill

½ tsp dried oregano

⅓ cup Mozzarella cheese, grated

olive oil, for drizzling

salt and pepper

sprig of fresh dill, to garnish

1 Roll out or press the dough, using a rolling pin or your hands, into a 10-inch circle on a lightly floured work counter. Place on a large greased cookie sheet or pizza pan and push up the edge a little with your fingers to form a rim.

2 Spread the tomato sauce over the dough base, almost to the edge.

3 Top the tomato sauce with the grated zucchini, then lay the tomato slices on top.

4 Drain the can of salmon. Remove any bones and skin and flake the flesh. Arrange on the pizza along with the mushrooms. Sprinkle the herbs and cheese over. Drizzle with a little olive oil and season with salt and pepper.

5 Bake in a preheated oven at 400°F for 18–20 minutes, or until the edge is golden and crisp.

6 Transfer to a warmed serving plate and serve immediately, garnished with a sprig of dill.

COOK'S TIP

If salmon is too pricy, use either canned tuna or sardines to make a delicious everyday fish pizza. Choose canned fish in brine for a healthier topping. If fresh dill is unavailable, use chopped fresh parsley instead.

Pissaladière

This is a variation of the classic Italian pizza, but is made with bought pie dough. It is perfect for outdoor eating.

NUTRITIONAL INFORMATION

Calories . . . . .612 Sugars 13g
Protein . . . . .12g Fat 43g
Carbohydrate . . .47g Saturates 11g

   20 MINS   55 MINS

SERVES 8

I N G R E D I E N T S

4 tbsp olive oil

5 cups red onions, sliced thinly

2 garlic cloves, crushed

2 tsp superfine sugar

2 tbsp red wine vinegar

12 oz bought puff pastry dough

salt and pepper

T O P P I N G

1¾-oz cans anchovy fillets

12 green pitted olives

1 tsp dried marjoram

1 Lightly grease a jelly-roll pan. Heat the olive oil in a large saucepan. Add the red onions and garlic and cook over a low heat for about 30 minutes, stirring occasionally.

2 Add the sugar and red-wine vinegar to the pan and season with plenty of salt and pepper.

3 On a lightly floured surface, roll out the dough to a rectangle, about 13 x 9 inches. Place the dough rectangle onto the prepared pan, pushing the dough into the corners of the pan.

4 Spread the onion mixture over the dough.

5 Arrange the anchovy fillets and green olives on top, then sprinkle with the marjoram.

6 Bake in a preheated oven at 425°F for 20-25 minutes or until the pissaladière is lightly golden. Serve it piping hot, straight from the oven.

VARIATION

Cut the pissaladière into squares or triangles for easy finger food at a party or barbecue.

Vegetable Calzone

These pizza crust packages are great for making in advance and freezing – they can be defrosted when required for a quick snack.

NUTRITIONAL INFORMATION

Calories . . . . . . .499 Sugars 7g
Protein . . . . .16g Fat 9g
Carbohydrate . . .95g Saturates 2g

 1½ HOURS   40 MINS

SERVES 4

INGREDIENTS

DOUGH

3½ cups strong white flour

2 tsp instant yeast

1 tsp superfine sugar

⅔ cup vegetable stock

⅔ cup strained puréed tomatoes

beaten egg

FILLING

1 tbsp vegetable oil

1 onion, chopped

1 garlic clove, crushed

2 tbsp chopped sun-dried tomatoes

¾ cup spinach, chopped

3 tbsp canned and drained corn

¼ cup green beans, sliced

1 tbsp tomato paste

1 tbsp chopped oregano

⅓ cup Mozzarella cheese, sliced

salt and pepper

1 Sift the flour into a bowl. Add the yeast and sugar and beat in the stock and strained puréed tomatoes to make a smooth dough.

2 Knead the dough on a lightly floured surface for 10 minutes, then place in a clean, lightly oiled bowl and leave to rise in a warm place for 1 hour.

3 Heat the oil in a skillet and sauté the onion for 2–3 minutes.

4 Stir in the garlic, tomatoes, spinach, corn, and beans and cook for 3–4 minutes. Add the tomato paste and oregano and season with salt and pepper to taste.

5 Divide the risen dough into 4 equal portions and roll out each onto a floured surface into a 7-inch circle.

6 Spoon one quarter of the filling onto one half of each circle and top with cheese. Fold the dough over to encase the filling, sealing the edge with a fork. Glaze with beaten egg. Put the calzone on a lightly greased cookie sheet and cook in a preheated oven at 425°F for 25–30 minutes until risen and golden. Serve warm.

Potato & Tomato Calzone

These Italian pasties made from pizza dough are best served hot with a salad as a delicious lunch or supper dish.

NUTRITIONAL INFORMATION

Calories . . . . . . .508 Sugars 8g
Protein . . . . .14g Fat 7g
Carbohydrate . .104g Saturates 2g

 1½ HOURS   35 MINS

SERVES 4

I N G R E D I E N T S

DOUGH

4 cups strong white flour

1 tsp instant yeast

1¼ cups vegetable stock

1 tbsp clear honey

1 tsp caraway seeds

milk, for glazing

FILLING

1½ cups waxy potatoes, diced

1 tbsp vegetable oil

1 onion, halved and sliced

2 garlic cloves, crushed

1½ oz sun-dried tomatoes

2 tbsp chopped fresh basil

2 tbsp tomato paste

2 celery stalks, sliced

⅓ cup Mozzarella cheese, grated

1 To make the dough, sift the flour into a large bowl and stir in the yeast. Make a well in the center of the mixture.

2 Stir in the vegetable stock, honey, and caraway seeds and bring the mixture together to form a dough.

3 Turn out the dough onto a lightly floured surface and knead for 8 minutes until smooth. Place the dough in a lightly oiled mixing bowl, cover, and leave to rise in a warm place for 1 hour, or until it has doubled in size.

4 Meanwhile, make the filling. Heat the oil in a skillet and add all of the remaining ingredients except the cheese. Cook for 5 minutes, stirring.

5 Divide the risen dough into 4 pieces. On a lightly floured surface, roll each out into a 7-inch circle. Spoon equal amounts of the filling onto one half of each circle.

6 Sprinkle the cheese over the filling. Brush the edge of the dough with milk and fold the dough over to form 4 semicircles, pressing to seal the edges.

7 Place on a nonstick cookie tray and brush with milk. Bake in a preheated oven, at 425°F, for 30 minutes until golden and risen. Serve hot.

Index